Voices from Heaven

By the same author:
Visions of Another World: The Autobiography of a Medium

Voices from Heaven

Communion with Another World

Stephen O'Brien

The Aquarian Press

An Imprint of HarperCollins*Publishers*

The Aquarian Press
An Imprint of GraftonBooks
A Division of HarperCollins*Publishers*
77–85 Fulham Palace Road,
Hammersmith, London W6 8JB

Published by The Aquarian Press 1991
1 3 5 7 9 10 8 6 4 2

© Stephen O'Brien 1991

A CIP catalogue record for this work
is available from the British Library

ISBN 1-85538-078-1

Typeset by Harper Phototypesetters Limited,
Northampton, England
Printed in Great Britain by CollinsManufacturing, Glasgow

For your Questing Spirit,
ever in Search of Itself . . .

Contents

Part Two
JOURNEYS INTO THE SPIRIT WORLD

Acknowledgements

My thanks to all those, from both sides of life, who have helped me spread the news of survival after death and the message of peace, love and brotherhood to so many millions.

I'm also grateful to everyone who has shared with others details of evidence they've received.

My thanks to Tony Ortzen and his staff at *Psychic News* for their encouragement and support, and permission to reproduce my poem 'Do Not Forget Me' from the anthology *The Still Pool* (The Psychic Press, 1990).

And a special tribute to Jeff Rees Jones, friend and manager, for his patient support and dedication in organizing my tours.

Death is an Illusion.
When a traveller passes hence
we grieve and mourn our loss: but those in the Realms of
Light shout for joy
for they have welcomed Home—a lost and wandering
soul . . .

Stephen O'Brien

Part One
A Servant of the Spirit

1

Voices in the Night

It was a dark and stormy winter's night. Black clouds covered the moon and trees lashed wildly in the gale, making ghostly shadows fly across the street. Lightning lit up the sky as we in the pathetic bus queue huddled together trying to dodge further rain whistling through holes in the shelter windows. How we cursed the vandals on that dark night.

Pulling up my collar, icy water ran down my back just as I spied a drunken man waiting at the corner of the road. Standing on the pavement's edge, he was swaying deliriously to and fro—quite unaware of the grave danger he was in. That corner had known many horrific pedestrian deaths: drivers just couldn't see around the blind bend.

Suddenly I gasped, as a flash of headlights shot over the hill—the old man was going to walk right out in front of a car. But just then, something strange happened—I stood transfixed, as a ghostly gleaming-white mist appeared behind him. It quickly condensed into the radiant form of a middle-aged spirit woman. Strangely unruffled by the gale, her hair was completely unmoved, not a drop of rain had wet it, and her flowing white spirit robes were bone-dry.

All at once, she stooped down, drew back her arm and delivered a swift blow to the back of the man's knees. My heart jumped into my throat as he fell backwards like a collapsing house of cards, landing on the pavement with his legs in the gutter. Just a second later, a reckless car hurtled around the blind bend at over 50 miles per hour, missing his feet by half an inch—then zoomed past the bus queue, splashing us with muddy water.

Brushing the rain from my eyelashes, I watched the ghostly woman kneel down, kiss the old man's troubled brow, smile, and then vanish into the dark night—fading back into the spirit world, from whence she came . . .

As people rushed to help him, I knew they weren't aware of what had taken place 'behind the scenes'. I knew they hadn't seen his spirit-wife save him from a gruesome end, for they were not mediums, but I am . . .

I've had these psychic abilities from my earliest years, visions of other worlds beyond death often coming to me in the strangest ways, and at the oddest moments. They usually happened without warning, yet each experience taught me something useful about life and its meaning. Some of them left such a powerful impression, they still haunt me, even today.

As a baby, just a few months old, I can vividly recall strange faces peering over my cot-gate at night. Sometimes they startled me by reaching out their arms to tickle my stomach or chin. They also spoke, of course, though I didn't understand them. But there was no need to worry, my spirit people were quite smiling, friendly folk and they never did me any harm.

As I grew older, I'd often wake at dawn in the hazy half-light to hear a beautiful children's choir singing that wonderful old hymn:

> All things bright and beautiful,
> All creatures great and small.
> All things wise and wonderful,
> The Lord God made them all . . .

The sound was marvellous, so real and crystal clear, that I'd join in with the happy singing, thinking to myself, 'Oh, I must be late for school, and they're singing in Assembly.' Then all at once I'd realize I was still in bed—and my voices in the night immediately ceased, earthly thoughts having drawn me back to this dull grey world again. I'd jump up and quickly go to the window, but of course, there was no one there.

Sometimes, the sounds were so very clear, as if coming from right outside myself, but more frequently they were silent 'voiceless' tones from within, which nearly always surprised me—for they often came when least expected. One such voice gave me a 'warning' as I swaggered home much too late one night, praying my father wouldn't clip my ear for staying out past sunset. I was ambling along when quite suddenly it ordered me to: 'Cross the road and go home a different way!' I quickly obeyed, and glancing back as I turned the corner, I saw a group of trouble-making youths bent on mischief coming along my previous path. It was a welcome escape, for which I remain grateful.

The spirit people were obviously watching over me, even at school. I remember the time I took an important biology examination, flushing red because I hadn't studied properly. I was sitting amongst all the other nervous candidates, fiddling with my pen and biting my lip, dreading the prospect of unanswerable questions, when—quite out of the blue—a clear voice said, 'Don't worry, you'll pass this test.' It was such a real sound, I turned quickly to see where it had come from. 'Face the front, O'Brien! No cheating!' called the headmaster from his big desk. When we came to start, my hand hovered above the paper, almost too afraid to touch it. But when I flipped it over, I was delighted. I knew all the answers to the set questions! And, of course, my inspirer was right—I did pass the test.

But perhaps the most mysterious spirit voice was the one which came at frequent intervals in a strange recurring dream. It began to worry me, so I shared it with my compassionate mother.

'Sometimes I get frightened,' I said.

'Don't be silly, Stephen, dreams won't harm you. Now, tell me what happens.'

I took a deep breath. 'It all starts with a pillar of golden light, set against a background of deep space and twinkling stars.

There's no end to this golden column, which stretches from Earth to heaven. And there are hundreds of sad-looking people walking endlessly around it, in a mindless procession leading nowhere. Then . . .' My mother leaned forward, as I went on . . .

'A deep voice says to me, "This is the Circle of Life." Then suddenly the people discover a gap in the pillar—and inside there's a broad golden stairway, ascending. They quickly start to climb it, as the voice says, "They are moving onwards and upwards, into the Light." '

There was a stunned pause as my mother searched the floor with her deep green eyes, then engaged them with mine. She looked quite concerned. 'Stephen,' she said, 'for the moment, try and put it out of your mind, and it'll soon fade away.'

No doubt she was startled by my dream's deep symbolism, especially as I was so young. But looking back now, I think the vision signified the monotonous round of daily life on Earth—with possibly many incarnations—until the soul realizes there's an eternal ladder of progression before it. It was such strange revelations, granted even in my waking hours, and confessions like this to my mother that led her, I believe, to realize I was slightly 'different' from other children.

The power of spiritual healing first manifested in me when I was still in short trousers. Rather embarrassingly, I grew a large unsightly wart on my right knee, which no one could remove. The doctors tried every medication under the sun, but without success. My mother, poor soul, was even on the verge of employing that old wives' remedy of rubbing raw bacon on it then burying the bacon in the garden, while our superstitious old neighbour, Florrie, twinkled with glee: 'I'll get the gypsies to curse it off next time they come round selling pegs.'

In the end I was so annoyed with everyone *and* the red monster, I shouted, 'I'll do it *myself*—leave it to me!' Then I gripped the tough skin tightly between fingers and thumb. 'I order you to vanish!' I commanded. But when I opened my eyes and looked down, it was still there. But, determined to the end, I kept my mind fixed on its removal.

The next day I was running through the park when out of the blue something made me glance down at my bare knees—just in time to see the ugly wart popping off my leg onto some nearby gravel. I stopped dead in my tracks, utterly astonished. And even though I scratched among the dirt and stones, I couldn't find the offender anywhere. There wasn't even a scar on my skin. 'Good riddance!' I thought.

I think I've always had an aura of healing around me, for even when I was a child, many youngsters, some older than I, often came to me for advice. They specially sought me out just to share their problems. 'You're calm,' they'd say, 'and we feel so much better after talking to you.'

Of course I realize now that Older Minds on the Other Side were inspiring me with the answers they needed.

But probably the most tangible evidence of the spirit people came in a photograph which my mother took when I was 11. I was sitting on the back garden wall. 'Smile, Stephen!' Click! And it was all over, until my twenty-second year, when I was given a message in a small Spiritualist church. The old medium pointed her bony finger at me and croaked, 'Get the album out, young man. There's a photo of you as a lad, sitting on a garden wall; and what's more, there's a spirit visitor peering right over your left shoulder!'

I couldn't wait for the meeting to end. I ran all the way home, jumped a flight of steps, dashed through the front door, flew up the stairs, pulled out the album, and there—*exactly as described*—was the cheeky spirit face, smiling for all he was worth! I was more than impressed.

There was never any doubt about the spirit people's closeness to my young life, as I recorded in my first volume of autobiography. One night, when I was just 10 years old, we were visited by phantom hammering on our front door at two o'clock in the morning. It was a hollow, eerie sound, but no one else in the house heard it, only me. It was a powerful message, which, in later years, the spirit people described as a symbol of their link with me. 'Behold, we stood at the door and knocked. We were waiting for you, Stephen,' they said. They were anxious I should discover my latent psychic abilities, which often went hand-in-hand with thoughts beyond my years.

As a youngster I remember looking down the terrace row where we lived, thinking, 'All these houses are made of cardboard, and the people in them are nothing but shadows.' And I often used to say, 'I don't belong on Earth'—for that's exactly how I felt. Like a goldfish forever circling a small round bowl, I stared out at distorted nightmare shapes which confounded me. It's taken a long time to come to terms with being in a physical body, in a physical world.

Now, of course, I realize Earth is just a training-ground for the soul to grow, learning through all its experiences. But throughout my childhood some deeper part of me had always been aware of this, and that's why I'd felt so terribly alone. Now I fully understand that I *don't* belong on this planet: none of us do—our true home is in the spirit world, from whence we came.

As a child, the dull adult world dismally failed to attract my attention, get inside my dreamy head, or understand why some of my utterances immediately silenced it. Whenever grown-ups fretted and moaned over (what seemed to me) unimportant things, I'd often say, 'Why are you worrying? Worrying won't solve the problem, and it'll make you ill.' They'd stand open-mouthed, glowering, uncertain whether to scream or take a well-aimed swing at my head. But more often than not, they'd admonish me with 'What do *you* know about it? Be quiet! You're only a kid!'

And of course, apart from my visions and voices, they were quite right: I was just another ordinary lad—but one who felt ill at ease amongst what he often thought was a cruel, unkind world.

Looking back now, in many ways I was rather a lonely little boy, always standing apart from the crowd, just a little outside life. I loved my own company and would walk on the hills or by the rolling seas in absolute silence, or perhaps I'd be caught in wonder by the beauty of the flowers; or maybe I'd be found sitting by a bubbling stream, thinking of the Mind behind

Creation. It's not that I wasn't interested in other youngsters, I just felt strangely misfitted amongst them—and such feelings led me to contemplate the Great Imponderables: Where have I come from? Why am I here? And where am I going?

A Voice from the Void

A Voice from the Void
Am I
A gathering mind
Forlorn

> A wandering soul
> Am I
> From yestermorn

Everywhere
Am I
Yet nowhere
At all

> A timeless sentient cloud
> Am I
> Omnipresent thought
> As yet unborn

A drifting spirit
Am I
With no fixed home

> I'm
> A wishing-star
> In someone's mind
> A liquid dream
> Of womankind . . .

> > . . . A blast of fusing light
> > I see
> > Beckoning me . . .

> . . . A folding darkness
> Covers me
> And memory is gone . . .
>
> A babe in the womb
> Am I
> Plasmic blood and bone
>
>> A cry in the night
>> Am I
>>
>> A wrenching form
>> And I am Born . . .
>
> Somewhere now
> Am I . . .
> Yet nowhere
> At all . . .

But who would have thought in those far-off days that 'little Stephen' would be known to millions through television, radio and the press, and take huge public meetings all over Britain, offering comfort, hope, knowledge and evidence of a life after death to the people? Who could have guessed that in my adult years I'd stand beside and mix with famous celebrities, household names, eventually becoming a celebrity myself? If some old gypsy had gazed into her crystal ball and forecast all these things then, no one else would have believed her.

But I might have; for as maturity came, I felt a deep call from within my own spirit—a call to serve. And before I was 21, I was already publicly representing the spirit world, fulfilling their prediction to me years previously, when they had said, 'We're calling you to represent us to millions. Unto you is granted the Power of the Word.' In child-like innocence, I believed my inspirers without question. And, indeed, their prophecy has to come to pass . . .

When my first book, *Visions of Another World*, was published I was taken completely by surprise by the whirlwind of publicity it generated. They say ignorance is bliss, and in this case they're right. I thought all you had to do was write a book and wait for it to appear in the stores. I couldn't have been more wrong!

Publication day passes quietly for most writers, who can sit at home with their feet up—but not when an author tour's been arranged. I soon found this out on a never-ending, catch-a-bite-to-eat-if-you-can-manage-it, whistle-stop tour of 20 major British cities. I was shooting all over the country like a jet that never stopped. Rising at dawn, bleary-eyed and only half-awake, I'd tell the singing birds, 'It's all right for you, boys! You can go back to bed and get some shut-eye!' Then I'd be off on a continuous round of TV, press and radio interviews.

For such a quiet man as myself, life soon became a living nightmare: I was dashing in and out of taxis, newspaper offices and TV and radio stations like a thing demented. Half the time I was so tired it's a living wonder I found the right buildings! Yet everywhere I went, the reception was the same—switchboards jammed with callers. The only light relief was some amusing moments chatting to celebrities like the rock group Status Quo, or bumping into famed cookery expert and author Keith Floyd. Our paths kept crossing at radio stations! He was always leaving as I arrived, and vice versa. 'It's all go, Stephen, isn't it?' he smiled.

It's hardly surprising I felt exhausted after my public meetings, because I gave my audiences everything—many of whom had travelled hundreds of miles to reach the most prestigious venues in Britain, just to share what I'd found.

I never dreamed just how *profoundly* my life-story would affect people: not just the media (who gobbled it up voraciously), but ordinary folk like you and me, whose lives seemed deeply touched by it. They were emotionally moved by my mother's tragic passing from cancer at 49, her deep love for me, and the remarkable night she broke the silence of death and returned from Beyond the Veil. They also cried at the touching meeting between me and my spirit guide, a magnificent North American Indian who gave his tribal name as White Owl. They were enthralled by his deep spiritual love for me, and his calling of my soul to serve those in need. Reading my story, the public were all at once stirred and fascinated by my life, and they wrote to me in droves. I did feel sorry for the poor postman delivering the mail; he had to climb three flights of steep concrete steps every day.

As soon as the first 500 letters arrived, I started the seemingly endless task of answering them all, scanning mail on buses, trains and park benches in every available moment—even in the bathroom! I read every single letter personally, and replied to absolutely *everyone.* It took me ages to add some personal messages as footnotes, and I was often up until the wee small hours replying.

Some thoughtful members of the public sent me extra stamps and envelopes to cope with the financial burden of postage, but I soon went broke, as hundreds of writers failed to include a stamped addressed envelope. This was always a particular headache: it's bad enough being faced with huge stacks of mail daily, but to reply, and then write out masses of addresses as well nearly drove me insane. Then *The Daily Star*, one of Britain's top tabloid newspapers, came to my financial rescue, paying for all the mail resulting from a huge two-page feature article they'd done about my life and work, and proving what my mother used to say was right: 'If God doesn't fetch, He sends.'

I lost count of the times my vision blurred behind a wall of tears as I read those emotional letters. Out of all the people in the world, I was the *only* one who could help them, people said.

What a frightening responsibility.

From deep inside their tragedies, men, women and children reached out and cried, 'Please, please help me find my loved ones again: my husband, my wife, my parents, my child. Although I know you're such a busy man, please don't desert me in my hour of need . . .' Or 'My baby is dead. My life is over, finished. I want to kill myself to be with him. Where is he now? Is he still alive? Who's taking care of him? Tell me, Stephen, will we ever be together again?'

I assured them all there would one day be a glorious reunion in another world, and plenty of opportunities to settle any misunderstandings or deep-seated guilts and regrets—for that is the Universal Law.

One young mother wrote to say her six-year old son had undergone major surgery because 'he'd been born with his heart back-to-front and on the wrong side of his body. The surgeons operated, but his heart swelled to twice its normal size, so they had to leave his chest open for 24 hours. Then they sealed his little body, and we prayed so hard for his recovery. Thank God, he did become fit and well again. But afterwards he caught a series of infections, and my darling little boy died.' Was there any news of him? Was there a message? I tried to alleviate this tragic grief as best I could.

Strangely enough, this young mum later stepped forward at one of my meetings in the north of England and gave me such a sincere embrace, and a kiss, and then said through the microphones to the 700 people, 'You'll never know what you've done for me, Stephen O'Brien. Your letter contained evidence no one on Earth knew. You brought my boy back to me, and gave me so much comfort. God bless you.' I immediately sent my gratitude to the spirit people.

Other writers also deeply touched my spirit, like the young man in southern Britain who'd lost his father. They'd been up on some scaffolding together, repairing the outside of the house, when the supports suddenly gave way. Plummeting to the ground, the young man landed on grass, but his father fell onto concrete. I shed tears as I read the emotionally-penned words, 'I cradled my Dad close to me, but there was nothing I could do. I just had to watch my wonderful father take his last breaths, while he died in my arms.' I pray some of my words may have comforted him.

But sometimes I was completely at a loss as to how to reply. One woman wrote to share her darkest secret: her father had sexually abused her in childhood, but with his last breath had made her reaffirm her promise never to tell another living soul. The pressures of this were too much to bear, and she underwent a mental breakdown and was admitted into hospital. 'Can you help me? Is there any word from my father? Is he sorry now? Does he understand?' Thankfully I was able to relieve some of her anxiety when relaying her father's 'plea for forgiveness'; he'd now realized his terrible mistakes and the torment and anguish they'd caused. After this, the woman regained composure and her life brightened considerably.

My spirit friend, guide and teacher, White Owl, is always nearby when I read my mail, and help is immediately despatched. Most correspondents don't realize that the aid they so desperately seek doesn't always come from me, as they request. Thought is mighty, and there are many great souls in the next life who are capable of bringing them relief; their one and only motivating force being the Power of Love.

Here's White Owl on the role of mediums:

> A servant of the spirit should educate and comfort, heal the sick, and uplift those who feel they stand in darkness.
>
> Go forward then, proclaiming from the mountain tops this timeless, glittering message: Love is the strongest power in the Universe. Love conquers all fear, and is even stronger than death.
>
> True mediums for the spirit world are chosen. They are marked out by the light of compassion shining through their works, brighter than the Spirit of the Sun.
>
> Our message is one of toleration and peace, and our task is to touch and awaken sleeping materialistic souls to the eternal power of the spirit within them, and the wonderful opportunities for growth and service this affords.

To those who think of spiritual mediums as 'fortune-tellers', White Owl's words may come as a revelation. But to the many already enlightened, they show that mediums are trying to effect a moral, ethical and spiritual change for the better in the human race. As a 'two-worlds team' we are still actively engaged in these tasks.

So far, the adventure of my life has contained many fascinating experiences. Glancing back, though the last 36 years haven't led me along an easy path (far from it), I do feel great rewards have come through being richly blessed by the Love of the Spirit. I've even been privileged to have known time-slips where I've visited the past or been granted powerful visions of the future. Along with my spirit friends, I've met, and hopefully helped, thousands of people in both worlds. And now I'd like to share what I've found with my fellow-travellers. Writing these books is a good way of achieving this.

Speaking of writings, hundreds of intriguing stories still pour through my mailbox: tales of sadness and joy, murder and suicide, blinding grief and ecstatic happiness—all proving that we're evolving through experience by playing out our parts in the great drama of life. I'd like to thank all those who've written, and I hope my words brought you some inner peace.

But irrespective of how my replies are received, I was soon left in no doubt about knowledge of my work spreading, for one letter arrived with a foreign postmark, only partly-addressed. It simply read:

To Stephen O'Brien
(medium)
Britain

And it arrived safely . . .

Then one day the telephone rang. 'Hello? Mr O'Brien?'
'Yes?'
'Would you please find time to help my aunt? She's in dire need of comfort, solace and evidence of survival. Please, Mr O'Brien, promise you'll help her.'
'Of course. What's her name?'
'Mrs James.'
'Ask her to come around next Wednesday evening . . .'

2

Between Two Worlds

The door knocked and Mrs Phyllis James, a small middle-aged woman in obvious distress, entered. She was accompanied by her daughter.

Glancing at her, I psychically felt my head spinning with dizziness, reeling under a blinding, inconsolable grief. Of all the people I've ever helped, I don't think I've met anyone so unable to cope with the death of a loved one; that's why I'd agreed to see her. With my psychic vision, I gazed into the electromagnetic fields of energy surrounding her—the aura—and there I saw recorded an endless string of lonely nights, and a powerful wish to die and fall into the arms of someone she loved. She'd spent many hours crying and struggling to come to terms with some deep and tragic loss—a fight that drained her of the will to live. She was a woman caught between two worlds, and she knew the pain of grief.

'Come on in, and we'll have a cup of tea first, shall we?' I said. And they slowly began to relax, as I explained how private consultations work.

'I can't guarantee anything,' I said. 'It's out of my hands. All we can do is wait and see what happens. No one can make anyone Over There communicate with us, and sometimes we don't get the people we'd like to hear from.

'*I* can't bring anybody back—only *you* can do that, because they love you. Some communicators try very hard to get a word through, but I don't always hear them clearly, and sometimes not at all. It's very much an experiment, and it works better if we can all relax and just wait and see what they can transmit.

'And remember, when they come through I can't govern what they'll talk about. They bring their own thoughts, the things *they* want to say—which may not be the things *we'd* like to hear. But we can't demand anything of the people in Spirit—they still have their own minds and free will.

'However, I won't bring any family skeletons out of the cupboard, and the only time I vet the messages is if they start using "choice" language! They don't change upon dying, you see, they're the same people one second after death as they were one second before it—though as time goes on people do progress and alter. It's all up to your loved ones now. Some find it easier to do than others—that's the way it goes.'

'I understand,' said Mrs James weakly, her voice trembling, fearing the one she wanted wasn't going to make it that night.

'Just relax, Mum,' said her daughter reassuringly. 'Stephen will do his best.' But conditions for contact were very good and there wasn't long to wait. I immediately became aware of Mrs James' 'dead' husband. Not only was he present, but he also began giving evidence in a rather surprising, clever way.

'I can see a man's hand here,' I relayed, 'holding what looks like a rug-making implement, and he tells me to "Thank you for recognizing I needed something to occupy my time; I felt so useless, there was no point in living the way I was." '

This made a great impact on his wife, who now perched on the edge of her seat, eager to hear more. It transpired that her husband had been brain-damaged and she'd nursed him for four years when he hadn't any knowledge of his plight. There were many sad weeks when 'I couldn't recognize my wife and children,' he said. This was particularly stressful, and his family bought him rug-making kits, hoping to bring awareness back and give further purpose to his days.

'And he gives the name of Brian here. Does Brian mean anything to you?'

'*That's his name*!' she tearfully replied, barely able to speak, her eyes darting across to her daughter who'd clasped her mother's arm on hearing the evidence.

They squeezed each other's hands and I went on, 'Well, he's telling you not to worry. "I'm alive and I was with you right up to the funeral, plus a few weeks afterwards, and then I went across to the spirit world where they taught me how to guide you to a medium." '

Visibly moved, his wife began to freely weep, but not with grief—these were tears of joy. 'Now Brian's showing me his passport,' I continued, which puzzled me. But the mystery was soon solved.

'Yes,' said Mrs James, 'he died abroad, while we were holidaying in France.'

Brian then kept showing me pictures of what turned out to be his last moments on Earth. He'd been swimming, then as he walked up the beach towards his wife he suffered a sudden massive heart attack—then collapsed and died immediately. He clearly remembered all of this, and also that his wife 'had to go through an agonizing week's wait before the French authorities could release my body and fly me home'.

'I came home without him,' Mrs James cried. 'I loved him with all my heart, but I had to come home without him . . .'

Brian was acutely aware of the pain this had caused his dear wife, and that for her it was just as though the light of her life had been extinguished. Then in an effort to stem her tears, he brightly mentioned 'a special cigarette lighter and a bedspread she's given away'.

'Do you know anything about these?' I asked.

'Oh yes, he never did like that old bedspread, and he used to take lighters to pieces and then he couldn't put them together again!' Brian had scored another hit, but not content with his success so far, he carried on by recalling, 'Yesterday, you were totally alone, and you got out every single photograph of me you possess, and cried like a baby.'

'Yes, I did . . .'

'And you won't let anyone touch my things, and none of the family can change the rooms around either.' Mrs James agreed. In fact, her grief had been so deep that she'd formed a kind of shrine, a place of remembrance for all of Brian's belongings, and no one was allowed to disturb them. Her husband then went on to show remarkable knowledge of her life and thoughts, and gave excellent, sensible advice, after mentioning, 'You prayed many nights for God to take you, so you'd wake up in the morning in another world, next to me.'

'Yes, I did . . .'

'But you can't come to me before your time. Just remember the kind of love we've shared—it binds us together. It's the kind that never dies. So go on living and fighting, love. Don't give up.'

'I wish I could, but I don't think I can.'

'Yes you can. Live for the children, look after them for me,' he said to her.

He then asked me to explain about the sacredness of life and that suicide solves no problems, so I did. 'If you did cross over, your husband would have your company, yes, but then you'd be further away from your daughters and grandchildren. Plus, "dying" doesn't remove our inability to cope with life—we take that with us until we learn to alter our way of thinking.'

Mrs James understood, and with a heartfelt cry said, 'Then, Stephen, please tell him I love him and miss him with all my soul. Tell him not a night goes by without my thinking about him or crying myself to sleep over his death.'

'He knows all these things,' I gently assured her, 'and often catches your thoughts, so just speak to him and he'll hear you, Mrs James. The power of love will link you together, no matter how far apart you might sometimes feel.' And these words brought her great relief.

Although his passing had been very sudden, it had not been altogether unexpected, for incredibly Brian then told us that his spirit family had been waiting for him: with their special kind of vision they'd seen his heart weakening. Still speaking of his death, Brian told his wife, 'Stop thinking of me as I was when I "died", with all the indignity.' She fully understood, recollecting the traumatic events as police and officials arrived on the beach where his body lay in public gaze, and all the painful formalities and fuss that followed before the body could be released. It was a dreadful time for her.

But from his new world, he was now sending all his love to his three daughters and mentioning some difficulties one of them had been through. Then I got the words, 'Sandra's baby was sickly.' For a moment this puzzled my sitters, but the mystery was soon solved. Sandra, one of his daughters, had lost a child, but her 'dead' father kept transmitting: 'I've got the little baby with me, and it's a boy!' he announced triumphantly. No sooner than this was said, Mrs James burst into uncontrollable sobs. Floods of crying and consoling followed, until she was able to explain. 'We always wanted a grandson, Stephen, but up to now all the children have been girls. The little baby's a boy! *A boy*!' she kept saying through tears of joy, utterly overcome with happiness.

'And we've named him Julian,' said Brian, 'so when you go to bed tonight, now you can also say, "And God bless Julian." '

It's impossible to judge the effect such a simple message like that can have. Brian James was a very good communicator. It's often the seemingly 'trivial' statements that provide the best evidence of survival. After all, what makes up our lives? If communicators spoke of Einstein's theory of relativity, ordinary folks wouldn't be interested. Their messages are usually packed with comfort and hidden meaning, or intimate facts known only to the two people concerned—*the one sending the message and the one receiving it*. Mr James was a clever man who brought plenty of these 'inconsequential' details through; things like 'the rug having to be picked up because she's always tripping over it' and a reference to the town Porthcawl, where they'd spent a lovely caravan outing when younger—or to 'the pair of shoes and a special suit' which he was especially anxious to transmit. I couldn't fathom why these items were important, until his wife explained: 'The undertaker offered to dress Brian in a suit for me, so I picked his wedding suit, shirt and tie, and one pair of shoes.

It's quite unusual to place shoes on those resting,' she pointed out, 'but the undertaker was very kind and understanding.' Brian had mentioned the items, fully knowing their significance: they were important to him and her—and *only* to them, no one else.

Towards the end of the sitting, he told his family, 'I'll often visit you at home—so watch out for me.' And even though he knew his presence wouldn't always be registered, he was determined his wife should 'see' him again. He then told us where he was living in the Beyond. 'It's a house in its own grounds, surrounded by country lanes, and it has a pink rambling rose bush on the trellis-work over the door.'

'We grew that very same rose bush before,' Mrs James acknowledged with a smile. 'That's wonderful.' His final evidence was quite clever too. When he spoke about 'a ship' Mrs James' eyes filled with tears. 'Brian was making a tapestry of a ship before he died. We've had it framed and it's hanging in pride of place on the living-room wall,' she said.

The ladies picked up their coats, but the grieving woman who left after that quiet sitting was not the same dejected soul who'd entered an hour earlier: uplifted and refreshed, renewed and grateful, Mrs James clasped my hands and squeezed them tight. Both she and her daughter kissed me, and thanked me profusely. 'You'll never know what you've done for me today, Stephen. I've fought so hard to carry on,' she said through her tears, 'and my strength was failing. But to know Brian is with me, still caring for us all, means the world to us. Thank you. Thank you so much, Stephen.'

'Please, don't thank *me*,' I said, 'thank God, and Brian. After all, he did all the hard work, I only transmitted his words. He made the effort because he still loves you all so very much.'

'God bless you.'

Mrs James and her daughter smiled as they made their way to the door. 'God will be kind to you, Mrs James,' I said. 'The sun will shine again, you'll see.'

Then, much happier than when they'd arrived, my two sitters left—*but not alone*. Following close behind them was Brian James, a man from another world, someone once thought 'dead'. And I dare say he was with them all the way home; *unseen* maybe, but walking beside them nevertheless . . .

Do Not Forget Me

Do not forget me when I go,
For go I must, I cannot stay;
But do not forget my face, my love,
Nor my life, I pray.

Yet, if you should forget awhile
When I am gone—do not despair,
But keep your tears at bay,
For the silver love we shared
Will never fade away.

And one dawn soon,
Together we will stand
Upon some silent mountain, in some silent land,
And gaze into each other's eyes once more;
Then, hand in hand
Along some distant shore,
We'll remember all the times that slipped our minds:

    Our fond goodbyes;
    The times we loved;
    The time we met;

My love, we'll not forget.

3

When a Child Dies

Picture a seven-year-old boy, lying unconscious in a hospital bed. Eyes tight-closed and unable to speak, he is dying of a rare form of liver cancer. Not even major surgery can save him. At his bedside is the father he loves more than anything else in the world. But his dad can do nothing but watch and pray. He is powerless to stop his young son's life ebbing away, out of sight, forever.

Then, the little boy dies . . .

What do you say to his dad? How do you comfort him? Do you tell him to have faith that one day there might be a reunion in some far distant heaven we know nothing about? Will holding a blind faith replace his boy's shining eyes, his fun-loving spirit and the wonderful, sparkling personality that made his son so very special? Should you maintain a cruel silence?

Or—if you could—would you throw back the gates of 'death' and offer him evidence of survival, proof that his beloved child is still very much alive in another world?

If *you* were the bereaved parent, which would you choose: blind faith or certain knowledge?

William Allen was lucky, because the spirit world solved all these problems for him; they carefully delivered the proof he so desperately sought. It was nothing to do with me, the Other Side organized it, because they loved both him and his son. I was just the channel young Jamie Allen used to contact his dad, who'd suffered endless heartache.

When Will, 40, lost his boy, the whole world fell to pieces around him. 'I prayed to die myself,' he said. 'Little Jamie was such a happy lad—so full of life. When he died, a part of me died with him. Suddenly there was a big void inside me; my life was empty. You see, Jamie and I shared something special, something very special.'

William started his search for news of Jamie after reading an article about mediumship in *Reader's Digest* which thoroughly intrigued him. 'If Jamie was still alive, somewhere, anywhere, then I wanted to know: I wanted to find him again.'

The night it all happened, Mr Allen was just another face in the crowd at my public meeting, listening to one of the thousands of messages I give each year. But strangely enough, I do remember the occasion quite well, for little Jamie was such a marvellous lad, and a lively communicator, full of fun and wicked grins.

In the middle of the demonstration, I suddenly became aware of a vibrant youngster—Jamie—who'd joined me on the platform. Spirit children always come to my meetings—they often misbehave and pull at my coat, prod my legs, or sometimes sit at the side of the stage playing with their toys until it's their turn to communicate. They're not always well mannered either! But there was nothing naughty about Jamie. In fact, there was something rather special about him. He was strangely 'old' and 'wise', and also brimming with vigour and a wealth of love, 'just for my Dad'.

Will Allen remembers the occasion far better than I do, so, here, in this interview, he can reveal all about his son's illness, remarkable bravery, his sad untimely passing, and that memorable night when Jamie pulled back the silence of death and proved his survival to the dad he loves so much. Will's story deeply touched and moved me. It's a remarkable tribute to a wonderful child whose short but fruitful life was full of light and happiness, joy, love and laughter, until fatal cancer struck him down in all the beauty of his youth.

As Shakespeare once penned: 'If you have tears, prepare to shed them now' . . .

Jamie
William Allen:

Stephen, I wanted to say thank you for the help and understanding you've given me in messages from the next world, from my mother and my son, Jamie, seven, who passed away in 1986. Jamie died of a very rare form of liver cancer, so rare that out of a million children, maybe just one might be unfortunate to contract it. I'd like to tell you about him, if I may.

For seven years he was really full of life, so active. He loved to run along the beach, laughing and shouting for all he was worth, feeling the wind blowing through his hair—and even in winter we had a terrible job to get a coat on him; he was such a wonderful son, and so loving, too.

If he hurt his head or leg, he'd come running to me saying, 'Dad! Dad, will you kiss it better for me?' And when I did, he'd cuddle me up, with his little arms wrapped tightly round my neck. We shared something very special, Jamie and I.

Then just before one Christmas, he was very tired and went to bed at midday. I had to wake him at 4 o'clock, which wasn't like him at all. At first I put it down to the Christmas excitement, but the following day there was no change in his condition so I called a doctor to examine him. It was then we were all shocked to find that his navel had swollen to the size of a clenched fist, and it was coloured black. The doctor hadn't a clue what was wrong, but quickly admitted Jamie to hospital. We were all very worried about him. Tests started immediately—blood samples and X-rays—and he was put on an intravenous drip to combat dehydration. The consultant told us it was 'a burst appendix, with solid pus'. I said to him, warily, 'You must mean tumours?'

'No,' he assured us, 'his temperature's fluctuating up and down, indicating pus infection.' This meant that still further tests followed but none of them drew any solution. Suddenly I got frightened, more and more scared as each minute passed—*cancer* began to creep into my mind . . .

Jamie was then transferred to another hospital for a complete body-scan, and the same tests all over again. It was then, for the first time, my heart broke as I heard my son pitifully cry out to me, 'Daddy, please take me home. I want to go home . . . Please take me home, Daddy. Take me home.'

I couldn't speak for a moment, as I was shedding silent tears inside. No one will ever know just how much I cried for my young son. Gradually, I calmed myself down and spoke gently to him, saying, 'Jamie, you're the bravest little boy I know, and when you come home you'll be wearing a gold medallion on a blue ribbon, with some words written on it:

> *To Jamie, the bravest boy in the world,*
> *With love from Mam, Dad and your little sister Emma*

To see any child suffering is terrible, but when it's your own child, you can't begin to imagine the agony and heartache you go through. It rips you apart inside, and shreds you to pieces.

We waited for the body-scan results, but still no answer was found. It was then we were told Jamie had to go into the operating theatre to discover the problem. On that awful day, his mum and I both walked beside him, our hearts full of love. We held his little hands in ours, and were kissing him over and over again. Little did we know then that this was the last time our son would be able to speak to us, for within two hours he was rushed into intensive care, having vomited into his lungs under the anaesthetic. My little boy never regained consciousness . . .

The surgeons discovered liver cancer, which has a good chance of being cured in some adults, but in Jamie's case it revealed itself far too late for successful treatment, and there was no hope.

I was summoned, alone, into an office where a consultant surgeon and two doctors gave me the news. It all happened so quickly. 'Your son is dying,' said the surgeon, as if it was just another everyday phrase. I was completely stunned. 'There's nothing we can do. He'll have to go back into theatre tomorrow.'

Then he left, and the doctors didn't really know what to say. I was offered some tea, and then they too left me alone. It was all over in a matter of 30 seconds—so cold, so hard and unfeeling, as if they hadn't time to sympathize because there were other pressing tasks waiting. I was totally numbed—and then I broke my heart and wept like a child, shivering with tears; I was going to lose my special little boy . . .

All the next day, we kept talking to him as he lay sleeping unconscious in his bed; and somehow, even though his eyes were shut fast, we both felt he could hear us, for as they took him to his operation, something wonderful happened. His mother asked for a cuddle, and Jamie, eyes tightly closed, held his arms up for both of us. It was so touching; a nearby nurse even dabbed her eyes.

Once again we walked beside our boy, placing his two favourite cuddly toys next to him on the pillow. Then the orderlies gave us a few more precious moments alone with our brave, blond, blue-eyed wonderful son. We embraced him, saying he'd be all right, and our eyes followed his little body as they wheeled him out of sight behind the swing doors. There was nothing we could do now, except perhaps one thing.

Alone, I went to the hospital chapel and sat in the quiet silence . . .and I prayed. I prayed and prayed so hard that Jamie would be safe and well.

Then at 11.15 a.m. a nurse came out of the operating theatre to tell us the surgeons had removed a large tumour from Jamie's liver. A flood of emotion filled my mind, and his mother and I hugged each other. Rather than seeing the black side of things, we felt it was a good sign. 'He's going to live,' we cried, 'he's going to live!' After all the worrying and uncertainty, now there was a flicker of hope, and I went back again into the chapel, and once more prayed gratefully, saying, 'Lord God . . .Jesus . . .thank you for letting my son live. Thank you for giving him back to us. Thank you.'

But by 6.30 that night, Jamie was back in intensive care again, when something went very wrong. Suddenly his tiny heart gave out, and they rushed him back to the theatre for emergency treatment and oxygen. After desperately struggling to keep alive for so long, he barely survived the stress, but by some miracle he pulled through, and then came a terrible week of waiting—but still there was no change in his condition. They were monitoring him day and night.

Unwilling to give up, we kept speaking to him and playing cassette tapes, specially made for him by all his schoolmates, saying, 'Hurry up and get well, Jamie, and come home soon.' Every child recorded an encouraging personal message for my son, in the hope the coma would break. But it didn't.

Through all these trials, and Jamie's brave fight for life, the nursing staff were truly angels, especially one who even cancelled a Spanish holiday to stay with him. 'If I went, I couldn't enjoy

myself,' she said. 'I want to be here and see him get better. He's so
handsome—he'll have all the girls chasing him one day, you'll see.'

I was very grateful for her kindness, but by now time and hope
were running out. Jamie's responses were slow, and much worse
than this—they discovered he was in pain. His teeth were clenched
tight, and I used to try and prize them apart for him with my finger,
fearful he'd bite his tongue, choke or hurt himself—and I couldn't
stand by and let that happen to him, not to my little boy. I spent
many restless, sleepless nights, haunted by my son's handsome face
and the terrible thought that he might never get better, and that I'd
soon lose him forever.

Towards the end, as our hope was gradually fading, we took the
unusual step of arranging a christening service at his bedside. A
vicar arrived, along with Jamie's grandpa and grandma, his mother,
a good friend of mine, and that special nurse who'd come to love him
over the weeks of his illness.

Everyone stood very quietly, stunned into silence and thinking of
the little boy in the bed, unconscious and helpless but with the face
of an angel. Silent tears fell from our eyes. I never thought I'd see
a clergyman cry at a christening, but I did on that day. There was
nothing anyone could do. And I remember thinking, 'Oh God, why
him? Why my Jamie . . .? Why?'

Shortly afterwards, at 7.2O p.m., his final moments arrived. I sat
and helplessly watched as my beautiful son's life slipped silently
away. I could see it happening, and as he was going, I leaned over
him with tears in my eyes, and found myself saying, 'Jamie, don't
fight anymore, just go to sleep, son . . . just go to sleep, Jamie . . .'
I tried to hold him close, but there were so many tubes and wires
in the way, I couldn't . . . I couldn't hold my son, so I just sat quietly
looking at him, crying and stroking his blond hair and kissing his
lips, knowing I'd never be able to do this to him again in this world;
this would be the last time.

Then suddenly, his breathing paused, stopped . . . and it was
finished. Jamie had died, and in those moments all my own life died
with him.

He looked so peaceful, so handsome and peaceful, and an
overwhelming feeling of love filled me, mixed with sadness and a
sense of great pride I had for him—and still have for him. But now
his young life was over. But why? He had never harmed anybody,

never hurt a soul. All he did was bring joy to everyone he met, and now he was gone, and I couldn't understand why. Why did God take Jamie from us? All I knew for certain now was that I loved him, my wonderful son—the bravest little boy in the world.

Then, quite suddenly, a sickening feeling of absolute pure hatred for God thundered right through me. He'd taken my son away—and I quickly rose, ran out into the corridors, and dashed back into the chapel and rushed up towards the altar. I stood defiantly and shouted out loud—I couldn't help myself. I spat towards the altar and violently shouted out loud, '*Don't tell me there's a God!*'

And I swore at Him, and stormed away.

Then the slow, painful months of endless grief started, and never seemed to finish.

Time rolled onwards.

Then William Allen attended one of my public meetings. Here's a letter from him:

I'd no idea I'd get a message that night. I just sat quietly amongst the people, waiting for the medium to start the meeting, wondering if there might be some news, some message or comfort from anyone belonging to me.

The hall was packed, yet during your clairvoyance, Stephen, you suddenly brought Jamie to me by name, with a great deal of love, and laughter too. It was a wonderful moment. My son gave proof of nearness and spoke of his 'yellow plastic ducks and submarine'. This was wonderful evidence, because when I bathed Jamie he used to spend hours trying to sink his ducks with his submarine, dive-bombing them and soaking everyone and everything! These were special moments we shared together, full of happy laughter.

I was more than impressed. As the messages came through I felt elated and deep emotions were stirred inside me. But it didn't finish there, Stephen, you also said Jamie mentioned 'two little dogs in stripey jackets'. This was remarkably accurate, for when my son was desperately ill, while they were wheeling him to the operating theatre for major surgery, my wife and I placed his two favourite toys beside him on the trolley pillow. These were Fluff and Scruff, *two woolly dogs dressed in stripey jackets*.

I'll never forget the memories those words brought back. Jamie was speaking to me through a perfect stranger, and I was uplifted and overjoyed. What's more, you gave his messages with such warmth, kindness and sympathy. Then, I remember my mother, who'd passed over, said she'd brought Jamie along to the meeting from the Other Side. She said she was taking care of him, and this brought me a great sense of peace. She told me, 'I know you've been through the mill for the last two years or so, but we're all proud of you, son.'

Stephen, you went on to describe Jamie's favourite police tricycle, the many hospital tests before falling into his coma, his passing, and how we'd both 'repair' his pedal-car by 'placing it on pretend home-made ramps'; all meaningless things to anyone else listening, but to me they showed my beautiful son was still alive. I was very comforted.

Jamie then said, 'Give my love to Emma.' This is his younger sister. And he asked you if you would 'Tell my Dad I love him, as he thinks of me so much. I love my Dad.' I was very moved, and could feel my emotions rising. 'Don't cry for me, Daddy,' my son said, 'and think of the good times. Look up, Dad, not down. I love you.'

I can't begin to say what those words meant to me. Up until then I'd often thought my life was useless without my son. There were many times when I just couldn't come to terms with his loss and I'd have been happy to die myself, to join him. But messages like this gave me great hope and peace, and I feel very privileged to have received them.

My only wish now is that other parents who find themselves in my situation will be lucky enough to be helped like this. To anyone like me I would say: don't give up, if I can find the child I thought I'd lost, you can find yours too.

Some sceptical people may say these messages might be 'untrue'. I reply, '*Rubbish.*' Those messages came from people I loved—and precise facts given through a stranger could only have come from *them*. There's no way anyone could have known those personal things. You even gave me my son's name.

I think I'm very fortunate because I've found Jamie again, through knowledge and love, and not just faith. And now I've come to accept he's not really far away from us all. I *know* he's alive.

Other parents in my position should hear my story; perhaps it'll give them hope, and knowledge that death is not the end. Of course, I still have my good and bad days, because you never ever forget. But I wish I could tell them to keep on looking for their child if they've lost one: I can only draw from my experiences and advise parents to visit good mediums and Spiritualist churches. Then perhaps they'll get the comfort I've found. In those small places they might find the love and support of people who not only understand death, but are also able to show it isn't the final crossing it's made out to be.

So, Stephen, thank you from the bottom of my heart for helping me in my great sadness to realize that my son's life is not over, not cruelly ended, but continuing in the next world.

Thank you for helping me to understand that he lives on and is being cared for in another life beyond death.

And God bless you in your work.

4

Through the Mists

Jamie's story touches me deeper than I'd care to admit, because I can't claim to have had such a close relationship with my own father. Although quite a lovable, determined child, who'd raise both his arms in the air and open and close his fists—which meant 'Pick me up and carry me' (hence the nickname 'Ever-Ready')—I can't ever recall Dad cuddling me. Neither did I sit on his knee, so it didn't take my young mind very long to decide he just wasn't interested in me.

He never came to school plays and recitals, or showed any interest in my schoolwork. I'd be so proud of pictures I'd painted, or my writings: I once won a nationwide essay competition, coming top in Britain, but Dad was unmoved and nowhere to be seen—unlike my mother who was as proud as punch and always ready to praise and encourage. I detailed my loving relationship with her in my first book . . . And so to Dad.

Very distant, cold and undemonstrative, from my tenderest years I felt he didn't love me. In hindsight perhaps I was wrong, but two horrendous scenes still freeze my blood when I recall them. It isn't easy to write of these, but they give revealing insights into why I now place such high values on love and kindness.

I was only a toddler when they happened, eager to learn of life and have fun exploring anything new. That's why the huge mud pool at the bottom of our street attracted me and my friend

Anthea so much. Kids will be kids, and we had a great time on that sunny afternoon, sploshing brown mud everywhere with our dried-out rhubarb sticks, until quite by accident, I fell in.

'Oh God, my Dad'll kill me!'

'Don't be silly!' rebuked matronly Anthea. 'Your mother wouldn't let him!' And she was right, of course—my mother worshipped the ground I walked on.

'But my Mam's out today,' I whimpered, desperately trying to scrape the mud off my bare arms. Then I ran all the way home, stopped in the doorway and crept silently past Dad reading his newspaper, trying my best to be completely invisible. But he saw me, turned and bellowed loudly, 'Stephen! Come here!'

My knees trembled, for I really feared my father's voice. I know the terror in a child's heart when it's truly afraid. I slunk pathetically back into the living-room where he stood waiting for me, hands on hips, feet wide apart, stern face frowning hard. Awkwardly, I tried to hide my muddy arms by twisting them around my back. This was the second time I'd got them dirty, and I feared the worst: I'd disobeyed my Dad. I felt so painfully frightened, all I could hear was the loud ticking of the clock and my thudding heart, pounding in my chest and throat. Beads of sweat stood on my brow and my knees were weak. And though what came next happened so very quickly, at the time it seemed as though each tick of the clock dragged by in a hundred years . . .

'Show me those arms!'

I weakly obliged, starting backwards as he caught hold of them with his strong hands. Suddenly his eyes flashed red with anger. '*What did I tell you*? I ordered you to keep away from that mud— and what have you done?'

I was trembling, too afraid to speak. Excuses only fired his temper, so I stood dumb, shaking with fear. His gruff voice rose sharply, louder and shriller, as anger increased its cruel grip on him.

'What did I tell you? I'll teach you to disobey me, once and for all!' Then he seized my shoulders and dragged me off to the kitchen. I scuffed at the floor with my feet in a frantic bid to escape, but he was too strong. Fear struck, and I panicked.

'Please Dad, I'm sorry. I was only playing . . . Please, I won't do it again,' I pleaded, struggling for release, but his mind was firmly set on punishment. Always a complete slave to his emotions, he instantly stripped me to the waist, grasped a dry scrubbing brush from the draining-board and scrubbed my bare back until it was red and sore. I sobbed and cried, and screamed for him to stop, but a flood of rage swept through him. My muddy arms were left well alone; my back felt the lesson, until his authority was once again stamped upon me.

'Please Dad, stop! You're hurting me! I won't do it again, I promise I won't do it again,' I cried pitifully, wriggling in his grasp.

'You'll do as you're told in future. When I say something, *I* mean it. I *demand* respect, and if I don't get it, I'll *make* you give it!' he shouted, scrubbing the hard bristles over my red skin. And all the while this was happening, some distant part of my mind rejected him out of hand—he didn't care for me. How could he, having done such a terrible thing to his own son? Surely fathers shouldn't treat their children like this? There and then, I decided I didn't have a dad, not like the other young lads. It was the only way to survive without further mental pain: better to live *without* a father, I reasoned, than exist with one who didn't love me.

A child's mind is so pure and trusting, yet millions of adults cruelly scar their little ones with a rash word, a hasty hand, unkindness or, worst of all the sins—the blatant rejection of innocent love. Children trust so completely; what a shattering, soul-destroying moment it is when their picture of caring adults as friends explodes in their faces. Having worked with psychologists and psychotherapists in recent years, I mourn because many adults who can't cope with life and their personality complexes fail to realize they were planted in their plastic minds by their own ignorant parents. The subconscious mind, where all past experience still 'lives', is easily programmed when young—and it's easily frightened in adulthood, which causes all manner of anxieties. We are creatures of habit.

But what a twisted, dark world many grown-ups live in, which brings me to another painful experience lurking at the tip of my pen, one that could only have happened while my mother was out—Dad would never have harmed me in front of her, she would have killed him outright.

He and I were the only two home, and he had to play a darts match in a local public house. But what could he do with me, a lively toddler? Our dear neighbour Florrie was out, so I couldn't be left there. He was in a dilemma, which he solved thus: he lifted me up, kicking, and thrust me into a high-backed chair. I was petrified, afraid he was going to hit me, and though I struggled, I was no match for his muscles. Forcing me against the wooden slats, he then took several of my mother's old nylon stockings and bound me hand and foot to the chair, after which he left for the pub.

I've no idea how long I tried to break my bonds. Painful experiences are difficult to time, and it's hard to recapture them through the mists of memory. I only know I was crying, frightened and alone. The whole house echoed to my sobbing cries, but no one heard them. In the end I fell deathly silent, almost in a semi-tranced condition: my mind's way of cutting off from something horrendous. I can't even remember who freed me, probably my brother, for if my mother had known, the roof would have been raised. A protective black curtain of forgetfulness blanks further details from my childhood mind . . .

Poor old Dad's always seemed such a sad man in my eyes. Growing older, I realized that because he wasn't brought up in a loving family home, he couldn't recreate this for his offspring.

Not long ago, someone who'd suffered similar treatment in her youth spoke to me with great bitterness against her father. She said she could never 'heal the rift'. 'You must learn to forgive him,' I said, 'as I have done.' And I only hope that one day he will learn to forgive me.

When Dad was in his early sixties and in hospital for an operation, I was working and got special extended lunch hours to trek all the way to his hospital bed before, during and after surgery. Yet each time I arrived he'd grumble and say, 'Oh, not you again! Why are you coming here every day, boy? There's no need for that, I'm all right—don't fuss about.' I guess he'll never change, and he's always called me 'boy', even in adulthood. I'll never be grown-up to him, always a child. Isn't it sad the way some folks refuse to change their thought patterns?

On the lighter side, one amusing clash still makes me grin when I think of it today. It wasn't funny at the time, of course, but now I can laugh at anything (and frequently do). After one of our shouting matches, he pulled me to the ground by my hair, and left me sobbing. More than upset, I left the house in tears. I couldn't return that night, he was so violently angry, so I sat alone at midnight on a cold park bench, gazing at the stars twinkling in a bitterly cold sky. Where could I go? Where could I sleep?

In desperation, I called on dear old Florrie. In her sixties, small, dark-skinned (pernicious anaemia and other problems), Florrie was dyeing her short white hair jet black, her wrinkled face covered with a million furrows, running with dye. She only possessed four long green teeth in her head—but I loved her, and still do, for her heart was kind and she thought the world of me.

'I can't go back home, Florrie,' I sighed, 'I wouldn't feel safe.'

'Shame on him,' she seethed through the gaps in her teeth. 'God never sleeps, and there's One above us all,' she warned vehemently. 'Stay here tonight, Stephen, in the spare bedroom. There aren't any sheets, but you can lie on the bed and I'll get some coats or something to keep you warm. If your mother was alive she'd turn in her grave.'

But I couldn't sleep, for in the next room Florrie was snoring like a steam train at full pelt; her shuddering whistles and wheezes shook the silent night and kept me awake for hours! Then just when I thought she'd had a nightmare and frightened herself into silence, off she'd go again: wheeze, rattle, whistle, snore . . . Finally, at 3 a.m., I slipped quietly from the house and walked 'home', still able to hear Florrie's grunts half-way up the hill.

Dad was fast asleep as I bravely sneaked into my own peaceful bed, grateful and undiscovered. When I told Florrie she snored like a trooper, she wouldn't have any of it.

'Never! Not me! Never in your life!' she said, quite affronted.

'It's all right for you,' I said, 'you can't hear it—you're asleep! If you got those teeth pulled we'd all have a bit of peace!' And we laughed together.

'You come down here any time you like, son. And don't let him bully you,' she said. 'Your mother was one of the best.' And I was grateful for the love she showed.

I think Dad and I passed through our stickiest patch just after Mam's death. Both of us were full of arguments, and these were my darkest hours. When I was out of work, confrontations were avoided by staying in bed until he left at midday for the pub. He assumed I was 'a lazy good-for-nothing'—which caused him to turn bright blue and rave at frequent intervals. 'Get up, boy! If *I've* got to work, *everybody* works!' Pulling the sheets over my head, I'd turn over quietly and pretend not to hear—difficult because he had a voice like a foghorn—and my silence got his goat. So next he issued bans. Though I contributed £16 a week for my 'keep', in those days quite a sum, I also did my own washing and cooking, and bought my own food on top. Yet still he screamed, 'I want you up at seven in the morning to make my breakfast!' I'm afraid I wasn't impressed or polite. I think I told him to 'Get lost!', then I ran for the hills.

But I lived to regret it. First he confiscated the small one-bar electric fire from my bedroom (where I now lived to keep out of his way). Then he banned me from taking showers because it 'burned electricity' and was 'too expensive'. (One shower a day cost less than two pence.) Then the washing machine was out-of-bounds. 'You're not burning money when you're not working,' was the gripe. This smacked of his own mother's meanness; she used to padlock the food cabinet to prevent her unemployed sons eating 'unpaid-for' food. So much for the sins of the fathers visited unto the next generations. But the final straw came when he shouted, 'If you're not in work by the end of the month, you're on the road—*homeless*! And I mean it, you'll be out!'

Devastated, I couldn't believe my ears. But he *did* mean it; his eyes were hard as flint. 'You'll be chucked out!' he repeated, shaking a stocky fist in my face, every syllable loaded with the threat.

At my wit's end, I trudged the town, pleading with three council officials who didn't give a damn about my problems (one of them couldn't even remember me from my first visit, two days previously). A deeply indifferent housing department didn't care where I'd lay my head at the end of the month either. So I visited a local Spiritualist church, but received no message from the Next Life. I sat in the front row and quietly cried like a baby during the stirring hymns. Silent tears rolled down my face and I sniffed and shook, while thinking of how I'd tried to help so many people, and this was my reward—homelessness.

But all my tears fell in vain, for despite the immense heartache, sleepless nights and walking the streets painstakingly trying to get another place (without result), at the very last minute Dad released his cruel threat. But it was withdrawn in deathly silence. Not a word passed from his lips; he never mentioned it again, not even to say he was sorry. How hurt I was.

But over the years we've now become much closer, understanding each other better when apart than we ever did when living under each other's noses. We're older, too, and that in itself helps. And to be fair to Dad, when I was in deep financial difficulties, my only brother, John, visited him and within a few days a substantial cheque arrived to ease the pressures. My mother, with practically her last breath, had made him promise to 'take care of Stephen'. But in earlier days we never saw eye-to-eye on anything. I still cringe when I think of that silly time we crossed swords not long after my mother's death—on the anniversary of her passing in fact.

'Go to the newspaper office, boy, and put a memory notice in for your mother.'

'But Dad, what's the point?'

'It's tradition, boy,' he returned with authority. 'People expect it of us, to show we've not forgotten.'

Not one bit concerned about what people thought of me, I argued back, 'But *we* know we've not forgotten.'

'Do as you're told!' he bellowed, and, even though I was 21, for the sake of peace and quiet I took his few shillings and sloped off to the newspaper offices, armed with bright ideas which eventually got me into more hot water.

Standing at the big desk, utterly ignored as usual, I thought, 'I've gone invisible again,' (something which always happens when I'm at a counter). When I suddenly became tangible, two bored assistants confronted me, one very big, the other painfully thin—but the strangest thing was, their voices matched their bodies. Miss Little twittered like a church mouse scampering over hot pipes, and Miss Large boomed like a foghorn over Swansea Bay. My notice was snatched away by Miss Large, whose plump eyes bowled across the lines with disdain. She then summoned Miss Little who squeaked disapproval, then they whispered in a huddle, after which Miss Large flumped back to the desk.

'We can't put this in,' she boomed.

'No, we can't,' echoed Miss Little.

Then the doors were thrown aside like they do in saloons in cowboy films, and in waltzed Madame Pink, the supervisor. In flouncy pink blouse, her brown hair set like a shiny football, and pink skirt swinging officially, Madame grasped the notice, skipped through the usual 'loved and sadly missed' bits, then waving the paper in my face, blurted out: 'Did *you* write this?'

'Yes. Is something wrong?'

'This part: "Loving thoughts *to* you". Have you some vague connection to the Spiritualists?' she said through tight-pursed lips.

'Yes, I have,' I replied firmly. 'What's the problem?'

This must have thrown her, for she lowered her curls, then flung the note at Little and Large, with an order to 'Print it!' Then she quickly glided out through the swing doors like the Duchess of Kent on a skateboard.

My father was far from pleased.

'Why did you put *that* in?' he grumped. 'Everyone at work's laughing at me. Your mother's *dead*, boy. How can you send thoughts to someone who's dead?!'

'Easy,' I said. 'You just do, and they'll receive them.'

But this was all too much for him, and his blood-pressure soared: 'That's the *last* time I'll ask *you* to do that!'

'Good!' I barked defiantly. 'I didn't want to do it anyway!' Then he muttered something nasty under his breath, stormed out, and I went to bed earlier than usual.

Snuggling into bed, I decided to get out the old photo albums. And there, in the glow of orange street lamps, I flicked through dozens of happy snapshots of bygone days, scores of wonderful memories: sunlit summer days of long ago; smiling faces; my mother holding in her arms the young grandchildren she'd worshipped; all our family's special moments recorded down the years.

I couldn't help an emotional tear when holding the very last picture of my mother, taken just before she grew too weak to stand, shortly after major cancer surgery. It was at my school's hundredth anniversary dinner and she was seated in a crowd of guests around refreshment tables; but her face was thin and drawn, her eyes glazed over with such a deep sadness. She was far, far away from the noise and celebrations, with the look of someone facing death, and knowing it. A cloud of sad memories enveloped me, as in the stillness something unusual was happening. I glanced behind me, fully expecting a voice to speak. *Someone* was watching . . .

Then, a gentle tapping sound came from the window pane. I swung round, but there was no one outside. Yet the tapping came again—at a different pace and rhythm, betraying an invisible intelligence—someone from the Beyond was present. But who?

Quietly naming out loud all the family who'd passed over, I drew no response until I mentioned my mother, Beatrice, when the window tapped once in agreement. A thrill of expectation quivered through me. I'd just been viewing images of her past, but now she was *here*, behind me. I could even smell her distinctive perfume. Excitedly I asked more questions:

'Are you happy, Mam?'

One tap for 'yes'.

'Were you looking at the album with me?'

One tap for 'yes'.

'Did you hear Dad and me talking about you earlier?'

One tap.

'Are you annoyed with us?'

Two taps for 'no'.

'So you're still close to the family?'

One tap for 'yes'.

And so it went on for over half-an-hour, my mother revealing many family 'secrets', things too personal to print here. And on occasions I also heard her soundless voice call to me through the mists, directing my line of thought. It was an incredible conversation with someone the world thought 'dead', filled with facts unknown to me which had to be checked. Needless to say, they all proved correct.

But my heart sank when eventually the tapping grew fainter, until it could barely be heard in the quietness of the night. Suddenly a flood of unanswered questions went racing through my mind.

'Please don't leave,' I said. There was a short pause, then one tap for 'yes'.

'Is your power weakening?'

A gentle, faint tap.

'Then before you go,' I whispered in low key, 'just know that I'm grateful you came; and I'm proud to be your son.'

I sensed her tears falling in the silence, just before one tap came, for 'yes'.

She then directed me to look at her well-thumbed autograph book, treasured by her when she was just 16 years old; it was nestling amongst old photographs. Opening it, my eyes fell upon some writing on the inside cover, lines she'd penned decades earlier, as a schoolgirl:

Beatrice Price is my name
Wales is my Nation
Tredegar is my dwelling-place
Christ is my salvation.
When I'm dead and in my grave
And all my bones are rotten,
Open this book and think of me
To show I'm not forgotten.

And in the dark bedroom I heard my mother's voice whispering through the mists: 'All my love to you, Stephen . . .'

I took a deep breath and sighed. 'And all my love to you, too, Mam.'

Then there was one more short pause, and one more faint tap at the window-pane, and she was gone . . .

Then I settled down snugly in my warm bed, wrapped in deep nostalgic thought, and gently drifted into the long and peaceful sleep of someone secure in the knowledge that there is no such thing as extinction: Love is Forever, Eternal, Everlasting and even Stronger than Death.

5

Flying High

One morning the telephone rang and Ulster TV was on the line: 'Will you come to Belfast and make a guest appearance and demonstrate your mediumship live on air in *The Gerry Kelly Show*?' This is Ireland's equivalent to America's *Johnny Carson* chat show.

I got quite excited, as I'd never been to Ireland before. 'I'm packing my bags!' I said.

UTV had booked an all-expenses-paid jet flight direct from London's Heathrow airport and reserved a luxurious suite for me in Belfast's lavish Europa Hotel. All the mod-cons were laid on: courteous room service, delicious five-course meals, unlimited telephone calls, even trouser-pressing and laundering! It was all so far removed from my own penniless existence and sounded so very swish, that I really looked forward to my appearance.

But on the day of the show I had a sudden shock! In the hazy morning light the telephone rang and it was my manager, Jeff, wanting to know if everything was all right. 'Of course it is,' I said, rubbing the sleep from my eyes. But when I glanced over my shoulder, my heart stopped beating and I gasped for air! The alarm clock had stopped (!) and I had less than 20 minutes to wash, dress, pack my bags, get a taxi, and speed to the railway station to connect with the *one* and *only* Belfast flight that day.

'For God's sake, Jeff,' I screeched down the receiver, at the same time as jumping out of bed and hopping about, struggling into my socks, 'Get me a taxi or I'll never make it!'

'Righto!' I heard, as I slammed the phone down and danced all over the rooms grabbing toiletries and clothes and shoving things into bags right, left and centre. The adrenalin rushed through my veins as I dashed around like a thing demented! I was absolutely exhausted and out of breath by the end of it, as I flew into the cab. I'm sure the driver thought I was going to scream 'Follow that car!'

I was totally breathless and panting, as red as a beetroot, and perspiration poured down my face like rain by the time I finally flung myself into British Rail like a mad dog with its tail on fire. I just managed to jump on the train, with my luggage knocking the carriage and jamming in the doors behind me, as it pulled out of the station towards London!

'What's the matter, love?' asked a very concerned elderly lady, perplexed by my colour and distress.

'Oh, man's trouble!' I wheezed, fit to collapse. She gave me such a funny look!

It took me ages to get my breath back, but there was plenty of time to do it on a pleasant coach trip into Heathrow from Reading station. I had never realized just how big the airport is; it was like a giant city in its own right: towering buildings, runways, lounges, restaurants, shops . . . It took over 40 minutes to reach the correct terminal for the flight. The vastness of it all overwhelmed me (I'm just a small-town boy). But I was even more surprised by the airport body-searches and security checks under the Prevention of Terrorism Act. An official shepherded a whole queue of us, one by one, behind security screens and searched our luggage: my suitcase was opened and meticulously rifled through—the officer even pushing his hands down inside my spare shoes. Then he seized my travel alarm clock and thrust it at me. 'Turn the hands around one hour!' he ordered. 'I must have one of those shifty-looking faces,' I thought. But before I could complete this task, meant to reveal hidden time-bombs, he'd snatched up my electric shaver: 'Open this and switch it on!'

I obeyed, noticing other men standing high above us on a raised gantry, scrutinizing every little twitch of our eyes as commands were given, looking for tell-tale signs of guilt. It was all most unpleasant, and I couldn't help thinking how embarrassing it must be for some shy passengers during these baggage checks. In my mind's eye I kept visualizing a rather short plump woman flushing crimson red as her vast winter bloomers were yanked into public gaze, rifled and hoisted aloft with the cry, 'This one's clean, Joe! She can go!' It's a good job all my briefs were neatly packed and bundled—some of them are nothing more than skimpy thongs!

After the predictable passenger-groaning delay we all trooped into the jet, and I must admit I was just a little conscious of a tiny inward prayer, the one that goes, 'Please God, no explosions over the sea, and I don't want to visit Mexico, thank you.' Well, you hear such strange stories about hi-jacks and terrorists on the news.

Soon the huge jet engines burst into piercing screams and suddenly I was thrust back against my seat as the plane sped powerfully along the runway then lifted from the earth like a giant rigid swan with its head towards the sky. But as we rose gracefully to heaven, I'm afraid I left my stomach on the tarmac! Then we juddered and shook through pockets of air turbulence and it felt as though I'd completely floated right out of my seat! One second I could feel the plane underneath me, and the next it had gone! It was most peculiar! My insides fluttered like a trapped butterfly and my breakfast nearly reappeared. I'd never experienced this weightlessness before, except fleetingly on fast roller-coasters at fairgrounds when you're just about to drop screaming to your death hundreds of feet below!

All of a sudden, my ears popped and clicked, quietened down, then popped again (!) as we climbed to 37,000 feet. Through the tiny window everything looked so small and insignificant in the early morning sun, but the smooth Irish accents of the attractive air hostesses eased tensions with, 'Can I get you a snack, sir? Tea, or some real Irish coffee?'

But the most breathtaking sight was when we sailed up through silver clouds and into a brilliantly clear electric blue sky. I looked out over the wings, and as the green fields got further away and the milky clouds got nearer, suddenly we were travelling through the morning mists, and then—my eyes opened wide to such an incredibly beautiful sight. In the crisp bright air, way out to the distant horizon, there was nothing but hundreds of miles of undulating white cotton-wool clouds, carpeting the vast heavens beneath us. They looked so solid, so tangible, almost as if you could step outside and walk on their glimmering fleeces; but another part of my mind kept wickedly reminding me that underneath them was far too much open space for my liking, miles of nothingness leading down to Davey Jones' Locker—the Irish Sea.

But the most frightening part of the trip was that dreadful tannoy announcement which crackled out menacingly: 'If there's a Mr Jackson aboard, will he please make himself known?'

There was utter silence . . .not a soul moved. A vulture's claw of panic suddenly gripped my throat, 'Oh my God, he's got a bomb,' I thought. 'We'll be blown to smithereens!' But of course, we were all quite safe—Mr Jackson was only a diabetic with special food requirements!

Soon the flight was over and we made our speedy descent through rainy grey cloud banks into Belfast International Airport, the whole jet shuddering again, its great shivering wings resisting the 120 mph head wind. For several minutes I went completely deaf; all my catarrh shot down into my ears and jammed there, whistling away merrily. Passengers glared across at me, wondering why my fingers had disappeared into my head, so I just chuckled inanely, and put my hands back onto my lap.

After dashing through customs as quickly as possible, where my baggage was once again rifled and X-rayed, next thing I knew, I was met by a chauffeur from the TV station carrying a card with *Stephen O'Brien—The Kelly Show* written on it, and we were soon speeding towards the luxurious Europa Hotel.

But I was completely unprepared for the devastating sights ahead. It all started with a huge green army helicopter blatantly keeping us under surveillance, closely hovering above the car as though we were spies. It followed us through plush green countryside for a few miles, and then—on into troubled Belfast . . .

I sat stunned and silent, hand over mouth in disbelief, as we did a round trip through the trouble-spots. I was horrified to see so many burnt-out businesses, blackened charred shells, destroyed because 'they failed to pay their protection money'. There were smashed and looted shops, and sharp barbed-wire on many buildings and traffic lights, defying terrorist attacks. Some of the streets were cordoned off by large guarded gates, reminding me of gruesome scenes from Orwell's *1984*. There was no trust in the air. But more shocking sights were to follow.

I saw British soldiers swaggering down the roads with automatic rifles primed and at the ready. They moved furtively through crowds of shoppers, their narrowed eyes taking in each street-corner whisper, any unusual movement, even every small child's progress along the street . . . It was a sickening experience, witnessing instruments of war paraded in public like that. Worse still, I was in no doubt that their bullets would have been fired if necessary. It left a warped and twisted impression in my mind, hard to remove—even now. And there was such a dreadful air of hatred between the soldiers and civilians; being psychic certainly has its price to pay.

I eventually broke my silence and said to the driver, 'It's all so sad. Why can't people live together in peace, despite their differences?'

'One of our staff was killed on this street last year,' he said. 'He didn't have a chance. The police were shooting at terrorists and caught him in the crossfire. His young girl passenger escaped, but she went into a mental hospital because she'd seen a man's skull blown apart in front of her eyes.'

I was stunned into horrified dumbness . . . I just couldn't visualize or comprehend the torment she must have gone through. It was such a shattering thought, such a wicked and senseless act. 'What on earth has happened to charity?' I finally said. Then we drove up the Falls Road and down the Shanklin Road—two of the hottest gang-warfare streets in Belfast. The psychic feelings there were terrible: oppressively heavy, with trembling fear hanging thickly in the atmosphere. Just witnessing the burnt-out shops made my mouth go dry.

'Young kids killed rival leaders here recently by dropping concrete slabs onto their heads from 30 feet up,' lamented my driver, and I groaned with him in the spirit, unable to understand the cruel minds which could do that to another living being. The thought of all the dreadful carnage, and the loss of so many innocent young lives, sickened me to my stomach. I could feel my insides churning. But then I'm a pacifist, and always have been.

'I could tell you some awful things about some of the "animals" living around here,' he said, 'for that's what they are. They don't deserve to be called human beings.' And he did relate several unspeakable horrific acts he'd witnessed, far too upsetting, blood-curdling and macabre to reproduce here. I wouldn't want them printed, for fear they'd cause innocent minds nightmares—or give wicked minds ideas.

As I gazed at the passing streets, all at once a searing sadness swept over my mind when I again realized this world of ours has a long long way to go before 'The Kingdom of Heaven' is enthroned on Earth, as preached by the One many religious groups claim as Leader, even in Ireland.

'Is it as dangerous here as we're led to believe on TV?' I asked.

'That depends on where you go. Don't walk the streets at night on your own.'

'Don't worry,' I said. 'I won't.'

We shortly arrived at the impressive hotel, where I was treated like visiting royalty.

'Let me carry your bags, Mr O'Brien.'

'I'll hold the door for you, Mr O'Brien.'

'If there's anything you need just ring and we'll send someone up immediately.'

'Please, don't fuss,' I said, being polite, 'I'm nothing "special". I've just left a council flat with a huge pile of dirty dishes in the sink!' Things lightened up a bit after that; the 'Mr O'Briens' ceased, but the star treatment went on. In the end, my shirt and trousers were whisked away along with my boots, and all returned an hour later, spick and span and with needle-sharp seams pressed into them. 'Can't have you looking like a rag-doll on *Kelly* tonight, can we?' laughed the attractive chambermaid.

'No,' I said, 'I suppose we can't!'

Everyone at the hotel was so posh, when I went downstairs they'd all dressed for dinner. I hoped I didn't look too out of place sporting my best black jacket and trousers, white shirt and red tie. (The whole outfit cost no more than £25, bought or donated from friends and colleagues.) I must have been 'passable', for the head waiter escorting me to my reserved table commented on 'how smart' Sir looked.

Dinner was lavish, but I'm afraid I felt too guilty to order such exquisite delights, and, being a vegan, settled for an avocado salad.

'The chef will make it *specially* for you, sir!'

I was embarrassed. 'Please don't put him to any trouble—'

'Nonsense! You shall have avocado salad with sliced mangoes and passion fruits, fresh greens and a special dressing!' and out he flounced with a triumphant swish of his coat. I'm not used to people waiting on me hand and foot—I feel like shooting out of my seat, seizing the cutlery, sitting the staff down and serving *them* instead!

In one corner of the restaurant a pianist and small ensemble were ensconced among plush green palms, and during my delicious special salad I was asked if I had any special requests.

'Why yes,' I said, 'do they know *Memory* from the musical *Cats*?'

'Indeed, I am certain they do, sir!' and off he went again in a little flurry of crumbs as he whisked away the bread basket. *Memory* was duly played while I ate like a king! But I felt such dreadful pangs of guilt as the sumptuous food was delivered and I was plied with further delicacies from the sweet trolley. I couldn't help it: I just kept thinking of the millions of starving children all over the world—I always do whenever such opulence is flaunted in my face. Then when I saw the bill, my heart sank at the amount, and it seemed so odd not having to pay.

'Courtesy of Ulster Television,' the pleasant head waiter said. 'Don't worry, sir, they will settle everything.'

I skulked out of the restaurant like a heretic released from stake-burning on a divine pardon, with waiters fussing around me, shaking my hands, and off I trotted for a quick freshen-up before my TV appearance.

When I reached the studios in another hired car, most of *The Kelly Show* guests had already arrived. I was ushered past a lively queuing audience and into a pleasant green-room to share some orange juice with the unusually-named new Australian film star, Yahoo Serious (!), there to promote his international box-office hit movie *Young Einstein*. He had such a great mop of reddish hair—but was thoroughly fascinated by my work. 'You're *amazing*, Stephen!' he said. 'Enough to blow my mind!'

I also chatted with famous British comedian Gorden Kaye, who plays French wartime cafe-owner René in the world-acclaimed BBC TV comedy series *'Allo 'Allo*. Gorden was charming and witty, and also held a firm belief in 'things unexplained', as he put it. When he spoke, I half-expected that famous mock-French accent to come out, but instead he was quite cultured. 'I once had such a devastatingly accurate prediction given to me by a clairvoyant, Stephen, it quite unnerved me!'

He and actress Madge Hindle, who for many years played Renée Roberts in Granada TV's famous *Coronation Street* soap opera series, were both charming people. Madge later told the millions watching that she'd been brought up in a Spiritualist home. There was a moment's silence. 'I bet that surprised you all, didn't it?' she said to the cameras. And, of course, it did!

After make-up had covered a multitude of sins, the show's host, cheery Gerry Kelly, wanted to know why I was named 'O'Brien' when I came from Wales.

'Well, my great-grandmother was called Elizabeth O'Brien,' I said, 'and in the late 1800s she came across from County Wexford in southern Ireland and took a job as a domestic in Swansea, South Wales. She was penniless.

'She fell in love with a publican called Billy the Boy, and had an illegitimate child, my grandfather. But she had to give her son away to the people she lodged with, Ned and Liza Quirk, because she found out she was dying of TB. Her only possession in the world was a small bureau she'd brought across with her, and this was her gift to the couple who raised her baby, William, my grandfather.'

'What happened to her?' asked Gerry.

'Poor Elizabeth died alone in the Union Workhouse, aged 26, and was buried in an unmarked pauper's grave,' I said. 'I did find Ned and Liza's resting place though, and planted blue forget-me-nots on it, just to say "thank you" for taking care of my grandad. But when I visited the grave again, the flowers hadn't bloomed.'

Gerry was very sympathetic. 'It's a pity we don't have time for that on the air,' he said, rising and dusting the make-up powder from his jacket. 'Well, we'd better make our way.'

Down on the studio floor, technicians quickly wired me for sound with my own radio-pack tucked neatly into my jacket pocket, and wires and aerials stuffed down my shirt front and into my trousers. I felt so silly, for after all that palaver I suddenly had an overwhelming urge to visit the bathroom! They grudgingly shuffled me out and pointed me down the right corridor.

'Oh, but wait a minute,' I said, 'I'm wired for sound. Can you switch me off, please?'

'Sorry, but you're plugged in now, Stephen,' smiled the cheery technician.

'But I want to go to the loo,' I complained, embarrassed. 'You'll hear everything!'

'Well, that's how it goes! Don't worry, we've heard it all before!' he cheekily replied.

So off I skulked, wondering how to disconnect my radio-pack. Then a thought struck me: pull out the trailing wire aerial. That should do it. But as I bent forward in the tiny cubicle, the whole pack suddenly lurched out of my jacket and I made a slippery grab at it but missed, and the electronics crashed to the floor with a resounding *bang*! I did feel stupid, and prayed to God that no one in the control room heard what I'd said! But at least the aerial had disconnected itself. Needless to say, I appreciated the privacy!

Shame-faced, I returned to the technician, proffering the ruins like Oliver holding out his begging bowl, half afraid to ask for more. My apologies were so profuse, they immediately gave me a new powerpack, seconds before Gerry Kelly announced: 'Ladies and gentlemen, would you please welcome the UK's top mystical figure, Stephen O'Brien!' And they did.

After a bright, successful and lengthy interview, during which I also answered a live telephone caller, Gerry openly asked outright, 'Is there anything fraudulent about what you do?'

'No,' I replied, 'nothing.'

'Well, Stephen, you'll have a chance to prove yourself later with our studio audience.'

I then left the set to make way for Gorden Kaye, Madge Hindle and Yahoo Serious, and later returned to make my spirit link. But first, Gerry warned the audience, 'Now you all know what Stephen's going to do. If there's anyone who wants to leave, please go now.'

No one moved. What on earth did they think would happen? My mediumship is all so natural, it's never frightened anyone before. But Ireland is a deeply orthodox country, so I understood the caution. I immediately began to tune in, hand to my forehead, deep in concentration.

'Please claim the connection if you understand it,' I said, 'or the whole link vanishes.' Then I felt a presence and heard a faint voice. 'Step forward, son,' I said to the apprehensive spirit lad trying to make contact. 'I have a young man here, about 16 or 17, and he passed very quickly and tragically to the spirit world. I feel he was thrown—catapulted over a bike.'

A nervous young lady in the front row raised her hand. The audience was silent and stunned. They hadn't a clue what to expect next.

'Someone's been lighting candles for him and praying in the Catholic church.'

'Yes.'

'And I get the name of Tom,' and the young woman's face lit up as her wide-open eyes glanced towards her friends nearby.

The lad went on to mention links with 'Anderson's town' and that his mother was to be told he was still alive and not to cry for him anymore. He sent so much love to his family, I felt my heart go out to the young woman accepting his link. But he kept giving me this sensation of being catapulted into eternity. I got some other details which couldn't be placed, so I advised they be researched. The whole connection was difficult to maintain, because of studio pressures and the emotion involved, but nevertheless I felt he was successful under the circumstances. The recipient was crying, and the audience applauded as I left, as Gerry asked her, 'Have you ever met that guy, ever before in your life?'

'No.'

'And was all that he said true?'

'Yes.'

It turned out my communicator was her young brother, who'd been killed seven years previously. He'd been blown up while on his motorbike. Thoughtful Gerry presented a large bouquet of flowers to the pretty young woman, who was obviously touched and a little shaken by the link. Audiences at my public meetings know what to expect, but she hadn't bargained for a message from the Other Side when she came to *The Kelly Show* that night, so it was quite understandable.

In the green-room afterwards, many people gathered around me, firing questions and showing deep interest in what I'd done. One man hailed it as 'amazing' and said he was 'gob-smacked'. I think that was a compliment!

Then, at the end of the evening, when I said goodbye to Gorden Kaye, all at once I had an overwhelming psychic feeling of impending danger: a powerful impact was crashing down right into me. I didn't want to worry Gorden with this, so I simply said,

'Drive safely, Gorden. Mind how you go, won't you?'

(Months later, he had a freak accident in London while driving his car through abnormally high winds. Billboard hoardings were ripped away and some wood smashed through his windscreen and into his head. He was on the critical list, in intensive care with severe injuries, while many of us prayed for him. And, thank God, he got well again.)

Leaving the Ulster studios, a flustered receptionist jokingly shook his fist at me, 'I've been on this damn phone for the last 40 minutes because of you, Stephen O'Brien! The switchboard's been jammed with calls from all over Ireland! You'd better give your tour dates to the researchers!' And with that, another set of flashing lights hurled him into furious activity, as I slipped out into the cold night, smiling.

At breakfast next morning, a stunning young waitress in the hotel restaurant recognized me and conducted several delightful chats. It was quite funny really. She kept passing my table, clearing things away, disappearing into the kitchens, then popping back to sweep invisible crumbs from the floor, whispering things like: 'So they *do* have bodies Over There then, and memories?' She was delighted that they did. But I soon discovered a more serious side: her 16 year-old boyfriend had been recently shot and killed in a sectarian murder, and she desperately needed to know if he'd survived his horrific death.

'Of course he has,' I assured her. 'It doesn't matter how we pass over, there's life for everyone beyond this world. Neither does it matter what religion we hold. We all belong to God.' She was so pleased, and deeply thankful that the 'Father in Heaven' she so fervently believed in showed mercy to all His children, irrespective of their creed.

'I'd kiss you if I could,' she grinned, pretending to clatter plates about, 'but I'm on duty!' So we passed that by, and instead both laughed at that morning's *Irish News* which had featured both me and film star Julie Andrews. 'Oow, look!' she wriggled, 'they've given you a much larger photograph and more coverage! Oow, you must be really famous! But if you don't mind my saying so, that mug-shot doesn't do you justice—you're much nicer-looking in the flesh!' Then against all the rules, she pecked my cheek, and even threw me a regal wave as I left for my taxi.

At the airport I was spotted several times—first by other passengers who nearly bored a hole right through my head with their curious staring. I overheard quiet whispers with the name 'O'Brien' interspersed amongst them, so I crept silently away and over to the baggage checks, only to find the red-carpet treatment continued at the customs desk.

'Oh, *you* can pass along with no bother, sir!' said the beaming official, without so much as inspecting my cases. 'Saw you on *Kelly* last night—great show!' And he gave me a wide-eyed smile and tipped his hat as I sheepishly moved through the barriers, wishing I was invisible, while other travellers swivelled on their heels and stood gawping, open-mouthed.

Then onto the jet I went, happily humming *Danny Boy* to myself. And for most of the sunny flight back home I relived the last two days. It had been a lovely time.

But, for me, the most important part of the whole trip occurred on the morning I'd left, when I plucked a single pink rose and knelt on Irish soil. The sun was misty and the earth damp. I looked into the quiet sky, and pondered on the thought that the great majority of Irish people were so good and kind, especially to me on my first visit, and that in these lay the hope of better times for tomorrow's Irish children.

Then, planting the flower in the green grass, I closed my eyes and gently whispered some thoughts within my mind:

> *Great Spirit, hear my prayer.*
> *As this perfect flower dies,*
> *So may its beauty touch the earth,*
> *And,*
> *In the touching,*
> *May Peace be born,*
> *Then flourish within this troubled land.*

6

Marilyn Monroe,
Sir Laurence Olivier and
Earl Mountbatten

The room was dark as we four friends gathered for a special séance which the Other Side requested we hold.

Quite by chance (?) one of our regular sitters at the psychic circle had suddenly said over Sunday lunch, 'I feel very inspired we should sit for the spirit people tonight.' We speedily agreed and arranged for the séance to be taped, each feeling some hidden reason would be revealed. And so the plan was set.

But at 8 o'clock, as we entered the dimly-lit séance room, instead of feeling excited I felt rather sleepy. My spirit guide, White Owl, was near, so I allowed his warm relaxation to overtake and free my mind, and I sensed him draw closer. That's when I lost touch with my surroundings, and White Owl's strong voice, deeper than my own, spoke among us.

White Owl:

Be still, and we can come near. Our world is very close to yours; it interpenetrates the Earth. We know your thoughts, aspirations and your innermost desires.

We bring you greetings from a world of eternal light which is blending with your lives, and is intricately woven into the very fabric of your being.

We bring good news for your world: where two or three are gathered in the name of Love, there shall we be in the midst. Through this power of your love we manifest in your plane of thought. Our untiring concern for the people of Earth brings us close to its grey, dark and often selfish sphere of life.

long pause

There will be great tribulation, great trials and also bloodshed in the years to come, in the East of your world, as people strive for freedom of expression. We are watching with interest.

Every birth comes through the pains of labour.

pause

Man has polluted his planet so much, now he begins to pay the price with many flash floods, hurricanes and disturbing weather-patterns right across the Earth.

He has poisoned and neglected the Great Mother. Her waters are polluted, her atmosphere full of harmful rays and gases. She must be cleansed and respected by those who dwell upon her. And until this time, she will react adversely against man's foolishness, to his detriment.

long pause, as though gathering strength, power

Now we wish to bring forward from my side of life a man whose name is not unknown to you. He, like many millions of souls before him, has discovered what Jesus spoke of as 'The Kingdom of Heaven'. He is a man of deep sensitivity with great heart and unbounding kindness. He is a man used to the public gaze, and his message, we think, is of vital importance to mankind.

Please be patient while he endeavours to speak, for what will happen is *my* mind and *his* mind, and my medium's mind, these three will blend in order to transmit. He will not be able to reproduce his voice exactly as known when among you, but his thoughts will be expressed clearly.

addressing the writers present

You may rest your hands and switch off the tape-machine until his blending is complete, at which time we can start again.

After a long pause, a faint voice speaks. It is Sir Laurence Olivier:

. . . Very hard . . . very hard . . . to . . . difficult, difficult to speak . . . clearly . . . very hard . . .

I was glad to die; not that I didn't love my people, because I did.

voice continues slowly, haltingly, right the way through

I'm not . . . I'm not inside this body . . . I'm close by it, trying to use it like a typewriter—it's very hard work. I never thought I'd do it, but I've done it . . . I never thought I'd speak, but I'm speaking. You'll never guess who I am.

I want my wife to know that I've survived. I made a promise once to her that if life continued beyond the cold grave, I'd be back to say so, *and I'm back*. My wife is Joan . . .

pause

in jocular mood: A horse, a horse, a kingdom for a horse (sic).

My speech is difficult. I was a grand old man. I can't blend my mind sufficiently to hold the communication, but if I could just say, of all the roles I played, of all the parts I undertook, this is the greatest role of all. When I died I made the most spectacular entrance of my whole career. I entered an eternal world, and fell into the arms of my former wife, my dear, dear Vivien. She's beautiful; she's taking care of me. And I want Joan to know that I will meet her when God calls her name to join me here. I want Joan to know I'm near, and I love her very much. I'm not dead, I'm *alive*, and I'm finished with make-believe, and I've just begun to live.

Vivien is taking care of me. She's so kind. She didn't mean to die, it wasn't a suicide—it was a mistake.

Tell Joan, Joan Plowright, my darling wife, there's nothing to fear: there's light, not darkness. She'll understand.

I slipped away so quietly. I'm so happy where I am. My love to the children. Don't move away. Tell her not to move away. How we would sit on the lawns and watch the sun go down. I know now that Vivien sat with us. Oh, and tell her not to worry about the finances, it'll be all right; it'll be cleared soon. She means more to me than anyone else alive.

I've been very busy speaking . . .

voice trails away almost to an inaudible whisper

Farewell . . . (?)

A long pause followed, then White Owl spoke again.
White Owl:

I'm afraid he cannot hold his contact. He is crying for those he loves. He speaks of a reunion between many friends, many people on our side of life. There has been a great party.

He wants his friends to know his love is with them, and he thanks them for the great honours and love they have bestowed upon him. There are no titles in our world, but he stands beside friends who were known in your world through their service to millions. Their names will be familiar to you. He has mentioned Vivien Leigh, he has spoken with Tyrone Power, he has met Marilyn Monroe.

He is saying that his wife, whom he dearly loves, is grieving still. She sorely misses his presence; she kisses his photograph by her bedside, and he wants her to know that her feelings and sensations of his presence are true.

'I want to pass through to you,' he says, 'the greatest news, the biggest Universal Contract I've ever signed, and the name of the picture is *Sir Laurence Lives*, not as a ghost but as a complete man.' He says, 'My legs are strong, my body is young again, my wrinkles have forsaken me. My time is endless. There are five major biographies accepted and in the writing now concerning me. Be kind to me. Tread softly . . . for you tread upon my dreams.'

Silence followed: the séance was over.

Sir Laurence sent us all off to the library to find out more about Vivien Leigh's passing. We discovered that she'd died of TB— but there had been some doubt about her intentions. One of her closest colleagues said of her, 'She didn't try to get well.' Another report told of Vivien speaking through a medium and saying she was very upset because she didn't want people to think she'd committed suicide. But without doubt, many close to her had reported she consistently failed to regularly take her medication, and continued 'smoking, drinking and entertaining, instead of resting'.

It was all very intriguing, but unless Sir Laurence returns to explain himself further, we won't know what he meant. One circle member thought there may have been some untrue publicity and lies about her passing created by certain gutter-press journalists after she died. If that's so, then Sir Laurence's statements do make sense.

Not long after that communication another startling link came from someone Sir Laurence mentioned, the late screen goddess Marilyn Monroe. I assume they must have talked together about me on the Other Side, and Marilyn saw the chance to communicate her sensible, controversial thoughts to our world. However they planned it, it was a complete surprise. And yet, some friends told me afterwards that she and Sir Laurence had worked together in a film called *The Prince and the Showgirl*, something I didn't know.

Marilyn's presence drew near on a train, of all places. Her voice broke into my consciousness in an idle moment. I recognized it immediately, though her speech quality was strangely metallic, like the crackling sound-track of an old movie, which—thinking back—makes complete sense now. But she displayed a radiant spiritual quality in her words and feelings. I scrambled in my pockets for a pen and wrote down exactly what I heard.

Marilyn—or should I say 'Norma Jean', for that's how she referred to herself during the link—had some tough uncompromising criticism of everyone currently making money from her celebrity status. She was, and still is, very conscious of the publicity value of her exquisite features, form and timeless sensual presence on multifarious items world-wide; from T-shirts and record sleeves to billhoardings and millions of picture postcards.

Marilyn was very unhappy about the way she's been treated since her 'mysterious' death on 4 August 1962, officially from 'an overdose of barbiturates'. The screen idol has different ideas about her passing.

Marilyn Monroe:

This is Norma Jean—Marilyn—here. It's been such a long time since I had the chance to send a message to Earth. I guess people still remember me so much. I keep getting many thoughts and, well, almost star-worship wishes from people down there I never even met.

I suppose you're wondering why I'm getting in touch? Well, I've got something to say. I want to set a few things straight about me and my life. So many people and writers paint me as tragic. Well I wasn't. How can they know these things? The answer is, they can't.

They know what makes a good story though, and far too many of them used me for that.

So many lies have been told about me . . . so many. Well I'm gonna tell a few truths now. First, I was a happy person—a little lonely on times, perhaps, but then how else can a person feel when everybody in the world wants a little piece of them? I never had a moment's peace from the media. They hounded me to death. Oh, and that's another sore point—my death.

It's been kinda veiled in mystery for a few years, hasn't it? *(chuckling)* Well, I don't much care now about it. It's gone, and it's the best thing that ever happened to me. This place is so much better than life was in America. But I wish people would stop saying I committed suicide, 'cos I did no such thing. I didn't take my own life, and that's all I'm prepared to say—nothing more. That's all over now.

Second, I'm kinda glad, very happy that my pictures still give people a great deal of pleasure. That's why I did them. I really tried hard to be a good actress—a darned good one, not just another name and another glamorous face flickering on the silver screen. And, if it's OK for me to say it, I think I made my point. *The Misfits* and *Bus-Stop* were my two greatest roles, and they give me a sense of deep pride and accomplishment when I think of them now.

There's something I want to ask of you. I want to say something to the media. I want my memory to generate money for children— kids down the block with no shoes on their feet, and others in the hot countries who don't have any hope, any food, or any love from anyone. It kinda grieves me that a lotta money is made out of my face and name, and though some of it does go to good causes, not all of it does, *and I want it to*. I know what it is to be unloved, without anyone to care for you; and if any money's being made, then it should go where I want it to. After all, it's *my* face, *my* figure, and *my* pictures that get the stuff in.

I wanted to say that. Tell everyone you can, and get it done. Can you do that for me?

(I said 'Yes.')

Good for us.

Oh, and there's just one more thing I'd like to say. I've found out a good deal since I came over here, and the best message I can give to everyone there on Earth is this: Be kind to each other. There isn't enough of that about. Be kind, and look after the hungry, the poor, the needy, the lonely and the grieving.

My life here is just great. I'm having a wonderful time, but I won't be far away from you, Stephen; I'll come and talk with you again.

Hold a good thought for me . . .

Marilyn blew two kisses to me, and she left.

I've kept Marilyn's words for over a year. This is the first time they've been publicly released on her behalf, fulfilling my promise to her.

Another controversial message came from Earl Mountbatten of Burma, for Prince Philip. Lord Louis had been killed in a terrorist bomb attack on his boat in Sligo, Ireland, while holidaying in August 1979.

Mountbatten spoke just before the funeral of Emperor Hirohito of Japan. Prince Philip was to represent Britain at the ceremony, but Mountbatten tried to persuade him otherwise.

Many servicemen were cruelly tortured or killed by the Japanese during captivity, and most survivors believed Hirohito was directly responsible for their suffering. They couldn't forget—nor seemingly forgive—his 'war crimes' and 'atrocities'. From the world of spirit, Mountbatten shared these intense feelings, and he wanted them heard.

As in all links involving well-known public figures, I'm ever loathe to publish. But in this case, because of his words in the text, I believe the time is now right for thousands of disgruntled servicemen to know Mountbatten's feelings on the issue. His statements also carry irrefutable evidence that he was closely in touch with the grass-root feelings of former British soldiers, now old-age pensioners, who eventually took to protesting, demonstrating and marching in streets all over the land against any representation at Hirohito's funeral. One pensioner even went on a hunger-strike to the death in protest: something which eventually drew a personal plea to end it from Her Majesty Queen Elizabeth.

As instructed by Mountbatten, I sent his words to Buckingham Palace.

Earl Mountbatten:

My dear Philip,

As the Family is aware, I am still conscious of the dealings and daily business of 'the business', and feel duty-bound to use any means at my disposal to reach you presently with my thoughts on a matter of international importance. I know your mind well, and it is strong and self-governed as mine is, but on this issue I cannot remain silent and have taken this opportunity to once again make my thoughts heard.

On the grave issue of the funeral of the Emperor Hirohito, I must say that I can fully appreciate the concern in the family as to its status in the public mind, yet I have tried my very best to communicate to Charles that for one of our family to attend this man's funeral would not be in the interests of the monarchy. While it is good and right and proper for us to be represented, I feel honour-bound to state—after much soul-searching—that I would not have gone, and would have preferred some lesser official to take my place.

International relations are, of course, of vital importance to the nation and its image, but I would have had before me all the horrific faces of the tortured and maimed that were given a dreadful termination to their earthly lives under this man's iron rule.

My love for you all is evident in my almost daily presence around you, but forgive me for my outspokenness on this issue; yet, do please, I beg you, think once more. It is never too late to send a substitute. I always maintained that, and still do now.

I have been anxious to communicate many things to you all, but have resisted the urge many times, believing that I should firmly stay in my place, in my world. But having suffered through the hands of terrorists myself, I cannot condone the support of similar acts. I cannot write too personally here, because it is my full intention, without any malice aforethought, to make known my plea; for the sake of those who died, for the sake of the grieving families hurt by any British representation at Hirohito's last journey, for the sake of standing up for one's viewpoint so that one's honour can be maintained, even from my world.

I have indeed spoken with Hirohito himself, and he still will not renounce his cruelty, believing—as he always did—that it was done to preserve a great and noble family line's status. Perhaps his viewpoint will change, Philip. Time alters one's mind so frequently, don't you agree?

I will end by thanking the man through whom I am able to communicate, and sending my dearest love and fondest best wishes to everyone 'at home'.

Your friend and adviser,
Louis

However, Prince Philip did go, but I think the public and media agreed with Mountbatten: it might have been better to have stayed away, for the rumblings amongst old soldiers continued for months afterwards. One ex-prisoner of war said, 'I don't think we'll ever forgive him.'

Feature articles about me have been published in different countries and languages around the world, and media attention has brought so many interviews I can barely recall them all, but the one for Britain's popular tabloid *The Daily Star* sticks in my mind. I'd just completed two days filming in London for two programmes in a paranormal series called *Stories in the Night*, which Thames TV was networking. Thames invited me to a press conference for private screenings with journalists. After sitting through the shows groaning (terrible to watch yourself on TV!), I met charming *Star* reporter, Liz Phillips. Petite and attractive, with a sparkly personality, dark-haired Liz viewed the programmes with interest and afterwards invited me to lunch in a French restaurant near the studios.

Liz was very interested, scribbling away furiously in her notebook, between mouthfuls of oysters. Two hours later it was all over. 'I'll ring you in Wales,' she smiled, as we parted company on a windswept London road.

Her phone call soon arrived: 'Stephen, the editor's giving you a double-page spread with photographs, but can I attend one of your psychic circles?'

'I haven't done them for years, Liz. I'm too busy touring these days.'

'Well, could you find the time for us?'

'All right,' I said, and immediately telephoned my friend, Clare, who runs a happy guest-house. 'I'm on the beg again, Clare!' I chirped, and when I explained, she kindly agreed to hold the meeting in her spacious lounge. 'I'm not bothered how you assemble the group,' I said. 'In fact, the less I know about it, the better.'

'Leave everything to me!'

And I did, which is just as well, because I was busy with a *Star* photographer. They sent him all the way from London just to take pictures for the feature. We trundled off to the Grand Theatre, which he *hired* there and then, on the spot! 'I want a smoke-machine,' he said, as though asking for a bag of sweets, 'and the full use of the stage and auditorium. Send the bill to London!' I was flabbergasted by the opulence. The administrator obliged, but made him promise not to mention the theatre, 'or we'll be inundated with calls asking about Stephen's next appearance!'

Within minutes, I was emerging out of smoky grey clouds, hands raised, as if I'd just landed from a UFO! But after all that trouble and expense, those pictures were never used! 'That's nothing,' said the photographer. 'Last year I spent three days in a village called Christmas, hired half the population in fancy-dress costumes and did shots of the entire *Twelve Days of Christmas*—even down to the lords-a-leaping and maids-a-milking. We really went over the top. In the end it cost us £2,000 and we never used a frame of it. Come to that, we didn't even run the story!'

On circle day, I met Liz at the railway station. With her was a mystery guest from London, Rose, a vivacious young blonde woman with a delightful personality. We arrived at Clare's guest-house, met the six circle members, and the test got underway. Successful from the start, the first link came from an elderly woman to a sitter called Susan.

'I looked after her,' she said.

'Well, she thanks you for your patience because she wasn't the easiest of people!'

'You're absolutely right!'

Then the old spirit lady pointed across to another sitter, Carol, at the opposite end of the room.

'She knows you, too,' I said, 'and asks if you remember the oven exploding?'

Recognition was instantaneous. 'Oh my Gawd! Yes I do!' laughed Carol, in her thick Lancashire accent. 'That woman was cared for by Susan, then I took over. So you see, she *does* know the two of us! And one night the stove overheated and caught fire!' Everyone in the room laughed. 'And you're quite right, she were a right old misery sometimes!' chuckled Carol wryly. 'But we all loved her for it.'

'Well, she's remembering you with smiles.'

Then I got a contact for our mystery guest, Rose, the attractive young stranger from London. It was her grandmother, who said she 'knew her when she was tiny', and spoke about a special shawl she used to wear, describing its pattern. Rose nodded in acceptance. Grandma then gave a warning about legal documents, saying, 'You're about to sign a partnership agreement which makes you and a gentleman liable for each other's debts in law, if the new business venture fails.'

'Yes,' said Rose, eyes widening in perfect understanding. Then she craned her neck forward, eager for more news.

'Well your grandmother's giving advice: "Think twice! It's a big step, and he might not be the right man for the deal." '

Rose was visibly impressed, and while Liz scribbled everything down, I went on, 'I can say two things about your grandmother's passing: it was sudden and peaceful.'

The young stranger agreed wholeheartedly. 'That's spot on. She died of a heart-attack in her sleep.'

'And Tom met her, and they walked off together into the light.'

'That's my grandfather!' said Rose, touched by the message.

The whole séance was pronounced 'remarkable' and 'amazing', and within days millions of *Daily Star* readers saw, if I might say so, an enchanting picture of my eyes with the caption underneath, 'These eyes can see Beyond the grave', plus a huge two page centre-spread feature with pictures, headlined '*The Star*

Puts Britain's Brightest Young Medium to the Test':

> Clairvoyant Stephen O'Brien is the man who has taken the crown from queen of the psychics, the late Doris Stokes.
>
> Stephen is different from most people you are ever likely to meet. Power seems to radiate from his fingertips. And when he speaks in his soft Welsh accent his followers hang on his every word.
>
> I saw an amazing example of his ability when I went along to a quiet terraced house in his home town of Swansea.
>
> It was the most ordinary of settings, but it was one of the most extraordinary afternoons I have ever spent. The atmosphere was one of a cosy tea-party until Stephen closed his eyes and muttered, almost to himself, 'Let's see what's here. I'll take what comes.'
>
> An elderly woman appeared to him, whom he felt was Rose's grandmother. He passed on messages about sorting out her jewellery box and that she must sort out her life too.
>
> Stephen mentioned a legal agreement Rose was due to sign, and pinpointed the cause and manner of her granny's death. He accurately described her clothes and appearance.
>
> 'Everything you said was spot-on,' Rose told him when he finished.
>
> Thousands of people pack out halls to hear him speak, many others travel hundreds of miles to visit him and he receives sacks of mail every week from strangers begging him to help them . . .

There was a tremendous response. Letters poured in from all parts of Britain and the Continent, and kept on arriving for four months afterwards. People wrote from places like South Africa saying, 'I've been sent this cutting from *The Star*. Can you help me?'

On the day the feature appeared, I was invited to Sky TV for an eight-minute live chat on *The Frank Bough Interview*—but they didn't realize I lived so far from London, so I couldn't get there in time. 'I'll come later in the year,' I said. Frankly, (no pun intended) I was relieved: I was so exhausted, all I wanted to do was relax and take things easy.

But, as my old grandmother used to say, 'There's no peace for the wicked!'

7

Dear Stephen . . .

Media interest in my mediumship means a high public profile, which makes my post-bag prolific. Stacks of letters arrive every week and every one is answered personally. They're so varied and fascinating I thought you might like to see some.

First, a selection of cheery tonic letters which brightened my day, some clearly showing what the spirit evidence given actually meant to the people receiving it.

Dear Stephen,

I must write to relay my gratitude for the message I received from you at Seaham Harbour.

You began by asking for someone in the back row who could recall the names 'Mr and Mrs Williams', but it didn't click. No one took this, and you said, 'I'll try for more information to pin-point the recipient later on.'

You then gave several messages to various people, all accepted; some through tears of relief, others with happiness. You showed such compassion in your attitude, and a great understanding of and a natural rapport with the people.

Then suddenly you said, 'Mr and Mrs Williams are back again and they're insisting the message is for the lady right at the back of the hall. They've brought Ethel with them.' I raised my hand, and you told me, 'Ethel worked with you many years ago in a fish and chip shop.' This was very true, but what startled me more was when you said, 'Ethel tells me Mr and Mrs Williams were your employers—they owned the shop.' I then remembered them, and was astonished.

Ethel advised me I needed medical attention—true, for I had suffered sleepless nights and was physically run-down. You even mentioned the exact names of several streets all around the place where my mother and father used to live. Then you explained, 'A lady called "Mers" is contacting you. This is her nickname.'

'Mers' was my father's nickname for my beloved mother who'd passed away 20 years earlier. I was so thrilled, I had to write. Travelling home that night I felt much happier knowing that my family were watching over me and knew my needs. I slept a lot easier too, better than I'd done for months.

Thank you once again, Stephen, for the caring and compassion you showed everyone that evening.

I do wish you every success for your future in this work, and good health—so you can continue with your calling.

Yours truly,

Mrs B., Tyne and Wear.

Dear Stephen,

I must tell you how wonderful your book *Visions of Another World* is. I bought it when I came to see you in Bristol. It took me ages to read it, the main reason being you wrote each chapter with so much emotion that I was crying near enough continuously all the way through!

I must say that your poem 'The Voiceless Ones' was written in such a way that the same day I read it I became a vegetarian. I haven't touched anything from animals since. Every time I read that poem I cry too!

I must add I don't often cry at all. It takes a lot to even produce one tear, let alone bucketfuls!

Bristol was the first time I ever attended a Spiritualist gathering. You were truly amazing and I am proud to have seen you 'in action'. I can't wait to see you again, nor can my family and friends. I have also seen you on TV in the *Stories in the Night* programmes. You defended mediumship well.

Please take care and be happy,

Love,

A. R., Bristol.

P.S. Have enclosed a stamped addressed envelope to save you both money and time.

Dear Secretary,

Psychic News in London printed what could have been a very nice photo of Stephen in their May issue, but it was all black and dark in my copy!

Hopefully you'll send me that photo of Stephen as I am a grandmother and find I feel so peaceful and comforted when I see his picture in my *Psychic News*. I would dearly love a proper photo; I'd love it to be signed by him, too, but I don't want to be a worry.

I've enclosed 40 pence for same if possible.

Yours sincerely,

Mrs L. F., Berkshire.

Dear Mr O'Brien,

My wife died of cancer at 62 and I felt so dreadful I must admit I didn't want to carry on living. I lost everything; we'd been married for 43 years and were very devoted to each other. When she died I felt so devastated, that's why I decided to come to your meeting, hoping to get some proof that she survived death somewhere.

I'll never forget the moment you brought a message from her—the proof you gave was so wonderful, I was elated. You told me things from my wife that only we two knew of; plus *my daughter*, you said, was with her. My wife had miscarried years before, and you reported the little one had grown up in the spirit world. And when you said they were both so happy together, it made me feel overjoyed, and impressed—for I'd never even met you.

I am now totally convinced of their survival, and I know that when my time comes, my wife, my child and I will live in eternity, which means everything to me.

Now, when I look upon death, I have no fear at all. The message changed my life. Your meeting was excellent, Stephen, and you struck me as a very likeable person. I wish more people could have the help that I've been privileged to receive, and I just can't ever thank you enough for everything.

Yours faithfully,

Mr R. P., Brecon.

Dear Mr O'Brien,

I have read and re-read your book *Visions of Another World*, and I know that I will continue to read it for many more times. It has given me so much hope, confirmation, so many things.

Perhaps you could let me have a list of your public meetings. Once again, thank you for sharing your feelings and beliefs, and please write another book before too long.

Yours sincerely,
Mrs I.C., Leeds

Dear Stephen,

You placed a very special friend of mine on your healing prayer list. I can't thank you enough. She is now a new lady! She *was* booked to have a heart and lung transplant at Harefield hospital.

She went for a check-up six weeks after leaving hospital in London and her doctors were absolutely dumbfounded, and said: 'We've never believed in miracles, but now I guess we'll have to start.'

She's been taken off the waiting list for a transplant altogether. She's been given the all-clear to do as she wishes, and now drives a car again, goes shopping and swimming, and has even bought herself a new mountain-bike and goes out on it every day.

Thank you again for your help and love, and your beautiful peace. Take care—I pray for you each day, that you might give out that peace to countless thousands as you carry on your wonderful work.

God bless, Stephen,
(name and address supplied), Sussex.

Dear Stephen,

I just had to write to you to tell you how much I enjoyed your book. I've never written to an author before, praising them, but I had to. Your book had me laughing in places and also wiping my eyes.

Enclosed are some poems for you, in the hope of helping you whenever you're down.

Tomorrow is Another Day

Today tears may have been shed
The pain so deep
While hearts have bled

Today everything may not have gone as planned
Not milk and honey
But instead a place of mud and sand

Today you may feel the darkness will never end
It isn't easy
Being alone without a friend

Today the hill may well have been steep
Knees scraped badly
But don't sit and weep

After dusk there is tomorrow
No more storms
Only a beautiful rainbow

Jan Castle, Hetton-le-Hole.

I'd be interested to see more reader's poetry, but regret I can't return them.

Dear Stephen,
   I'm writing to say the message I received from you at your meeting last night was brilliant. I was totally amazed.
   I should have been going on holiday that day, but strongly felt the urge to cancel and, instead, go along to see you. When I arrived, the hall was packed with hundreds of people, but I was just happy and contented to sit and listen, yet was astounded when you said out loud, 'Someone has postponed a holiday date to come along to this meeting.' Of course, the message was for me!
   You told me how I'd sat quietly and decided to cancel, then brought me superb evidence from my darling daughter, who died as a baby, mentioning the final arrangements we made for her, even telling me 'she was buried in a special vault at the hospital, with all the other babies', which was absolutely correct. You also gave her correct name and a perfect description.
   Then love came from my grandad, after you rightly said he'd committed suicide, suffering from cancer. Grandad showed how close he was to us all by talking about 'car tyres needing attention'.

My son's car was stopped by the police *that very night*, but luckily they overlooked them!

It was all so remarkable, I really can't put into words what it meant to receive it. And it most certainly made my holiday the happiest ever! I can't believe how fortunate I was.

God bless and take care,

Love,

Mrs C. J., Wales.

And now some fascinating psychic experiences, selected from shoals of them (!) proving we're all psychic. Each one of us has the ability to see, hear and sense the next world through the powers of the mind. 'Psychic' stems from the word 'psyche', meaning 'soul'. Therefore psychic powers are soul powers. We all have a soul, and so we're all psychic to greater or lesser degrees.

The world of spirit is nearer than hands and feet.

Dear Stephen,

I was reading an article about you in the daily newspaper. I'm an unmarried mother with a little boy called S. aged six.

When he was four he had a terribly ulcerated mouth and he was really suffering, so I gave him a *Rinstead Pastille*, and he was sat there sucking it when suddenly he looked at a chair next to him (which was empty) and a puzzled look came over his face. And he said, 'What?' and then he took the pastille out of his mouth and said, 'Nana, children's not supposed to have them.' And she asked, 'Who's told you that?' And he said, 'Andrew,' and his nana said, 'Well, where's Andrew?' And S. pointed to the empty chair.

When I asked the doctor if I should give him *Rinstead Pastilles*, he said, 'No.' I'm Roman Catholic and I'm reading your book and it's really interesting. If you write any more I will surely buy them.

Good luck and God bless. Thank you for being so patient in reading my long, long letter.

Yours sincerely,

Miss S.D., Lancashire.

Dear Stephen,

A few years back I had an abortion. It was my choice. I was four months pregnant at the time and the sex of my child is not known. Anyway, moving on, I sometimes see a little boy in my bed, aged about three, holding out his arms to me with a smile (one in a million), but as I try and get closer he seems to fade out like a light. This child even brings me flowers. Could this be the little boy I aborted?

Please could you reply to my letter,

Yours in need,

T. L., London.

Answer: Yes. Your family in spirit brings your boy to visit because you're his mother, and he loves you. Both aborted and stillborn children continue to develop and grow on the Other Side. Next time he comes, why not speak to him?

Whenever we feel like sitting down and moaning about our lives, if we turn to these next correspondents we'll realize just how fortunate we are, and perhaps next time we'll sit down and count our blessings instead.

There's always someone worse off than ourselves, as these heart-breaking, tragic letters prove:

Dear Mr O'Brien,

I would like to know if my husband's spirit is at rest. My daughter's boyfriend murdered him three years ago. Not a day goes past that I don't think about it, worrying in case he's not at peace. My husband was only 41, and the man who did the murder got just four years. After 18 months he's free, and trying to come back into our lives again, for access to his two children.

I know my husband would be livid at the cheek of him, and frustrated he can do nothing to prevent him. I would dearly like to know how he is.

Hoping to hear from you soon. Have enclosed a stamped addressed envelope,

Mrs —

(name and address supplied).

Dear Stephen,

I listened with interest to your broadcast on BBC radio today, and I must say, listening to you filled me with a sense of well-being.

I have a severely mentally handicapped daughter, 34 years old. When her time comes, will she be normal in the next life? She was brain-damaged at birth, and is so very important to me.

Yours faithfully,

Mrs M.F., Liverpool.

Answer: Yes, she'll be fine. When the physical body dies, the mind and spirit express themselves clearly through the spirit body, in which no handicap exists.

Dear Stephen,

My 18 year-old brother X. got stabbed to death, just round the corner from where we live as he stood talking to some friends.

My Mum and the rest of the family are terribly upset, as my brother was stabbed straight through the 5th and 6th ribs, into the heart, and he died straightaway; and now my Mum is blaming herself and no matter what people say she still says it's her fault, and we're all scared in case we lose her as well.

I have told my Mum X. will always be with us and he's safe, but she won't listen. All she keeps thinking about is him dying in pain, without any of us being there with him.

Could you get in touch with our X. and tell him we all miss and love him so very much, and reassure my Mum if he did or did not die in pain, as she's going through so much pain herself thinking about it.

All my thanks,

(name and address supplied).

I gave a confidential reply to this correspondent.

Dear Stephen,

I am 16 and still at school. I was reading about you and hoping you could contact my Dad, as he was killed in a car crash. But with me being only 7 when I lost him, I can't remember much about him.

I'm just getting over leukaemia, which I developed at 10. At first it was pretty rough, but I'm nearly through it now and I believe and hope my Dad was with me all the way, just as Mam was.

Please tell my Dad I love him and not a day goes by without me thinking about him, tell him Mam also feels the same.

Ask him to say hello to Nana X. and Nana Y., and to my Grandad: tell him I miss him also.

It doesn't matter too much about those little messages, as I send up my prayers each night. But please just tell my Dad I love him and want to know how he is. PLEASE, if my Dad is contacted, please write back to me and tell me what he said.

God rest your soul, Dad. I'll love you always, and so will Mam. Love you,

(Christian name)

XX

Thank you very much

Stephen O'Brien.

Yours faithfully,

(name and address supplied).

Note: Just send your thoughts to your loved ones, and they will be received.

Dear Mr O'Brien,

3 years ago my boyfriend died in – Prison, by hanging himself. The following Friday I had my baby girl. I still cry most nights. I can't understand why it happened.

I'm now living with my mother, as I am uneasy staying by myself. Even though my boyfriend's spirit is in Mum's house, she's talking about moving. I don't want to, I don't want to leave him.

Mum's seen him 3 times, in different clothes, and my sister has seen him once. They say he looks as though he's still alive but with a shimmering glow around him. I've heard him calling my name. Could you please help me to understand?

(name and address supplied), North England.

Note: He will be beside the people he loves; the location of the house doesn't matter. When our spirit friends visit us, they 'home-in' on our personalities, our minds, by the power of thought.

And Now For Something Completely Different!

Dear Mr O'Brien,

Over the years, various astrologers have forecast 'sums of money coming my way', 'you will have a windfall' and so on!

Had all this money arrived I'd have been worth Billions, and wouldn't have lived long enough to have enjoyed a spending spree.

Result of these predictions: No windfalls, and all I did was pay out again and again.

The next forecasts were that I would get a well-deserved promotion and a large increase in salary—that was 10 years ago!

What happened? I was hit by a 300-weight lawn-mower, was laid up for six months *and* lost the job as a gardener!!

Another forecast was that I would win large sums at bingo and on the horses, none of which happened.

Then I was told of 'a fabulous job offer' coming my way, this never happened *at all*. Finally, after a number of years of being unemployed, we had to sell the house we lived in, and get a council flat.

A great come-down, is it not?

After all these forecasts, it seems something's bringing me bad luck, but I don't know what it is.

That's about it then, and the best of luck in your work,

Yours sincerely,

Mr M. E., Oxford.

Note: That's life! I'm not a fortune-teller, but good luck!

Dear Stephen,

I cannot possibly go on living, I'm at my wit's end. You see, I've lost 8 pieces of jewellery. Can you tell me where they are?

Sincerely,

Mrs —

(name and address supplied).

P.S. I've also lost my husband, do you think *he* knows where they are?

(!)

[no date or introduction]

Reading your rubbish in the local paper you and your Doris are a load of old conns there is lots of your kind jumping on the bandwagon the only spirits you get intouch with are in bottles if you are what you say you are ask your spirits to tell you how to find this lost baby, and you and your Doris tell us who will win the Derby and FA Cup also tell us what you charge you must be laughing all the way to the bank, like your Mystic Meg and TAROT, my mother was conned for £40 by one of your sort, you look a couple of conns I shall look for a reply in the paper, by the way the one who conned my mother what used the same paper as you told my mother that my farther and her would have long and happy life three week my farther was killed, both OAPs and easy minded people fall for your patter stars and spirits are lot of rubbish all this rubbish you wrote you have only you to believe any body can write that you asked your spirits give me the Derby winner and I will give you half

Mrs S., Norwich.

I was unable to answer, as no address was supplied, which is a pity, for I'd liked to have helped this lady. (By the way, I wish I did know the Derby winner, I could do with the money myself!)

And now, with your indulgence, a letter *I'd* like to send:

An Open Letter from Stephen to the Picket Line Protesters

Dear Pickets and Protesters (singers and shouters),

Please would you be so gracious as to exhibit kind manners, and not hassle the public queuing to get into my meetings. After all, they haven't chosen to hear your message, but mine. If you would be kind enough to keep away, this stops an already over-worked police force being laden with extra duties.

If you *should* feel the sudden urge to hurl condemnations at me, or sense an overwhelming attack of converting others to your beliefs outside my venues approaching, please would you:

1. Go immediately to bed with two aspirin;
2. Go to a Revivalist Meeting;
3. Take a cold bath.

With many thanks for your kind co-operation,
Yours sincerely,
Stephen O'Brien.

(Those wishing to write to Mr O'Brien, please be thoughtful enough to enclose a stamped addressed envelope, without which he cannot reply. Stephen also welcomes donated stamps and envelopes to aid answering his many correspondents. Vast quantities of letters means mail can take a while to receive attention, so please be patient. Stephen also wishes to thank the many people who have sent him gifts, and especially for the teddy-bears, which he has given a good home.)

8

Bouquets and Brickbats

'Fame ain't easy.'
Stephen O'Brien

Fame, of course, is a two-edged sword, which not only knights but also cuts. And, flattering as it may be, I don't cope well with being renowned. Intrinsically shy, deep down inside I long to fade away from public gaze. There's a heavy price to pay when the world knocks at your door. Some people revel in the limelight, but I'm not one of them—though I've learned to accept it now as part of my calling. But sometimes the stress is unbearable, and all that keeps me going is the thought that millions may benefit by hearing the Truths of the Spirit.

As *New Zealand Woman's Weekly* quoted:

> I live almost as a recluse, in a small place of my own. I prefer the quiet stillness of the mountains and hills of Wales to parties and pubs. The first love of my life is silence and I enjoy going for days without talking to people—except my spirit friends.

But as well as some nasty brickbats I've had thrown at me, there have also been lovely bouquets, such as meeting people I'd never have known if I'd remained in the shadows; people like professional composer Philip Greenwood who presented me with a specially-recorded musical tape in London:

I was so moved by your book, Stephen, especially the part where you met your Spirit Guide, White Owl, that I sat down and composed this music for you both.

I was deeply touched. And with the tape came an inspired poem:

The Meeting

Borne on the Wind, he came.
That same Wind which had
Carried a Host of Winged
Messengers throughout Eternity.

He came to meet his Earth Brother,
By the cool waters, he stood.
The Light in His eyes, and the
Warmth of His Smile,
Said simply—'I Love You.'

> (With thanks to the Guide and his great medium,
> Stephen O'Brien) Philip H. Greenwood.

I also made a 60-minute digitally-recorded stereo cassette which was released to the public. It was exciting to do, and I know it helped many people. I spoke of the soul's journey through birth, life and into the Beyond—and I also gently answered many frequently-asked questions about several aspects of the paranormal. [For further information see p.256 – Ed.]

On the other side of the coin, however, my work has not escaped some dramatic moments. One stinging brickbat was hurled at me in a Welsh venue. And I regret to report, it hit me right in the eye! Just hours before the meeting, young religious fanatics telephoned the hall, demanding cancellation. But the complex manager replied, 'As long as Spiritualists pay rates in this town, they have a right to the amenities.' So the meeting proceeded, the hall filling to capacity—500 people, with another 150 turned away for lack of seats. But backstage I felt very uneasy, pacing back and forth and twiddling my thumbs, unable to get a spirit link. This is so unlike me: I'm usually very calm and collected. At that time I'd no idea there were 75 protesters outside, singing, chanting, hassling and shouting abuse at the public. Eventually they were removed by the police.

After a specially enthusiastic welcome, I was about six minutes into my opening talk when three young women suddenly stood up in the front row and marched towards the stage, screaming abuse at me, such as, 'Renounce the devil!' Then one of them actually spat into my face.

No one could believe their rudeness. Then all at once the audience retaliated, and started shouting at the women, ordering them to 'Get out!' 'Shut up and go home!' 'Stop peddling your religion!' and various other choice phrases, too coarse to repeat here! It was like a nightmare, especially when the whole 500 started clapping and stamping their feet in rhythm, chanting loudly like a mad forest tribe: '*Out! Out! Out! Out!*'

Stewards removed the demonstrators to hoots of derision and fist-waving from the angry crowd. But even as they left, one still screamed, 'Repent!' to the gallery. Grossly ill-mannered, they were lucky to escape unharmed, the audience was so furious with them. If they'd stayed, I'm sure there would have been a fight. That sort of thing's fine in a Clint Eastwood movie, but certainly not at one of my evenings. But such is the fate of all those who'd like to disrupt my meetings, so beware! The crowd is on my side, not yours.

But as well as such unpleasant memories, there have been many amusing episodes too. One happened when the Southampton Guildhall rang: 'Do you want the tower clock silenced during your performance?'

'What on earth do you mean?'

'Well, on the stroke of every hour the clock chimes out deep and loud that lovely old hymn *O God Our Help in Ages Past . . .*'

I was highly amused, but didn't think those ghostly strains would help the demonstration, so we paid the few pounds to keep it quiet!

Southampton provided further merriment, too, when I provoked a major incident by losing my black briefcase. Panic suddenly set in, for everything of value was in it. Then a brainstorm prompted me to ring the restaurant where I'd had my tea. They were laughing uncontrollably. 'We've just had the bomb squad in! We were all petrified to death!' I'd left it under a table, after having burnt my chin on one of their hot apple pies!

There was another funny occasion, this time at BBC Radio Nottingham, when the transmitter signals went haywire from the moment I entered the building. 'Stephen O'Brien, this is your fault! It's your psychic powers!' admonished the presenter.

'Sorry,' I smiled. 'When I was photographed recently for a magazine, the shutter wouldn't budge because my house was in the background.' This was something I'd been unhappy with, considering it an infringement of my privacy. When *I* had tried the camera, the shutter had obliged, and we got some nice shots of the photographer standing on the exact same spot she'd tried to picture *me* on! But she still couldn't capture *my* image there. 'Come on,' I'd said, 'let's go to a park.' And there the shutter worked every time, the pictures appearing in dozens of countries around the world.

When I left BBC Radio Nottingham, everything clicked back to normal again! (Sorry, chaps! There's a message there somewhere for a disbeliever at the station!)

Speaking of unusual happenings, after one demonstration my manager, Jeff, came into the dressing-room wreathed in smiles.

'Something really funny's just happened out there. I was sitting next to a white-haired old man who'd hobbled into the hall on two sticks; he looked about 150! Half-way through the first half he mumbled something to me. I couldn't understand a word he said, so I just smiled back.

'Later on he did the same thing again, and I just smiled. Then in the interval, when I could hear him properly, he leaned over and asked, "*When is the wrestling coming on?*"!

' "Oh, there's no wrestling here tonight," I said, and he hobbled out again on his sticks!'

Well, I couldn't help laughing. 'Sometimes it feels like a wrestling-match when I'm trying to place my connections!' I said—which brings to mind that horrendous episode at Glasgow City Hall. I'll never forget it as long as I live.

Just before I started, absolute uproar broke out in the auditorium. Several 'ladies' challenged some people in the front stalls, accusing them of occupying their seats. The first group disagreed and refused to budge. Public outcry immediately broke out, tempers steaming-hot and fists clenched in readiness. Arms were waving around menacingly. Then suddenly the air was blue, full of four-letter swear-words, which included every known expletive, and other incensed audience members started booing at the 'fishwives' to stop—without success. It was more like a pack of football hooligans than an audience!

All this time I was perched high out of sight behind curtains, 30 feet from the stage, powerless to stop the screaming. As the shouting reached its peak, a kilted official defiantly screeched at the trouble-makers down the microphone: 'Sit down and shut up!'

This further enraged the white-faced 'fishwives' who bellowed their contempt over 'his bloody silly rules', while I stood stunned, and gasping, 'I don't believe this is happening, it's a nightmare,' and telling myself to remain calm or there'd be no clairvoyance at all that night.

Then the official blurted out: 'If there's a message for you, you'll get it no matter where you're sitting, you silly woman!' To which she angrily replied, 'I'll give *you* the ******* message, sonny!' (It began with an 'f'—Glaswegian slang, later translated as 'I'll slit your throat.')

There was a stunned pause. Thankfully, the hall manager then seized a microphone. 'Please! Be quiet and behave yourselves! People don't want to hear you shouting at each other—they've come to see Stephen O'Brien.' At which point the packed crowd wildly applauded, cheered and whistled.

When I finally entered, 15 minutes late, there was a tumultuous greeting, and once I started speaking, absolute silence descended—you could have heard a pin drop in the auditorium. An unearthly calm swept through the crowds, who sat almost entranced, hanging on my every word. The spirit people did not let me down, the messages flowing as though nothing had happened. The links were clear and detailed, and the meeting was a roaring success.

Looking back now, I can only see the funny side (a priceless gift I've always had!), especially as the troublemakers were eventually seated *in front* of the first rows. All night long the microphone leads kept catching in their handbags and stockings!

Seated in the gallery was the much-respected veteran Spiritualist medium, Albert Best, who later invited our party back to his home for supper. 'Stephen,' he said, 'I've done these big meetings for decades, and I don't think I've ever seen such disgraceful behaviour in an audience. Yet I must tell you, *I* couldn't have worked after that fuss tonight, but you handled it beautifully. If you can use your gifts in conditions like that, you can work anywhere in the world.' Then he gave me some helpful advice on how to improve my mediumship, for which I'm very grateful. Thanks, Albert.

Glasgow brings to mind another 'peculiar' event which happened further down the coast, on Tyne Tees Television in northern England. It was one of the oddest shows I've done. There was the usual interview, audience and sceptics, but I can only describe what followed as a 30-minute free-for-all bun-fight. Everyone interrupted, and no one—not even the other studio guests—had a fair chance to answer points. I told the producer, Thelma McGough (incidentally an ex-girlfriend of the late Beatle John Lennon), 'Thelma, you might as well have bought a huge plate of sticky buns, plonked them on the studio floor, then shouted 'Go!' and let everyone have a throw!'

If only they'd allowed me to work with the audience, as they'd originally asked, I might have been fortunate to make a link like the one I gave at the prestigious Royal Liverpool Philharmonic Hall: one of the many messages which recipients say improved the quality of their lives. It was a particularly touching contact that fell to a woman in the crowd. She'd worked with the wife of a man who'd died in the tragic Hillsborough Football Stadium Disaster—that dreadful British tragedy, in April 1989, in which 95 people were crushed and suffocated to death. It was England's most horrific football accident, and news of it stunned the world when TV pictures appeared across the globe. Police had allowed hundreds of extra enthusiastic fans into an already-packed ground; old and young alike had their bodies crushed under the immense pressure of the crowds, and they died against the high wire barriers near the pitch.

My spirit communicator found his wife's workmate and relayed a most moving message, which included his name and recalled his last precious moments of life when, as he put it, 'The pressure of the crowd crushed the life out of me and two girls, one at either side. We three must have died at the same time because when we climbed up over the barriers together, standing on people's shoulders, and ran onto the pitch and pulled at the gasping bodies against the fences, our hands just passed through them. We were completely helpless, everyone was.' Then I heard him take a deep breath, as though sobbing at the memory of that horrendous scene.

He conveyed his love to his grieving wife, 'who couldn't come to tonight's meeting', and then he mentioned his family.

'He has three children,' I relayed.

'No, only two.'

'Oh, please forgive me, but he's adamant he has *three*, not two.' Then she gasped out loud.

'Yes! They adopted a son!'

Needless to say, that message brought a grieving woman tremendous comfort. I owe my spirit friends such a lot.

But I think one of the most touching 'bouquets' in the way of spirit contacts they've given in recent years was the time when a youngster with special needs came through one night in Bognor Regis. It was so emotional, and came from a young lad who'd been crippled. 'I was starved of oxygen as I was born,' he told me. He'd suffered great physical handicaps as a spastic, and couldn't speak or stand, but as his link came through he touched everyone's heart with his exuberant joy and enthusiasm. He gave his name, then the connection started.

'This young lad's Carer is here, and there's a strong memory of "a Sunshine Coach". "I belonged to PHAB," he says—The Physically Handicapped and Able Bodied Society.' A young lady immediately stepped forward to accept him, and his joy was instantaneous.

'I'm free!' he shouted to me. 'I'm free, I'm free! I can move my arms and legs, I can speak, I can stand up tall on strong feet, on my own! I've got a wonderful body with no pain, and my tongue is loosed, and I'm free!' Everyone was deeply moved. Then he gave a succession of correct names of friends, including his social worker, Jayne, and told his Carer, 'Thank you so much for taking time to look after me. I now realize that by coming into the world, I learned patience and self-control. And as well as mastering my mental and physical difficulties, my condition taught many others who knew me how to love.

'And I do thank God for those lessons, and you too, for your concern and loving care. But I'm so happy now, because my new body gives me so much freedom! God bless you. I'm free!'

I was told later that a similar young man seated in a wheelchair elsewhere in the audience that night, with his mother beside him, listened avidly to that message. As this wonderful link came through, the boy's mum leaned across and wiped freely-flowing tears from her son's eyes. He was obviously greatly comforted to know that one day he too will be free to move and speak. Please God, my words may have brought him a sense of peace and further purpose to his days.

On a different tack now, my Other-World friend, White Owl, who doubtless helped that young spirit lad communicate at that meeting, hasn't escaped some unkind brickbats, despite all his good works. His existence has sometimes been 'doubted' by sceptics. But he's proven his reality so many times, to so many people, that their arguments don't hold water. Here he is, speaking of his critics:

Sceptics want to prove either I do not exist, or else I am a fragment of my medium's imagination. But if I were to give my true name, birthplace and time, plus other 'relevant' information which could be proven 100 per cent correct, they would only accuse my medium of researching the facts.

Those who wish to believe will do so—the others must be left to themselves.

I am not concerned with personalities. *What is important is my message—nothing else matters.*

The mission I have undertaken has once again brought me into close association with the Earth, where I am trying to teach eternal spirit truths, touch souls, and open man's understanding to the Greater Realities of the Spirit within him, and the endless opportunities for growth and service these afford.

These will be remembered long after I am forgotten.

And of course—he's right. And many other accounts he's transmitted concerning his short time on Earth seem to really touch a pure note of authenticity. He was murdered by a jealous brave from his Indian tribe at the tender age of 21, as fully told in *Visions of Another World*. A tomahawk blow to the base of his skull took him over into the next life, leaving his soul-companion, Running Deer, to tell the tribe of his murder.

Here's what he says about the 'burial' of his body:

From a clearing through the tall pine trees, I watched the celebrations for seven days and nights over my mortal body. My people commended my spirit to the Great Heavens, as I stood beside my beloved woman, Running Deer. So brave was she, not one teardrop fell from her eyes, but she was hurt beyond repair; her grief was stronger than the bright sunlight which blinds a desert-wanderer's eyes. Her deep and lasting love for me will always be branded in my mind.

On the dawn of the eighth day, I witnessed my useless body carried high up into the Singing Mountains, by torchlight procession, near my tribal home. Many valley braves and their squaws paid homage to my last climb; and there, upon a verdant hill, my body was placed upon a tall pyre of forest wood, mighty and strong.

And a young brave said, 'Here we lay you to rest, true friend of the weak and the lonely. May the Great Spirit receive your soul into the Hunting-Grounds of our fore-fathers with gladness. May the moon shine bright upon you in the Land Beyond Sunset. For as long as the rivers flow, and the Great Snows fall, we shall not forget the courage and warmth of our friend and leader, White Owl, the Wise and Brave.'

Then the women wept and rent their tunics, and threw dust into their faces, and departed with heavy hearts down into the valley of my people.

For many months my body lay wrapped in the soft blanket specially woven for it by Running Deer, who climbed alone each day to sit and pray next to me, pleading with the Great Spirit, hoping that my soul would be allowed to wait for her beyond the Land of Dreams.

'As I raise my hands to the skies,' she said, 'may my prayers follow until they are carried on the Great North Wind and heard by my beloved one. Come back to me, my friend. Do not leave me comfortless. I am young and strong now, but I do not have you to warm my days. Do not let me age without your warmth. Come for me, White Owl—carry me across the Divide!'

My tears could not be contained. I was so near and yet so far away from her. I tried to show her my radiant new form, but her suffering wrapped a grey cloud of blinding grief about her psychic vision, and I remained unsensed . . .

So I whispered into her mind, 'I will always love you, my little one . . . always . . .' but the water from my eyes did not even wet the brown earth . . .

Over the seasons, the spirits of the air and water, and the birds, claimed my corpse as their own. The birds grew fat upon my flesh, and thereby carried part of me way up into the Great Spirit's Domain. Every full moon, when the squaws sat around the watch-fires and sang their songs of thankfulness, I appeared to my woman in dreams and visions, and only in this way was her sadness dried and her faith bolstered.

Then, a few years later, some young braves travelled to my resting-place, and from my bones they made ornate necklaces and tools for use in the encampments below.

Nothing is ever wasted in the Red-man's world.

So, rightly understood and properly viewed, death isn't a morbid subject at all, as White Owl's story shows.

In fact, returning to the lighter side of events, one of the happiest bouquets given to man is laughter. And one of the funniest things I ever witnessed, believe it or not, happened at a crematorium several years ago.

Before the cortege and mourners arrived, my dear old friend Kitty Jones, a bright-eyed mature woman of ample proportions, was investigating the pulpit button, which, when pressed, sent the coffin downwards. She'd climbed the four tiny steps and was just coming *down* when her driver, John, a heavy man with a walking-stick and a gammy leg, came hobbling *up* the steps to poke his nose into Kitty's business. He shouldn't have been there at all—and then it happened! As they collided on the narrow steps, John's walking-stick slipped and shot out between Kitty's legs and they suddenly lost their balance, swayed, then clasped each other like dying lovers as they twirled ungraciously on the stairwell and crashed to the ground in a twisted tangle of arms and legs!

Weak with laughter, I dropped to my knees, utterly helpless with my sides aching—especially as they both tried to be so polite and graceful about it! Normally they would have filled the air with blue threats, but instead they said silly things like 'Good gracious me!' and 'Oh my leg!' and 'Dear, dear, dear!' as they writhed in a red-faced mass of embarrassment. There were limbs everywhere, and you couldn't tell where one lot finished and another began! I only just managed to unscramble them, seconds before the mourners arrived.

'Kitty,' I said, wiping tears of laughter from my eyes, 'you and John are the only two to have been laid out at the crem and got away with it!'

But little did I think then that I'd be back in that very same place to take Kitty's mother's funeral service shortly afterwards. Maggie Edwards, Kitty's lovely mum, was a wonderful character, full of life, always joking and cheerful, and she was 90 when she died! At the house on funeral day, Kitty said, 'Would you like to spend a few moments alone with Mum in the other room, Stephen?'

'Yes, I'd like that very much,' and I went into the drawing-room, stood by cheery Maggie's coffin, gently rested my fingertips on the closed lid and sent out my kind thoughts to her. 'God bless you, Maggie,' I said. 'They won't know what's hit them Over There now you've arrived!' And I sensed her near, chuckling with me; she still had her wonderful sense of humour.

'Maggie,' I said, 'if you had your chance, what would you say to everyone today?'

And back came her voice, as clear as a bell: 'I'm grateful for the love of all my family and good friends.'

So I took her words to the service with me and faithfully conveyed them to the people—and what wonderful, comforting thoughts they were. If only all the world, especially those who fear death, could have heard them.

Reaper, will I dream?

Death Approaches . . .
Tell me, Reaper, will I dream?

> *In pictures*
> *and in thoughts*

Tell me, Reaper will I die?

> *Not in essence*
> *but in form*

Through misted haze the spirits come,
each face etched with deepfelt care;
and across their gaze
'Death Approaches'
is clearly written there

Tell me, Reaper, is it Time?

> *There is no time,*
> *there is no break*
> *there is no sleep,*
> *there is no death*

Then calls the grave?

> *None can wait*
> *and all must cross*

But will I feel a desperate pain?

> *Only in the loss of bones,*
> *only in the world of sense,*
> *only when alone.*
> *And the Brilliant Lights*
> *are those who've come*
> *to take you Home*

And tell me, Reaper, will I dream?

> *All Life is such—*
> *dream it there, or dream it here,*
> *it matters not*

Then may I choose?

> *The choice is made*
> *the moment's spent—*
> *you came to me*
> *not longsince—*
> *The Veil is rent . . .*

But I'm alive: I feel no death

> *There is none*
> *only Light . . .*
> *Welcome to the Higher Life*

9

Body, Mind and Spirit

I had a big shock.

Stripped off, I glanced in the mirror, gasped in horror and there and then decided to get myself back into shape! I'd been working out in a multigym for over a year and though muscles had grown, recent inactivity had bulged the waistline! Instead of being sylph-like and slender, I was now 28 lbs overweight. So I immediately joined aerobics classes—where our nubile instructress contorted herself into the most incredibly eye-boggling positions!

'Right!' she shouted above blasting pop music, 'Do the splits!' And with that she'd immediately drop to the floor in half, while we flabbies gawped in horror! The eyes of the man next to me stood out on stalks: 'Good God! That woman's made of elastic!' he said. And the girl behind muttered, 'If I could do that, I'd be laughing!' Nevertheless we all took a brave shot at it, grunting and twisting ourselves into unrecognizable shapes and wrenching our backs. It was great fun though—and so good for us. We were supposed to gain 'added grace and poise', but most of the older women were escorted blue-faced from the hall, and even some youngsters left panting for breath. But because of my clean life-style—no smoking or drinking and a healthy vegan diet—I felt fighting-fit, though desperate for a glass of fresh orange juice. And by the way, anyone who thinks aerobics are only for women should try it! Even the toughest men couldn't keep up with the music!

I've always believed in keeping fit—in Body, Mind and Spirit—especially as a spiritual healer. We're not bodies with minds attached, as some people think, we're minds registering through temporary physical shells. We're *Mind*—first, last and everything. The physical is but a shadow of the Essence. The body is the Temple of the Spirit; and if we keep it healthy, fit and strong, we may remain on Earth to gain valuable lessons in soul-growth.

Two truisms guard and guide physical and mental health:

● We are what we eat.
● We are what we think we are.

The recent huge boom in health foods shows humanity is finally getting the message: natural wholesome products are better than frozen or processed varieties. Meat purveyors are now suffering a powerful body-blow to their blood-red industries, as the public demands 'cleaner' sustenance.

One amusing incident concerning a Spiritual Healer and food always sticks in my mind. She was a rather well-fed buxom woman, giving a public prayer at a meeting: 'Please God, bless and keep from harm all the little furry creatures of the Earth, all the lovely animals, our dear friends—' when all of a sudden she produced an almighty belch. 'Ooops, sorry—that was my bacon sandwich!' she said!

Another chuckle came later when an elderly woman patient was ready to receive contact healing from her. The patient looked awfully worried. 'Pssst!' she whispered seriously to the healer, 'I've got me curlers in under me 'eadscarf—will the 'ealing still work?' The poor woman thought the power might 'perm' her hair instead of cure her!

Leading such a hectic life-style, it isn't surprising that I often crash into bed in the early hours of the morning, utterly exhausted, only to sense healing presences gathering around me. My mother is often among them, acting, she said, as a 'nurse' to me. When I questioned White Owl about this, he gave a revealing insight as to how some people in Spirit administer healing to their charges on Earth:

> Your mother is a good soul who re-energizes your spirit. She achieves this by attending specially-prepared places in my world, where energies have been generated, gathered and stored. These batteries of psychic energy are extra healing sources from which many healing guides can obtain their power.
>
> She concentrates on absorbing the rays by a disciplined act of mental will. When enough has been imbibed within her aura, thus charged, she makes her way to Earth by the power of thought.
>
> On arriving, she waits until you are gently resting. Then, along with others similarly self-charged, she directs her thoughts towards you. Her great love enables the rays to flow into your auric fields of electromagnetic energy. Rather like a sponge, your auras drink in and hold her emanations.
>
> Just as lightning jumps from one highly-charged cloud to another of lower charge, so do these rays transfer, but more gently. Gradually you then feel renewed and refreshed.

Spiritual Healing works because the spirit of the healer attunes itself to the God-Force (The Great Spirit) then channels these energies to the spirit of the patient. *From* Spirit, *Through* Spirit, *To* Spirit.

The patient's spirit body then transfers these powers to the physical, and the ailment is treated or corrected. Many healers, like myself, also have highly-trained spirit guides on the Other Side who help direct these intricate processes. And you don't need Faith for success, for many have received Spiritual Healing without knowing, and have fully recovered. Even animals respond. But Faith certainly helps. 'According to your faith be it unto you'—if you believe it will work, you allow the invigorating rays to enter your spirit, and you also get your own healing mechanisms working, all of which aid your recovery. Everything is Mind-controlled, especially our health.

I do a great deal of Absent Healing these days, another branch of this psychic science in which power is sent via the spirit world to the sufferer, who's not physically present beside me. Love knows no bounds, and God is everywhere—so, if the healer's operating correctly, the power reaches you no matter where you are. Distance is no obstacle. This is how I now provide my healing services, because there are so many requests and no time for me to visit people personally.

But whenever we need to, we can do a great deal to help ourselves get well. When you feel 'drained', 'tired' or 'under the weather', why not try this: by just lying on rich green grass you can mentally draw upon the vast energies in the ground, filling your psychic being—your soul—with new vigour.

Trees also have powerful energy fields around them which can be tapped. It's purely a psychic exercise, of course, which requires sensitivity to feel the upsurge of strength pouring into your spirit. But the spirit of the tree is usually quite willing to give, yet, like all good gardeners, recognize they are living entities, and *talk* to them first—and don't forget to ask!

Considering harmony and health are *our* responsibilities, it's amazing how many people still run to their doctors, expecting them to take charge of their well-being, delegating this task. While I always advise patients to keep their ailments under medical supervision, for I believe healing and the medical establishment should work hand in hand, ultimately our health is *our* responsibility.

Mental health can only be maintained when the mind contains positive, calm thoughts. Negative forces behind agitated emotions create mental whirlpools of swirling energy which disquiet the mind. These eventually cause disease in the body, because the physical body is a reflection of the Mind: it is nothing more than Mind made manifest, or thought solidified. This is why holding a good self-image is so important for a healthy life.

Selfishness, greed, avarice, egotism, bitterness and grudging attitudes of mind 'cripple' mental balance and pave the way for dis-ease. Violence, anger and raging tempers are, without doubt, the biggest causes of ill-health. Even jealousy has a detrimental effect upon the body.

I've frequently used my psychic vision while working with emotionally-ill people, especially when helping psychologists and psychotherapists with their patients. The constantly-moving auric fields of 'unbalanced' personalities are darker in colour and more agitated than those of the average 'normal' person, whereas balanced minds radiate brighter hues and appear far more gently undulating and serene to my clairvoyant vision.

Mental health, therefore, comes when we maintain a general quiet peacefulness, when we become a character based on outward-flowing concern for others and *not* on inward self-interest alone. A 'middle-of-the-road', 'moderation in all things' attitude towards life helps create inner harmony. But harsh, aggressive and reactionary emotions repel health, and don't belong to truly spiritually developed people. Perfect love not only casts out fear, it also obliterates disease.

The human body is such a living miracle, so complex and intricately designed, with every cell motivated by Mind, which therefore responds to mental directions. The body heals itself, as proven when a cut is sealed or a bone mended, but delivering powerful mental directives influences it to speed up the healing processes. Creative visualization in cancer patients frequently works, the sufferer visualizing the malignant tissues reducing or being killed, with remarkably successful results.

So why not try it? It can work on any ailment.

Whenever my healings have been 'unsuccessful' and the patient has passed over, the spirit people have taught me never to view this as a failure—for death occurs only when the time is right. No amount of healing can stay the transition; but it *can* be made pain-free, and endowed with greater dignity. Besides, the ultimate purpose of spiritual healing is to touch the soul of sufferers and awaken them to their true selves: who and what they are, where they have come from, and whence we all go.

And speaking of the future, these days I'm increasingly concerned about the health of our planet, which is our Mother. If we take a leap in imagination and visualize Mother Earth seen from a distance, she would appear as a glowing light, filled with sentient life and surrounded by vibrant energies. Seen from space—something I've been privileged to witness—highly sensitive observers would be aware of every Living Mind moving over her surface, under and above it; a vast panorama of teeming consciousness. Even rocks, dust and air have their own life-force.

Mother Earth is a Living Being, and it's time we recognized her as such. She is a part of us, and we, a part of her. Our bodies sprang from her womb, and back to her they must eventually return, slowly breaking down into the elements from which they formed. Her rocks are our bones; her rivers, our bloodstreams; her fertile soil, our flesh.

Our bodies belong to Mother Earth and our spirits to the Great Father, God; and this isn't a new concept. Many centuries ago, a Brotherhood known as the Essenes were active in the areas around Palestine at the time of Jesus, to whom these teachings were a reality. Jesus was one of their sect, wearing the white robe of the *Therapeutae*—translated as 'physicians', or 'healers'. He learned the gentle healing arts from these peace-makers, who loved the silence and tried to live a pure life. They understood the necessity of clean living and tending the Great Mother with loving hands.

Here's White Owl again:

If we look to Nature, everything is held in a state of constant change, yet perfect balance. But once man interferes with Nature's equilibrium, disaster results.

Man is the greatest slayer of life-forms; he threatens to make the Great Whales extinct, chops down vast atmosphere-regulating forest lands, and continually pollutes rivers and seas with dangerous toxic chemicals.

Untold harm is daily tilled into Earth's soil, while life-threatening sprays and fumes are dispersed far and wide into her atmosphere, now thinning out and enlarging the gap in her protective ozone layer. This will result in harmful rays penetrating man's skin and causing all manner of problems and virulent diseases.

Harmful poisons in the earth are absorbed by plants which are eaten by animals, and unwise individuals who still consume meat welcome them into their bloodstreams. Even compassionate vegetarians and vegans cannot completely escape these frightening side-effects.

It therefore comes as no surprise that humankind suffers with widespread 'incurable' diseases, cancers, and generally poor health.

Man is now literally reaping what he has sown—no more, no less.

But if we just changed our habit pattern, stopped and consciously *thought* about what we're actually doing when purchasing chemical solvents and household cleaners which will destroy marine life, and subsequently, us—it wouldn't take a second to leave the poisons on the supermarket shelf and choose the environmental-friendly brands—at least, then, we'd be helping our planet's slow recovery towards health and harmony. And if man returned to a natural way of life, eating clean chemical-free food, breathing fresh unpolluted air and drinking pure water, superior physical health could be his.

The body of the Great Mother is daily damaged by hidden nuclear waste materials; sealed in concrete blocks and metal drums, they are buried in secrecy, deep in caverns under the sea. But the Earth is still evolving, and its movement will one day burst open these highly radio-active time-bombs, releasing into the planet's veins a life-killing poison. Then there will be no escaping the harmful radiation. How unthinking and careless can man be? Each day he slowly destroys the very source of his physical well-being. There will be a heavy price to be paid, for we can't hurt the planet without eventually damaging ourselves.

But the only way Mother Earth will be understood as a Living Being is through educating the ignorant—by us raising our voices and shining the good examples of our lives. If we protect our wildlife, beautiful countryside, rain forests, clear bright seas and all the wondrous pageant of the natural world, we shall not only heal the planet but also improve our quality of living.

But if we *don't* cleanse our Great Mother, the next generations may suffer horrific diseases and unspeakable miseries.

And so now to the many requests for Spiritual Healing I receive. Let me say that from the moment your letters arrive help is sent out. Distance is no obstacle to the Power of God's Love and His Presence; the Healing Light is Everywhere, without and within.

A Simple Exercise for Self-Healing

If you sit quietly for 15 minutes each day, thinking of being healed, or God, or colourful flowers and trees, rolling countryside, a candle flame maybe, or any restful pleasant thoughts which ease your mind and achieve that quiet attitude of 'building castles in the air', then my prayers and healing thoughts will reach you. You will also be placing yourself in a receptive frame of mind to absorb the Cosmic Healing Powers all around us. There is an endless well of life-giving energy to be tapped at will.

If it helps, select a photograph of me in this book, look into my eyes, and draw upon the Healing Power of Love, a Golden Light which soothes, refreshes and heals the spirit, mind and body.

And never despair—always keep bright, positive and cheerful. Expect improvements and await them with eagerness, never placing limits on what can be achieved by the Power. The lame have walked, the blind have seen, and oh so many people have been greatly helped.

So, may God bless and aid you to find your Peace Within, for when your mind is at ease, your body will reflect this, and all dis-ease may be removed. And remember, this healing exercise needs no religious creeds or dogmas to activate it, and no special intermediary—it's just between you and your God.

And according to your Faith, be it unto you.

Morning-Light

Rising in a timeless lake of dreams
To conscious power,
Eyelids flicker and inwardly glean
The final fragments of a passing world.

He breathes again on Mother Earth
As nightlight fades, eager to be dawn.
And moving to the window, he feasts
Upon the coming of the morn.

Tactile trees, black-horizoned, still unmoved
As their tranquilled breeze desists and dies,
Know something wonderful is immanent.
And before his marvelled gaze,
Magic lanterns stream across the skies:
Gleaming, dying;
Starlight rods reaching out to God.

A distant skylark, spirit-moved, opens its throat
And brightlight sings,
While violet moves away for blue;
And the naked Watcher slips the latch, unseen,
And softly treads the dankerous earth,
Drawn by resplendent hue.

With outstretched arms and face to the sky,
In nakedness, he's
Washed in mystic energies on the height;
Alive again, reborn again,
To feel again and know again the Power of the Light
That wakes and breathes and touches him
And heals world-aching sight.

Purple to green, to orange to gold,
Till yellow daylight ignites his soul
And whitens the tranquil sky;
Imbibing and reviving,
Till every portion feels and knows
From whence it came,
And why.

> *'No man can paint*
> *Nor picture hold*
> *Its incandescent sigh.'*

Watcher, stand bare-breasted,
Beating At One with the Greatest Heart, and rejoice
Lest you forget that from out of this
Came every lustrous shining part.

Feel the wind embrace your pristine soul, and
Bathe in glorious floodlit gleams;
Let body thrill with penetrating wonder:
Let loins and arms be totally engrossed
By the Cleansing Touch of the Highermost.

Pounding joysounds infuse with mighty awe
As the Watcher sparkles and glows divine;
Dazzling threads of visible Godlight, thrill
To him and through him and from him again.

It caresses trees and parklands; birds and houses;
Fixing dusky shapes apart;
Tickling awake longsleeping grasses that stretch up
To touch a Universal Heart.

Naked,
I behold the naked light,
Fashioned by Mind Omnipotent:

Naked,
I behold the fading of the dying night,
Composing magic strains fresh-lent—

For I am the Watcher,
And my soul from pure Omnipotence was sent.

Rise then, o sun, in beauteous sight—
But touch me not no other living thing—
These Watcher's tears are not for sorrow shed,
But for the magnificence of Morning-Light:

And naked they will stand and drink with me
A myriad glistening rainbow rays; at this,
The birth of another sunblest day.

10

Northern Lights

August '85 saw a big Welsh send-off for me, days before I moved to England. There was a public presentation at the Psychic Centre in Swansea, which I'd helped to establish, and where I'd served for three years as Vice-President and trained many new mediums for the platform.

After a service of Psychometry—where psychic sensitives hold objects and sense accurate details from them about their owners—the presentation was made, the audience applauding as I was handed a large wrapped gift.

'Now come on, Stephen,' said the Secretary, 'you've just been teaching us Psychometry. Show us how it's done! What's in the parcel?'

Without hesitation, I replied, 'A copper plaque of the *Desiderata* writings.'

'Ooh my goodness, *he's got it*!' she yelled—and everyone laughed!

After sad goodbyes, spluttering from exhaust fumes while locked in the back of a truck with my meagre possessions, I sallied forth from my native Wales to live in north-east England. After the 400-mile, 10-hour journey came all the frantic unloading. Then my Welsh drivers pulled away, shouting, 'Be happy, Stephen! Be HAPPY!' Little did I know then that a great deal of my life up North would prove anything but happy: it was two years of unmitigated hell.

Though the move was predicted by the Beyond, they didn't reveal I'd be living in the poorest area of Gateshead with many soul-crushing hardships lying in wait. My council flat was a most peculiar place built on three split levels, joined by four flights of noisy wooden stairs, 28 in all, and I didn't have a brass farthing to carpet them.

I was still unemployed and penniless, but chirpy friends said, 'Make ends meet.' 'Listen, I can't even *find* the ends to join them together!' I said.

Then I launched a brave effort to make my flat feel like a home—but failed dismally. It never was a home, just somewhere to live, in the worst estate I'd ever seen in my life, and there was to be nothing but trouble for me there.

Most nights the indescribably disgusting smell of burning paraffin oozed up into the rooms from beneath, as well as other smells. Sometimes I could hardly breathe; the choking fumes were stifling. God knows what they were cooking beneath me, but *I* wouldn't eat it; the stench was foul. So I borrowed masking tape, then on hands and knees tried sealing the gaps in the floor, to no avail. Every smell reappeared somewhere else and, like Marley's ghost, they wouldn't go away. I was physically sick, breathing the putrid air.

But worse still, I was trapped in a rabbit-warren of filth. The shared walkways were disgustingly dirty: full of litter, unrepeatable graffiti, rotting garbage, and urine. I was amongst people who cared for nothing, not even themselves. Their households were riddled with debt, crime, ignorance, and no respect for life. The children were plentiful and abusive, and living in squalor. When the government says there were no poor in Britain in the 1980s, I cringe at the shameful lie. I lived near youngsters with no shoes on their feet, dirty faces, twisted minds and neglected bodies—an all too sad reflection of the widening class gaps at that time.

There was no telling what you might find on stone stairways linking different levels—that is, if you could stomach the vile stench of human waste plastered over the filthy walls. The tenants behaved like animals, ripping down and burning garden fences for 'fun' and 'something to do'. It was a living nightmare that I prayed I'd wake from. Every door along my walkway was firmly locked, empty flats boarded up, bolted and sealed with padlocks and six-inch nails against looting, arson and vandalism, which were all frequent occurrences. Robbers wrenched out electrical sockets, doors and windows, and disconnected copper water boilers for sale on the black market. It was a frightened community, living in fear of itself.

At night, unable to sleep, I'd listen to fights outside my door: people reeling about drunk, smashing windows, swearing like troopers, and punching each other until blood was drawn and left where it fell. There were frequent fast chases with victims flung headlong into passageways. People screamed, but I'm afraid *my* doors remained tight-locked; they deserved each other. One night a couple were fighting beneath me and there was a thunderous bang and the smashing of glass: he'd thrown her through a plate-glass door. 'Stephen,' I moaned, 'what are you doing here?', half-suspecting it was another soul-learning time.

But worse was to come: one night a drunken man tried to break down my front door. Hammering, he threatened to kill me with a knife if I didn't let him in. I dashed to the phone (not a luxury, a necessity) and within minutes two police officers arrived, but by then he'd made his escape. They seriously advised: 'Take it from us, you're too good to live here.'

'But I've nowhere else to go. I'm from Wales—400 miles away. Besides, I've no money.'

'Take our advice: *move*. Didn't you see the fire next door? Someone tried to burn the people out. Nobody decent lives here, it's full of tax-dodgers, debtors and all sorts. They run here to get away from troublemakers, but the troublemakers come and get them.'

For the first time I felt a little frightened. 'Are many incidents reported?'

'Hundreds each year: burglaries, fires, grievous bodily harm, malicious woundings, abuse and slander—'

'There's no need to go on,' I interrupted, rubbing my forehead in dismay.

'Take a fool's advice—get out, and the sooner the better.' Then they left.

In the early hours of that morning I considered their warning, but decided because growth comes from challenge, I'd stick it out as long as I could. But how I prayed for the house of my dreams—somewhere silent, far from noisy cities; somewhere in the country, nestling in a green valley where birds perch in the hedgerows and the rustle of autumn winds sing in the giant trees. How wonderful it would be to wake in the morning to the glorious sounds of God's country: humming bees and birdsong, the scent of summer flowers gently wafting through my window. I've always needed somewhere to walk alone in the silent hills; alone with my thoughts, alone with God. Peace and stillness would refresh my spirit. Then, at night, when the red sun sets, I'd be at perfect peace. But these were all dreams—and still are—and unless by some miracle a kind soul bequeaths me this haven of rest, I just can't see how I'll ever achieve it.

Something else I couldn't swallow—or perhaps I did swallow them—was the toughened strain of northern germs. Within a week of arriving I was flat out with the worst virus I'd ever experienced. My chest felt as though an iron band had been welded around it as I wheezed away long into the night. Shivering hot and cold, vision blurring, delirium blanking my mind, there wasn't an ounce of strength in my body; I couldn't move. The lonely dark bedroom swam before me. I'd always fought illnesses, even working in public through them—but this time I was beat. Like a limp lettuce leaf, I hung over the bedside weeping like a lost child, with no one to care for me. I cursed the northern bugs, and felt utterly sorry for myself.

It took ages to get well again, then I ventured out to explore the big city, and what I found cheered me up no end. Newcastle was a lovely place—curiously old yet young, full of ancient and modern architecture. My breath was taken clean away by the buzzing city activities: clowns and agile acrobats on the quayside of the River Tyne, accompanied by skilful street musicians and a one-man band, whose music filled the sharp air with lively sound. In the heart of the bustling crowds were thousands of black squealing starlings, circling far above the town, then huddling warmly together on high buildings, to fight off the biting cold winds. And every day a ragged old gypsy birdwoman came to feed the hungry wild pigeons, who cooed around her like grateful children. What kind eyes she had.

In Eldon Square, a massive undercover shopping mall, thousands of bobbing heads hypnotically swayed, and I was still very weak from my illness and got so flustered by thronging strangers jostling against me that I almost fainted away.

When normality returned, I boarded the 'Metro'—fast electric trains linking most of the North-east together. They were marvellous. But on that day, shooting through underground stations at lightning speed and whizzing out into blinding daylight across huge steel bridgework over the cold River Tyne made me dizzy. When I got home, I went straight to bed.

On the cheerier side, there was a magnificent breath-taking vista of Newcastle City from my window: buildings as far as the eye could see in the blue hazy light, with the River Tyne snaking in and out between them, glinting in the cold August air. The crispy newness of everything sent a thrill right through me as I realized there were countless new places to explore, fascinating people to meet. After all, a great part of this marvellous adventure was to get away from everything stale and make a new life in a new land.

One of my first major hurdles was to understand the local dialect: Geordie. It was very peculiar! People would say: 'Whyaye man, weerya gan noo?'

'Pardon?' I'd frown, knitting my brows together. Roughly translated, what they'd said was: 'Well yes, man, where are you going now?'

I really loved the Geordie accent! I once stood at a bus-stop for over 10 minutes, sympathetically nodding my head in seeming agreement while an elderly Geordie woman prattled on and on about something or other, at the end of which I broke the awesome silence with, 'I'm sorry, but I didn't understand a word you said!' And another of their funny habits was to precede everything with an outburst of '*EEeee*!' delivered loudly, accompanied by a twisted simian grimace, with jaw stuck out and no real meaning attached. It's the equivalent of 'Well, I never!' I loved it, and was soon scuttling around expressing my '*EEeees*' right, left and centre—even in places where they weren't really needed!

But as the months tumbled over, things got miserably worse, and something else began to depress me: the North's atrocious weather. I thought I'd perish through hypothermia. While twisting winds whipped and whirled outside, my now-famous cat Sooty and I curled up in a warm blanket before the one-bar electric fire.

'Never mind,' I'd say, as she looked up at my blue nose, 'at least we've got our love to keep us warm!' But outside the crisp frost glistened on bleak moonless nights as we pricked up our ears at the relentless wind howling through window frames. With icy legs and freezing feet, I cursed that old saying 'And the North Wind doth blow, and we shall have snow.' The chilly air froze my exhaled breath, and this was *indoors*! Outside, people rushed like lemmings into warm shops, snorting steam like dragons as they clicked along hard stone pavements. Furious windspeeds often dropped the mercury even further down the thermometer.

Down in the blustery road one night, I watched a windswept polythene sheet pinned around a lamp-post. Flapping wildly in the gale, its clapping noise frightened an elderly woman nearby. Suddenly it loosed itself, flew across the road and wrapped right around her legs. She kicked and pulled at the ghostly parasite, but it wouldn't move. The more she picked at its skin, the tighter it clung, until she fell under its ragged tentacles. The mighty wind then whipped away her headscarf, blowing it right up into the night sky, over the trees and out of sight, as she freed herself and scurried off after it in the darkness.

Tin cans were always bouncing noisily down the streets,

clanking past black trees, long since stripped bare of every leaf. Even birds deserted the skies to cover their hungry young inside cold nests and the trees housing them lurched violently back and forth as the wind screamed through their bending branches.

'No wonder the Romans banished people to northern Britain,' I said to Sooty, 'it's the worst punishment there is!' Gale-force winds dropped the temperature to six below zero on some nights, and when it rained *it meant it*! I'd battle uphill against what felt like freezing cold ice-bullets piercing my skin. A clinging dampness seeped through even the thickest clothes—but my only outer coat was a thin plastic anorak, much the worse for years of wear and tear. Even the cat's fur felt cold, and on bright sunny days we'd get what I called 'arctic sunshine'—a brilliant blue sky and blazing sun, yet freezing winds gnawing at your bones like shark's teeth.

Shopping was a regular fiasco. I'd struggle against the gales, moving 45 degrees into the cyclone, with two carrier-bags catching the full blasts like plastic parachutes! I'd be wildly blown over the roads all the way 'home'. Flopping exhausted into a chair, I'd sit listening to winds howling round the building like screaming banshees. I just wasn't used to it. People told me it would be cold all year round, and I now believed them!

Soon news broke that Stephen O'Brien had arrived 'fresh' from the South, and work started pouring in, fulfilling the Other Side's prediction of supporting many charitable ventures through venue ticket sales. I was soon busy taking Spiritualist services as well as larger public meetings and lectures on the paranormal and mediumship training. Before long my time was full of enterprise, and I became one of England's Northern Lights!

During one seminar I psychically selected two promising students and got them working with the public under my watchful eye, delivering messages from the spirit world. One of them was Adrian, and this led to a lovely friendship with him and his wife, Moira, and mother-in-law, dear Lily. I also met Isobel and Joyce, two platform mediums, and eventually I took two private psychic circles in different towns. Along with my old friends Sheila, Graeme, Keith and Elizabeth, these people formed my close circle of friends, and I soon had plenty of spiritual work to occupy my time. There were many people needing help.

Despite all the hardships and depressions at the flat, my psychic powers weren't adversely affected. In fact, they increased! One day, standing before a juke-box looking at the selection, I simply *thought* I'd choose *The Crystals* singing an old classic, and while fumbling in my pockets for a coin, the machine suddenly started clicking and whirring, and I stood amazed as my record played all by itself—*twice*! 'How's that for psychic power!' friends said, as I popped the coin into a collection-box for blind children.

At another meeting, where I'd been speaking about the Nazarene and his work, I was suddenly surprised when a weighty black leather-bound Book started waddling down the lectern towards me of its own accord. 'We've got a walking Bible here!' I announced, as everyone leaned forward in their seats to watch it. And when I told someone, in a message, that they'd visited a fortune-teller, but 'You'll get the *truth* here!', there was an almighty cracking *rap* on a nearby mirror. Everyone in the front row ducked! They thought someone had thrown a coin at the platform! But, of course, it was the spirit people. 'Someone Over There agrees with us!' I smiled. 'It's all right, you can sit up now!' To which someone shouted back from the congregation: 'That always happens when you're here, Stephen!'

I know I feel very close to the Other Side sometimes, but I nearly joined them at another meeting, when I got a thunderous electric shock as I touched a faulty microphone. I crumpled and let out a yell as the searing pain shot up my left arm, and the audience gasped. I cringed, recovered, then wittily said: 'The messages should be much clearer tonight after that power-boost!' But I was lucky—I could have 'died' and been *giving* the messages, instead of *receiving* them!

The months rolled by, and the work poured in and I was kept forever busy helping countless strangers understand the great truth of everlasting life. Now it was nearly Christmastime, my first December living far away from home. All the festive sights and sounds buzzed in the air. Newcastle came alive with thousands of bright Christmas lanterns and smiling shoppers who gathered around the famous animated figures in Fenwick's shop windows—that year several scenes from *Pinocchio* were enacted by life-size mechanical puppets, accompanied by songs and a taped story. They even had a huge whale in one of the windows (!) and the sparkling Blue Fairy with her magic wand enchanted all the children and adults crowding around the spectacular show, until another street attraction caught their eyes: the Dancing Waters, where huge water-spouts and fountains dazzled and danced to music, spurting 20 feet into the air, lit by bright-coloured lights—silvers, blues and golden sprays. The 30-feet long display made every passer-by stop and stare. Children cried out gleefully, 'EEeee, look Mam! It's magic! EEeee!'

Yet despite these marvellous sights, something else struck at my heart: the deadening pain of homesickness stifled my throat and overtook me. Me! The self-sufficient being! A hollow raw emptiness was eating through my mind and emotions, numbing my actions. At these times, I found no pleasure in solitude. New friends were busy and I was out on a limb, totally alone and longing for my roots, my homeland. Some nights it was so bad I just wanted to run as fast as I could, back home to Wales.

The only way to forget was to burst out into the crisp, empty Sunday night streets. And there I'd pass silent terraced houses: every door locked and bolted fast against the bitter Christmas winds, every stranger passing swiftly with covered head held down, shoes clicking by uncaringly. How I longed to find some open door on those lonesome nights, how I ached to see smiling familiar faces beckoning in friendship to sit by a blazing coal fire. I had plenty of friends in Wales—a lifetime's worth—but not here, not now, not tonight.

The shadowy tight-packed terraces were long and unwelcoming, the streets were endless, the park gates padlocked, and not a living soul was anywhere in sight. At such times, I'd sit anywhere—in cafés, outside chip-shops—anywhere people gathered so I could hear their muffled chattering. Then, cold and lonely, homeward I'd go. But sometimes I just couldn't face it: the dirt and grime, the selfish tenants and filthy surroundings, they'd all get to me, and on such nights I'd go anywhere but 'home'. I'd be off on some spontaneous journey or other, a mystery tour. I didn't care where, as long as it wasn't back to my flat.

One night I ended up miles away, down in South Shields, a small coastal town with a ferryboat dock. Silently, I boarded the lonely quayside ferry on the banks of the Tyne. It was a purple-skied night and the boat was empty of passengers. Despondently, I climbed the iron stairs to the upper deck and stood with my whitened fingers clutching the rusty guardrail as the ferry chugged its way out onto the chilly black waters. I was feeling sad, depressed and miserable. Christmas was coming, and I felt so alone.

Here and there some squawking seagulls were diving for bread scraps bobbing on the dark undulating river. And as *The Shieldsman* powered its way to the opposite dock, I no longer felt the numbing cold on my face, for I pondered on the great imponderables—why, where and how—just as I'd done when I was a child in my homeland.

Somewhere a distant ship's foghorn split the night, and a dog barked in the hidden streets far off. They were lonesome, hollow sounds, stirring my own loneliness deep within. A single seagull floated on the rippling black water, his wings folded, his head tucked well down on his chest—and I knew he was just like me, facing the purple sunset and the brisk night breeze on his own. His body broke the twinkling sky's reflection on the river and I couldn't help thinking: 'We're two of a kind, you and me; both completely alone—only, you belong here, but I'm 400 miles from my roots, from my home . . .'

It was then I realized I would 'die' in the North-east—not *physically*, but the man who'd eventually leave wouldn't be the person who'd come from Wales. These experiences would challenge me *spiritually*, and help me grow. I was passing now through a twilight land; a place of deep uncertainty; on a restless black journey through the caverns of my inner self, where the spirit is tested and assailed by doubts and temptations, and unkind influences.

Not the first visionary to suffer these torments, still I wanted to fling away the mantle of service, throw aside my spiritual work, reject my pathway and lose my purpose. And devious spirit voices gathered around my depression, encouraging this. My faith and loyalty to the Spirit of Love were tempted and tested. I was out in a wilderness. Face to face with my life, my work, my future and past, I fought to decide them all. And I was utterly alone. The Dark Night of the Soul was upon me . . .

It was in this spirit of thoughtfulness and longing that Graeme, Sheila and I, three friends together, walked the following evening to a weatherbeaten church for a Christmas Eve midnight carol concert. The gentle breeze turned cold and the first frail snowflakes of winter suddenly began to fall, pirouetting, dancing on the air and carpeting the gloomy streets. 'It seems we'll have a white Christmas after all,' said kindly Sheila, brushing the crystals from her long black hair.

'I wonder if it's snowing in Wales,' I replied sadly, deep in nostalgic thought, as we made our way through the glistening streets and took our places at the back of the cold church. Most of the seats were full, for the service was already underway.

The grand swell of organ music rang out and richly filled the ancient building with spine-tingling sound. Then the people stood tall and opened their hearts and loudly sang their praises to the Prince of Peace. And as the congregation and choir harmonized the beautiful strains of *Silent Night, Holy Night, All is calm, All is bright*, I felt a wall of tears filling my eyes in remembrance of a life and land long-distant, a place which seemed so far out of reach now. Christmases of long ago gently floated before my mind's eye: happy memories of when I was a boy and mother was alive and full of festive smiles and love; and then I could see my dearest friends in Wales, and I cried for the many kindnesses they'd shown me over the years. My song was for them, and my heart pounded loudly to go home again, in that pensive hour, on that snowy, freezing night. As the beautiful music surged and my thoughts ran free, I made no effort to wipe away the tears on my cheek.

Yet, from that Greater World Beyond came only Silence . . . there was no call of my name; no sweet sound of comfort from the family I loved; no vanished hand upon my shoulder; no heavenly presence nearby. My spirit wandered through a vale of sadness, unaccompanied.

So there, amongst the singing throng, I was strangely alone with my thoughts and precious memories, haunting me through my trials; solitary in my longing for my distant loved-ones—and gently weeping, on this, my first northern Christmas, so very far away from home.

11

'Suffer the Little Children . . .'

It happened every morning at 6 a.m: THUMP! THUMP! THUMP! THUMP!—kicking and knocking on the walls and floors of the flat above. I'd be rudely woken at six on the dot, half-dazed and grumping for sleep. But I never got it, the noises just got louder and worse. THUMP! THUMP! THUMP! THUMP!

Leaning out of bed, semi-conscious, I'd pound on the hollow walls, then the dreadful noise momentarily stopped. 'Ahh, peace . . .' I'd sigh, turning over and covering my grateful ears with the sheets. Then it would start again, banging and knocking, kicking and the rattling of bed-supports. THUMP! THUMP! THUMP! THUMP!

Then one morning, my patience finally cracked. 'For God's sake, *be quiet*!' I shouted furiously. 'Give me a break! *Let's have some peace and quiet!*' Then an almost shocked, stunned pause followed, and silence reigned. But the awful noises started up again. With a banging headache to match the din, I dismally buried my sleepy head under the blankets, the infernal racket clattering on and on, and on and on and on, every sunrise for several hours, for weeks on end.

Finally, there was nothing for it but to seek out the culprit and deliver a piece of my mind, but (predictably) no one knew anything about the disturbances. Everyone denied causing them. 'Well, it isn't ghosts,' I yelled, knowing I'd have seen them, 'nor mice!' thinking that if it was, they must be wearing hobnailed boots and slugging back the whiskey each night. '*I* don't know nothing about it!' snarled one hefty female resident, sporting for an argument. Then she slammed her door in my face.

The trouble was, the flats were built in a most peculiar way: everyone slept at the back and lived in the front, all piled high on top of each other. But certain living-rooms were lower than their bedrooms, plus the stairways connecting backs to fronts were all criss-crossed in an impossible-to-untangle maze. If it sounds confusing, it was! I hadn't a clue whose bedrooms were above mine. So I wrote to the Housing Department complaining about the din, then crossed my fingers and hoped for the best. But time dragged on and the noise grew louder, earlier and more belligerent, and now entered a new phase: vocals. Occasionally there'd come a shout—a wordless grunt, an angry cry. I began to get concerned, thinking it was a young distressed child. But why didn't he or she speak?

Silence came from the Civil Service (no shock there, judging by years of past experience), so I tried a spot of Other-World medicine: *The Power of Prayer.*

My spirit friend, White Owl, had often taught me:

> Prayer is a stream of Living Thought. It radiates outwards, rippling the atmosphere, and is registered by people in the world of spirit who exist on roughly the same frequency as the person praying.
>
> Prayer is 'heard' by sensing the Language of Thought. If it contains good and noble requests which, if granted, benefit both parties involved, we do what we can to materialize the desired results on Earth.
>
> However, selfish greedy prayers are often ignored by evolved souls in my world. Thoughts are *alive* and great care should be taken to regulate them, for they will certainly draw the response they deserve, once the time is right. 'Like Attracts Like.'

With all this in mind, that night I transmitted a stream of thought to invisible friends (I never bother them unless unable to cope myself). 'I've done all I can,' I lamented. 'I think someone needs your help, and if you can also solve this dreadful noise problem,

I'd be grateful.' A simple request for aid, I left it in trust to the spirit world, planning to be very patient.

A few days later, there was a knock on my back door. I was sitting in a makeshift living-room I'd set up in a bedroom at the back of the block, the residents' televisions being too loud to bear in the proper living areas. I gingerly peeked around the door, and there stood a cultured mature woman, immaculately dressed in pale matching colours, something quite out of place on our estate.

'Hello,' she smiled. 'May I please speak with you, Mr O'Brien?'

'Certainly,' I replied, immediately warmed by her gentle countenance. She settled comfortably on the settee, introducing herself as Mrs Smythe.

'What can I do for you, Mrs Smythe?'

'Well, I've come to ask if you've heard anything unusual, anything at all, small disturbances in the area maybe? Or anything else . . .?' Her kind voice trailed away, begging for response, and her eyes were strangely full of hope.

'Why yes,' I chipped in enthusiastically. 'Are you from the Housing Department? I complained to them recently.'

'Really?' she asked, moving to the very edge of her seat. 'Can you tell me why?'

'Well, because of the dreadful noise above these bedrooms.' Then I gave a blow-by-blow account of the early morning fiascos I'd suffered for months. I don't think I've ever seen such a relieved expression appear on anyone's face—she heaved a sigh of shivering proportions and raised her eyes to heaven, uttering: 'Thank God, oh thank God . . .' I was more than intrigued. 'I can't believe it,' she murmured, seemingly stunned by my innocent remarks.

'Is something wrong?'

'Oh no, Mr O'Brien, quite the opposite,' she said, regaining composure, 'everything's *right*. You see, I'm a social worker assigned to a problem family here, and for months now my department's suspected them of maltreating their son. He's three years old but only looks about 18 months, so painfully thin and neglected. He can't speak a word, because no one's ever spoken to him properly, or spent time teaching him. Then, last week we found a cigarette burn on his frail little body—'

'My God, you mean—'

'Yes, but cruelty's hard to prove. You see, we have very little evidence. Whenever we confront the father he says, "How do *you* know what goes on in my house?" Our hands have been tied.'

'Until you read my letter at the housing offices?'

'What letter is that?'

'But I clearly stated I thought a distressed child was involved.'

'I'll get on to it straightaway,' she said, rising urgently, obtaining my promise to report any further noises, for the sake of the little child. I also said I'd visit her superiors about the case, which I immediately did.

Interviewed by a kindly Mr Davis, he profusely thanked me for the help I'd given. 'Your testimony is invaluable,' he beamed. 'Now we have something concrete to go on. If the case proceeds to court, would you be a witness?' I agreed straightaway, thoughts of that poor child locked in his bedroom haunting my mind. Mr Davis continued, 'We've been unable to prove the father's aggression, until today. Our suspicions are now substantiated, thanks to your concern, Mr O'Brien.'

'Whatever you do,' I pleaded, 'please don't close the files on this case; anything might happen to the little boy. I'll give you all the help I can.'

'I can now reveal,' he said, consulting his notes, 'we're trying to get this family moved, somewhere more conventional, with bedrooms at the front. In such a place this problem would never have occurred; the tot's cries would have been heard and reported much sooner.'

I was delighted something was being done, and a few days later, warm-hearted Mrs Smythe called again, and confirmed, 'They've been locking their son in the bedroom all day, not even changing his wet underclothes. He hasn't been toilet-trained. These flats are death-traps for children in problem families. If it wasn't for your conscience, we would never have known the

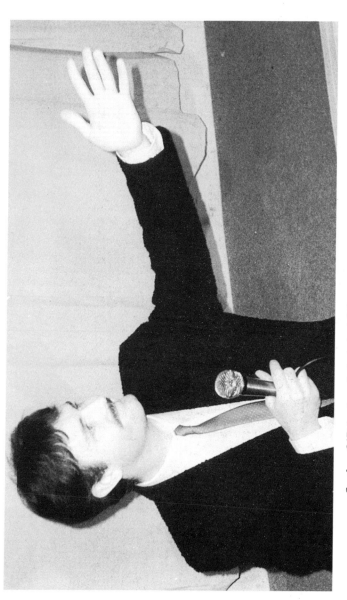

Stephen O'Brien 'caught in action' delivering one of the thousands of messages from Beyond he gives each year.

Young Jamie Allen, seven, died of liver cancer—but returned to his father through Stephen's psychic gifts with 'remarkably accurate' evidence.
'Don't cry for me, Daddy. I'm still alive and I love you.'

Stephen outside the old English mansion house where he crossed time zones and came face-to-face with a woman from the past.
'I could have stretched out my hand across the misty centuries, and touched her . . .'

Screen goddess Marilyn Monroe. Through Stephen, she gave startling, controversial messages from beyond the grave.
'Dying's the best thing that ever happened to me.'

Lord Olivier and Vivien Leigh. After his passing, Sir Laurence relayed comforting personal messages to his wife.
'There is Light, not darkness.'

Earl Louis Mountbatten of Burma, killed by terrorists, sent urgent pleas to Prince Philip at Buckingham Palace.

White Owl, a North American Indian, Stephen O'Brien's spirit guide and teacher.
'Take my hand, and I will show you what life is like in the next world . . .'

'Over two thousand people applauded and cheered, as dazzling flashlights exploded in all sections of the vast stadium.'

Stephen and his now-famous cat, Sooty.
'I'm only an ordinary man; Stephen, the boy next-door, who sometimes just happens to hear voices from another world . . .'

truth.' She sighed deeply. 'God alone knows what might have happened to that little boy. He could have starved to death, or something even worse.'

We sat for a silent moment, unable to comprehend how people could be so cruel to the little ones sent from heaven to bring us joy and happiness, whom we're supposed to love and respect all our days. Then the kind woman discovered her speech again. 'Thanks to you, these people *will* be moving soon to a better house, where we'll keep an extra-special eye on their son. He'll even get nursery school training and speech therapy.'

I was overjoyed. 'Tell me, Mrs Smythe, what made you knock on my door the other day?' I quizzed.

'Well, I'd almost given up hope on the whole case, then I . . .' she fidgeted with her handkerchief, then raised her face and looked into my steadfast eyes. 'You see . . . The night before making my housecalls, I prayed for some help. It was a last desperate hope, a final chance that something might be done. Then, as I passed your back door the next day, I suddenly felt inspired to knock. I'm so glad I did. Does that sound very silly?'

'No. For you see, I too prayed for help. It seems someone, somewhere heard our requests and granted them, thank God.'

'Do you really believe that's possible?' asked gentle Mrs Smythe, her kind eyes shining with interest.

'Yes, I do. Even the toddler's cries were answered, weren't they?'

There was a long, respectful silence between us.

'It's amazing really,' she said at last, those big eyes now twinkling.

'Tell me, Mrs Smythe . . . do you believe in the Power of Prayer?'

And there was only a further moment's pause for thoughtful consideration, after which she smiled back at me, leaned forward slightly in her seat and said quietly, 'You know something, Mr O'Brien . . . I think I do.'

12

'Oh Great White Spirit . . .'

[White Owl delivers an Invocation.]

Oh Great White Spirit,
we open our hearts and souls unto Thee
in innocent trust, like children
seeking
refreshment for our spirits,
knowledge for our minds,
and light for our pathway.

We are grateful for the challenges which beset us
and test us through life—
for these are the priceless jewels of spiritual progression
disguised as torment,
trial and hardship,
which,
when faced, overcome and defeated,
have made us richer in the spirit.

Through pain we have come to know compassion;
through sorrow, joy;
through blinding darkness, effulgent light;
and through wandering in confusion and despair,
we have come to know Thee.

We thank Thee for the great truths so far vouched-safe to us,
and now reaffirm our promise
to shine them into the Mind of Man
through any means at our disposal.

May channels for the Power of Thy Spirit
present themselves for service,
with hearts full of gentle compassion,
that together we may spread the love of brotherhood
wide throughout the Earth;
destroying barriers of
materialism, creed,
racialism, intolerance,
ignorance and selfishness,
(which steal away freedom and happiness).

Sweeping these aside with Thy Mighty Understanding,
we pray for strength to deliver these revelations,
and encourage minds to
love all
help all
and care for all Creation.

May peace reign
in the hearts of all Your Children,
wherever they may be.

Oh Great White Spirit,
May the time come quickly
when men know Thee for what Thou Art—
not a vengeful deity, shaped as a jealous man,
but a Great Power of Consciousness which
Sees,
Hears,
and Knows all things.

Thou Art in the burning sunshine,
behind the sparkling eyes of a little child,
in the beauty and splendour of flowers
and in flights of feathered birds.
In Majesty, through Immutable, Eternal Natural Laws
are Thy wondrous works seen:
Laws which wheel the stars in spiral courses,
ebb and flow the endless tides;
Celestial Rulings which fill us with wonder at the
secret forming of a child, and the miracle of its birth,
and the Mystery of how Thy Consciousness
breathes into common clay,
begetting Life.

Thou Art within,
and without;
beneath, above, alongside,
and through all forms and expressions of Life.
Thou Art the Divine Architect,
The Lawgiver,
The Unfolding Creator;
Our Father
And Our Mother—
and We Are All Thy Children,
Each One.

And for all Thy Many Blessings,
hidden and seen,
accept now
our grateful thanks.

13

Circles

Tuesdays and Fridays were special nights up North, when friends and I sat in the Power of the Spirit in two psychic circles, in much the same way as Jesus and the disciples did in Biblical times, awaiting Other-World manifestations. I was asked to lead both classes.

Every Tuesday tea-time I'd arrive at Sheila's in Jarrow, swinging a cumbersome overnight bag, my cat Sooty clawing madly at her cardboard prison-box, and a massive sporting umbrella knocking everyone sideways on the Metro. Usually drenched, I'd fall onto Sheila's sofa, exhausted by the long trek from Gateshead.

After tea the other sitters arrived, and Graeme, Joyce, Isobel, Sheila and I would all exchange amusing gossip about the latest 'goings-on' in psychic organizations since last we met. After a miserable week in my filthy estate, I really did look forward to these soirées! Laughter was always present, but we knew the serious business of the Physical Circle followed, where the spirit people drew much closer to Earth than they would normally do. Ours was psychically strong: the five sitters were all platform mediums, all powerfully psychic, so the sittings were never boring, but always lively and fascinating. We also got some startling results.

At exactly 8 o'clock we'd sit in a semi-circle in the blacked-out séance room, all freshly bathed, in comfortable clothes. With telephone unhooked to avoid disturbances, I'd then dim the red light, plunging the séance into pitch blackness. Physical manifestations are best created in darkness—just as white light destroys developing photographic images, and babies need darkness to form in their mother's womb, so these special spirit energies are harmed by powerful light: red is the lowest frequency light visible on Earth. But we always started in blackness, followed by a sincere prayer, then happy taped music to help us all relax.

Have you any idea what it's like to sit for a whole hour in pitch blackness? Your eyes are open yet they see nothing but a dark impenetrable shroud. There wasn't any firelight, because of its glow, and on cold nights we were each so tightly wrapped in blankets, it's a living wonder we sensed anything at all!

Then came absolute silence, while we kept our thoughts as spiritual as possible and waited upon 'the messengers'. And we were never disappointed, obtaining some remarkable results: supernormal sounds and visions, spirit messages, rappings, small blue and golden discs of spirit-light floating in the air, or columns of silver energy building up then slowly dissolving into nothingness, plus spirit gifts, and disembodied hands touching our faces and moving around the room. Friends from the Other Side were trying to physically materialize themselves, for us to see what the 12 disciples must have experienced when the Nazarene appeared to them at similar séances in centuries past.

Isobel frequently reported spirit hands touching her shoulders, as indeed I did. The Other Side had withdrawn sufficient psychic power from the sitters to clothe their spirit hands in a substance called ectoplasm, taken from body fluids and tissues. Once this was done, their hands became physical for a short time, but after the séance the power was always returned to the mediums, and the forms disappeared, or dematerialized.

Poor Isobel, she was also plagued quite often by another strange occurrence. 'Stephen? Did you just get up and walk past me?'

'No, I haven't moved.'

'Well, I'll eat hay with a donkey! Who was that then?!' And we'd all laugh. 'Somebody's been hoofing it around here tonight—the little blighter went right past my face! Blooming cheek!' But of course, none of us had shifted an inch. It was a guest; an angel, a visitor from eternity.

Another time she felt a spirit person's breath warming her cool face and heard a man's stertorous breathing gliding around the séance room. Both Joyce and I also reported this (Graeme was asleep, and Sheila had a hearing difficulty).

'If I never move from this spot, that heavy-breather was snorting *right into my left ear*!' quipped Isobel, and there were more smiles all around. 'What a nerve!' She was a marvellous tonic, always ready with a joke, and so good-humoured about the Other Side's frequent pranks, especially when they tickled her nose. 'I don't mind you *itching* it,' she'd haughtily announce, 'as long you *scratch* it as well!'

On another occasion, we all heard something odd high above the fireplace. 'Sheila, I think they're scraping at the wallpaper,' Joyce said.

'They can redecorate it if they like! It needs doing!' grinned Sheila. Then I was quite startled—stretching out my tired legs to get the circulation going again, suddenly my foot touched something hard, on the floor, right in front of me. Under my bare toes it felt like a large man's foot, where only seconds earlier there'd been a clear yard of empty floor before me. I quickly withdrew a shaky leg—but no spirit voice said 'Ouch!'

But the most tangible happening came when the Other Side presented us with a spirit gift. One Tuesday, after the séance, we were clearing the room when I found something lying on the floor. It was a small piece of blue paper with German writing on it, about the size of a postage stamp, quite old and worn. It definitely hadn't been there when we started; the room was always cleaned and checked each week.

Our spirit gift, known as an 'apport', had a German town written on one side, and on the other printed letters reading *Tabak*, which none of us understood. There was something very significant about this, however, for the evening before it arrived, Graeme and I had attended an art evening class where there'd been a sharp disagreement between the lecturer and ourselves. She'd allowed smoking in the tiny room and Graeme had announced emphatically, 'If that continues, I'm not going again.'

'Nor me,' I said, the two of us badly affected by cigarette smoke.

Nipping along to the library, we translated the German word *Tabak* on the spirit gift, and found it meant *tobacco*! Furthermore, the lecturer's name was *Greta*! It all tied in so marvellously, showing just how clever the Other Side had been to bring our gift all the way from Germany to Jarrow! 'Thank Gawd it made sense. I was beginning to think they were all "dead" Over There!' quipped Isobel.

But as well as these manifestations we also received wise teachings, personal messages from our loved ones, and sound thoughts on which to build good and fruitful lives.

But the most unusual occurrence happened one bitingly cold winter's evening. 'Eeee! It's freezing in here tonight!' wailed Sheila, clasping her blanket firmly around her legs.

'My feet are like ice-cubes!' added Isobel, while cheery Joyce just turned blue. Other-World draughts were stirring the air and making it colder. The room temperature had already fallen considerably—a frequent occurrence when physical phenomena are developing.

'We should be used to these psychic breezes by now,' I chimed in, my whole body quivering in the icy chill.

'We are, but I'm still nobbled, pet!' chuckled Isobel.

After going into the stillness, all at once the entire room was lit up by a brilliant flash of intense white light, just as though sheet lightning had zipped through the atmosphere. It was a blinding flash, which made my eyes smart, and then it faded out as suddenly as it came. Then there was complete darkness, and absolute silence. No one moved or commented on it. Thinking back now, we must have been a bit nonplussed. Later, Joyce piped up, 'It was definitely a spirit light.' Sheila agreed, and

Isobel sat open-mouthed and dumbfounded. But I wasn't entirely convinced. It *was* a manifestation of energy, certainly, but was it from the spirit world? I wasn't so sure . . .

Over refreshments, I questioned Sheila's son Ashley, who'd been in the next room along the landing with his girlfriend. I noticed a small camera on the coffee table. 'Ashley, did you take a photograph when we were in the circle?'

'Yes.'

'How many?'

'Just the one.'

'And was the camera pointing at the séance room, by any chance?'

'Well yes, it was. Why?'

The mystery was solved. The light was the camera flash, yet a solid wall and passageways lay between the two rooms, and we'd been sitting in pitch darkness—there was no way on Earth it could have got into the circle, not by normal means. The next time we sat, I questioned White Owl, who confirmed my suspicions:

It *was* the flashlight you saw. Not only did it take *you* by surprise, but *we* were also caught unawares! It was unexpected.

When you sit in circle we sensitize the atmosphere, quickening it so that your energies can be used for manifestations. The whole area, even the space beyond the séance room, is quickened, which is why the light penetrated the bricks and mortar: it passed through the atmosphere which was vibrating at a much higher rate than its physical surroundings.

Think of sound waves. When you are in one room, you can sometimes hear speech in the next, reaching you through the walls because the waves pass through them.

In future we will be more careful—but you must remember that we are learning just as you are.

Afterwards, Sheila wittily mused over her cheese flan, 'I don't mind them vibrating the walls, as long as they don't knock them down! They're not paid for yet!'

'I hope you're all listening up there!' laughed Joyce.

One Tuesday night White Owl treated us to a remarkable piece of evidence. I suddenly heard him talk about one of my acquaintances back in Wales. 'Tell Gladys Brooks her mother has arrived safely on our side of life,' he said, following this with a personal message from her mum, which I memorized word for word. Incredibly, later that night Swansea was on the phone about a future booking, when I asked the lady, 'Have you seen Gladys Brooks lately?'

'Yes, she's right here in the room with me!'

'Will you put her on the phone?'

'Certainly.'

Gladys was absolutely amazed when I relayed White Owl's words. *'My mother's just passed away with cancer, Stephen, and I'd asked the Other Side to give me evidence of her survival through someone who knew nothing about it.* Thank you so much.'

And when I told Gladys her mother's exact words, she was over the moon. They were: 'I've arrived safely on the Other Side. And it's just as you said it was. Look after the family, and I'll be through to you again when I'm rested. Love, Mam.'

Gladys replied, 'Stephen, that's remarkable, because I'd sat with my mother as she was dying, whispering to her all about what I thought she'd find after her passing. So her words "It's just as you said it was" mean such a lot.'

White Owl's voice also spoke to me privately at the circles, regarding how miserably trapped I felt in disgraceful living conditions at Gateshead. 'Be patient, my son,' he'd say. 'All will be well, but you must be patient.'

But still I couldn't settle, and suffered many nights robbed of sleep and rest . . . Oh so slowly the agonizing months tumbled over one another and, as I watched the seasons come and go, I couldn't combat the depression. So I threw myself into my mediumship 150 per cent. On the go all the time, I did anything to occupy my mind and get me out of my miserable flat, busying myself with the two circles, taking a course on Moral Philosophy at Newcastle University, gaining a 'distinction' in music examinations, and appearing in many public meetings for worthy causes. Keith and Elizabeth often organized these, and hundreds of pounds of ticket monies were sent to places like Mother Teresa's Mission for the Destitute and Dying in Calcutta. I tried to completely lose myself in service to others, thinking, 'While Mother looks after earthly needs, I'll support her financially by meeting spiritual needs.'

There was an endless roundabout of work whizzing around me all the time. Meanwhile, Sheila kindly eased the pressure by acting as telephone secretary, filtering out my calls—a thankless job she performed brilliantly. Always courteous, she was the epitome of patience. Adrian and Moria, Lily, Graeme—all my new friends rallied round to support me through my dark times. I'll always be grateful for the kindnesses they showed me. Whenever they could, they cooked me meals, invited me to the warmth of their firesides and expressed true friendship to one who often felt like a fish out of water. I'll never forget their greatness of heart.

Even though I was in my late twenties I'd often curl up at night with Sooty purring, crooked into the back of my knees, and say in childlike gratitude, 'Thank you, God, for the love of my special friends, and my warm bed. Thank you for not forsaking me. As troublesome as my flat is, at least I have a roof over my head tonight, which is more than some of your children have.' And I'd drift into troubled sleep, warmed only by the dream-voices of my friends saying: 'If ever you're in the area, don't walk by, pop in and see us. Never feel alone, so far away from home.'

My new friends were so very important to me: without their love and support I don't know what I would have done. Seeing I was on edge, Graeme pulled me out of despair by introducing me to nearly all the Spiritual organizations in the North-east. Sometimes we'd trudge through ankle-deep snow or piercing winter winds and rain, miles on foot or public transport, to what seemed like the outer edges of the known universe, just to help out at a meeting. Some societies were housed in nothing more than small tin sheds set in barren fields. But the welcome was always big.

I lost count of how many comforting messages I delivered to people in need all over the North-east. And everywhere I went people stopped and stared, treating me like a celebrity (I was already well-known in the UK), but I didn't want that: all I needed was a friendly smile, and to be accepted as one of their own.

Sometimes chairpersons would pick me out in public and make a fuss, saying incredibly upsetting things like: 'Welcome to you, Stephen. We're so pleased to have such a famous medium in the North. I understand you live in the swish part of Jesmond and run a guesthouse, is that right?'

'No,' I'd reply quietly. They were convinced I was wealthy, joyously happy and wanted for nothing. Isn't it amazing how people make assumptions? Just because I'd often appeared in *Psychic News* and other publications, they thought life was sweet.

But back on the home front, nothing could have been further from the truth: my life was utterly miserable. The grime and filth of the estate hadn't improved—in fact it was worse: vandalism was rife, and the cruelty of the children completely horrified me. I daren't let Sooty go outdoors for fear of her life. The local newspaper had front-paged a story about a woman who'd caught some children throwing large bricks at a half-drowned kitten in a pool of muddy water, just outside where I lived. I was sickened, loving animals as I do.

'If I hadn't frightened them away,' they reported her as saying, 'they would certainly have killed it. This society's ill.' And with a heavy heart, I had to agree with her, for only the previous week there'd been a blazing fire-ball at the top of the bank nearby: malicious, idle teenagers had set a car alight. The vehicle was completely gutted, leaving only a blackened steel shell. Thankfully it was empty, and no one was hurt.

Behind the car was a recently vacated government building, a modern extension attached to brick offices, and no sooner than it was empty, the thugs moved in and literally kicked it down.

They destroyed everything: they tore out all the electrics and stole them, made off with radiators, lead and copper piping, Venetian blinds, and even ripped out doors and, just like the car, left nothing but a useless, gutted ruin. Then, incredible as it seems, they actually *kicked* the walls down until there was nothing left but a huge pile of dusty bricks and rubble. I just couldn't believe my eyes. Yet worse was to come.

A few days later, when I asked noisy 10 year-olds if they could 'please play in the park, away from the corridors and windows', as well as an unrepeatable gush of foul-mouthed language, the next morning I also received a disgusting reward. At first I thought Sooty had had an 'accident', but further inspection revealed the vandals had pushed dog excrement through the letterbox. I had to throw away the little mat and scrub everything spotlessly clean with disinfectant and boiling water. But it was no use complaining to anyone. Who cared? Who'd do anything about it? No one. And this was how I lived. So much for the guesthouse in Jesmond.

At each Tuesday circle, White Owl's advice kept coming: 'Be patient, and learn. You are never given a cross to bear, without the strength to bear it.' And though I love him, it was hard to believe. Then I remembered that police visit months back, and instantly decided enough was enough. I was going to act on their advice and search for a new home. But the local council delivered a quick shock: 'Some people have wanted to leave your estate for more than 16 years, Mr O'Brien, and they're still waiting.'

My heart sank into my boots. They were saying I was stuck with it: there was no way out. But biting my lip in determination, I promised, 'Well, not me—I'm *moving*!' Then I took matters into my own hands and set about seeking a house exchange with any willing party. I walked miles, visiting all the area housing offices, making notes of anyone listed for swaps, then I tramped the streets for weeks on end until my feet were sore and blistered. I walked and walked until I was fit to drop, knocking on doors and asking for an exchange. 'Where's your flat?' the tenants asked. And when I told them, the usual reaction was cynical laughter and, 'You must be joking! I wouldn't live *there* if you *paid* me!' But the sad thing was, they really meant it, and I understood why.

On what seemed like my hundredth freezing-cold misty-day excursion to some seedy-looking flats in north Newcastle, I bumped right into one of the circle, cheery Joyce. 'EEeee, Stephen! Fancy seeing you here! Where are you off to then, with your A–Z tucked under your arm?' And when I spilled out the whole sorry tale she cooed sympathetically, 'EEeee, that's a dreadful place. What on earth are you doing there, man?'

'All I want is a quiet, decent home,' I groaned emotionally. 'I've walked the streets for weeks, and I feel I'm just going round and around in circles and getting nowhere.' Joyce sat with me on a nearby wall and we rested our aching feet.

'Whey, cheer up then, Stephen, there's a cemetery up the road, that'll be quiet!' she joked in her Geordie accent, trying to cheer me up. But I couldn't raise much of a smile on that day. 'Stephen,' she said seriously, 'you'll never get out of that hell-hole, man. It's my job to collect debts from places like that, and I'm telling you it's a dead loss.' And I feared she was quite right, as all of a sudden a thick dark cloud of hopelessness descended upon me, and defeat set in.

I sadly replied in a lost, pathetic voice, 'I feel so miserable and trapped.'

'Listen, I'll keep an ear open for news of anyone wanting an exchange. But it doesn't look very hopeful, does it?' said Joyce sympathetically.

'No, it doesn't,' I sighed, dismay welling up inside me. 'And it looks as though . . .it looks as though I'm stuck with it.' Joyce patted my shoulder, and we parted on the road. I can't describe the terrible feelings of helplessness which swept right through me on that day. It was as if the whole world had collapsed at my feet, and I had no place to call my own.

I turned my stooped shoulders towards Gateshead, heavy-hearted, dragging my aching sore feet all the way back to the flat—where the widespread grime, disgusting graffiti, rotting trash, and the self-centred thugs and vandals awaited me . . .

14
Time-Slip

It was a roasting-hot July day, even inside Newcastle cathedral. Noticing the ancient doors were open, I'd gone inside, drawn by the peaceful tranquillity. It was as though I'd entered a sound-proof box; busy traffic and bustling shoppers just didn't exist anymore. All around me stood towering stone pillars and centuries-old relics of times long past. Brass and marble plaques decorated the walls in silent tribute to the famed of yesteryear, and grey slate tombstones paved the floors, covering their mortal remains.

Bright sunshine streaming through beautiful stained-glass windows created shafts of rainbow light across the old wooden pews, making the distant altar visible only through this glowing veil. But it was the tangible silence which struck me most—the empty church seemed immersed in it, until I heard clicking footsteps. Turning, I watched a young man enter the organ loft, as I decided to leave, having savoured the cathedral's magical calm. But just as I reached the exit, a spirit voice spoke. 'Rest awhile,' it said. So I did, taking a seat right at the back of the empty church, directly on the aisle near the flat blue tombstones.

Suddenly the magnificent organ pipes deeply sounded a most wonderful hymn: a very old piece indeed, composed and sung in some bygone age; and its melodic strains, coupled with the peacefulness and my exact location in the church, triggered off a Time-Slip, an unexpected journey, way back into the Past. As the still air echoed with joyous chords, my eye-sight blurred and the Present Now slipped away. Then somehow came the sights and sounds from a Now in the Past . . .

Instantly the empty pews were full of worshippers. In the packed church everyone stood tall as the music played. These were people of another time, another age altogether. The women wore coloured ribboned bonnets and long capes with many folds, and the men dressed darkly in rough clothes. I sat there, transfixed, afraid to move and disturb this unique experience. I could hear the blood pulsing in my ears and throat.

Then I saw the procession: moving slowly up the aisle towards me were about 30 silent nuns in black habits, each sister carrying a lighted candle in a brass holder or a glinting lantern, gradually approaching my seat at the back of the church. 'Why nuns?' I wondered. 'I thought this was a Church of England cathedral.' Nevertheless, they were gracefully walking to the majestic music, heads half-bowed in reverent prayer.

Then the most curious thing happened—one of them, a very tall woman, turned her head and stared across at me in my chair, right into my face. She looked terribly surprised (my modern-day clothing, no doubt). Instantly, it dawned on me I'd been *seen* by this woman from a Past Now. *Both of us were at the same place, but the ghosts of ourselves had crossed Time Zones*. She was witnessing a Future scene, while at the same time I was looking into the Past. It seems we both shared the same space in eternity, but at different Times.

Then the oldest nun, supported by two others, must have felt her leg give way, for she dropped to her knees directly in front of me. I half leaned forward to assist, but restrained myself for fear of breaking the link. She was helped to stand again with dignity, and the halted procession continued on its winding way, lanterns and candles shimmering as they filed steadily past me . . .

In a twinkling of an eye, the Past quite suddenly slipped from sight and I was back once more in my Present Now, in the twentieth century. Strangely affected by my experience, I sat perplexed, stroking my chin and staring around the empty church. All the 'ghosts' had gone and the aisle was now deserted. I was firmly back in the 1980s, and the music had stopped.

Puzzled by why I'd seen nuns in the time-slip, soon details were revealed by a cathedral official. 'This has been consecrated ground since 1091, when the first church was built here in Newcastle. But before the Reformation, when Henry VIII ransacked the churches, this was a Roman Catholic place of worship.'

There was the answer.

Somehow I'd travelled back into history, but not a 'dead' picture, but a 'living' Past Now in the cathedral's life. So the Past isn't over and gone—how could it be if I'd just seen it, and been seen 'in it'? Our idea of Time has to change.

Another strange step backwards came one peaceful night in Gloucestershire, near the mystical Cotswold Hills and rambling Severn River valleys. I was staying with friends in a stunningly gorgeous mansion house, built in 1584, which still retained much of its original structures, despite being converted into several apartments. The breathtaking house was set against dying purple sunlight as brilliant stars were just appearing high above. I was sitting in the gardens on a hot August night, drinking in the stillness and marvelling at the dramatic mansion's silhouette against the darkening skies. Its old towers jutted up towards the star points as if to say defiantly, 'I've been here centuries, while fickle humans have come and gone . . .'

Then it happened—

First, quiet ethereal strains of waltz music and violins faded up within in my mind—and the dark ballroom overlooking the gardens was now lit inside. An orchestra was accompanying ladies and gentlemen of fine breeding as they danced romantically together. The house was full of laughter and chattering which drifted gently across the lawns. Then, near the weather-beaten stone balustrade where I sat, I spied two exquisitely-dressed young women sauntering along the grasses, occasionally supporting themselves with one hand upon the stone—but it was no longer crumbling, ancient stone, it was now in perfect condition.

The pretty young belles giggled, wafting the hot air from their faces with delicate bamboo fans. One of them particularly caught my eye: she was very slim, had sandy-coloured hair parted in the centre and pulled back into bouncy ringlets which cascaded over her slender white shoulders. Her tight-fitting apple-green bodice shimmered in the fading light and her full wide skirts and petticoats gently swayed in the evening breeze. It was such a remarkably clear vision, I could even see the ladies step in time to the waltzes pouring from the ballroom. I felt I could have stretched out my hand across the misty centuries and touched them.

And then, for a fleeting moment, she glanced in my direction. A strange quizzical look flickered across her face as our eyes met. Then she turned away, for I felt she'd *seen* me, caught the 'ghost' of my reflection on that balmy August night, as we both faded out from each other's world . . .

My host informed me the mansion had indeed smiled through many fine soirées, when pretty women and dashing young men gathered in its fine grounds at parties. It was owned then by an extremely wealthy family, the Marlings, very affluent people in that area many years ago.

If we can experience the Past, what then of the Future? Can that be glimpsed too? Is it pre-ordained, unchangeable? If so, then air and sea disasters would have to be planned by someone, somewhere. So would child abuse, torture, rape, murders. All these would have to be thought out and planned beforehand if our Future is fixed, and who among us would undertake those duties? But if the Future *isn't* preordained, how on earth can we explain this next experience?

Suddenly the department store faded away, and in its place I saw the Shuttlecraft launch pad in America, and heard the Mission Controller's voice, 'Three—Two—One—Ignition! Lift off! We have lift off!' And the gigantic space shuttle rose majestically from its pad. I could almost smell the burning fuel and sense the great excitement in the distant crowds, just as though I was there myself. It was wonderfully clear, truly magnificent.

The huge shuttle climbed high into the blue skies, leaving its long white smoke-trail behind it—everything was so sharp, so well-defined, it took my breath away. I could even see the yellow-white fire shooting out from the exhaust rockets. Then suddenly two giant numbers superimposed over my sight, large golden numbers: 25. They hovered for a moment, then I felt a most sickening feeling as I spied short trails of igniting fuel running up the fuselage, seconds before the shuttle exploded into a fireball before my horrified gaze. Stunned and dumbstruck, I couldn't speak—as the dreadful vision vanished, leaving me back in the department store where I worked.

Someone asked, 'Are you all right, Stephen? You look as though you've seen a ghost.'

'No, I'm fine,' I muttered. But she was right: I *had* seen a 'ghost', so I explained what happened.

'Perhaps you imagined it. Try and forget.'

'But I saw it clearer than I can see you now. But what did those numbers mean? Why 25?' I wondered out loud.

That coming week saw the first ground-launched voyage of the *Columbia* Shuttlecraft. I felt so sure it was doomed to explode 25 seconds into the flight that I didn't watch the news. 'Thank God I was wrong!' I said, when it went without a hitch. In fact, two dozen flights were made over the next five years. Then, one day, watching TV in Gateshead, my nightmare vision materialized. The *Challenger* Shuttle exploded *exactly as I'd foreseen it five years previously*. It was correct in every heart-breaking detail. My stomach turned and sickened. People all over the world saw it 'live', including countless schoolchildren who supported the young mother of two, schoolteacher Mrs Christa McAuliffe, due to broadcast lessons from space. Even her husband and children stood and witnessed the horrific explosion, stunned into disbelief—and millions of others, including me, were deeply upset by it. The emotional shock-waves travelled right across the globe on that sad day.

But news reports had finally solved the riddle of those golden numbers: this was the *25th* shuttle flight.

But how could I have seen it five years before? The only explanation I can offer is—*the Future casts its shadow before it. Somewhere, right now, the Future is already taking place.* These are mystical concepts, very difficult to grasp. But if they're correct, then we should be able to forecast anything. Our own time of death, for instance. But can we? Is our Moment of Passing known? Is it written somewhere in minds far more aware than our own? I believe this is more than a possibility.

This next amazing memory gives evidence of this. It concerns one of my dearest friends, Phyllis, an honest, kindly woman in her late sixties, whose experience happened when she was terminally ill. She'd been placed in a hospital side-room to die after having five major operations almost simultaneously, the main one being to remove a massive cancerous growth from her abdomen. Her family were told she had 48 hours to live, so they gathered silently around the bed, waiting for the end.

She was in a deep coma and, as far as this world was concerned, 'dead' to all hope. But what her doctors and anxious family didn't know was that she was undergoing a remarkable Out-Of-The-Body Experience in her spirit form. I will never forget her incredible recollection. But let her tell us herself:

I remember floating out of my body, light as air, and the next thing I saw was a white marble pathway leading up to a large marble arch, covered in green heather.

I was suddenly taken aback when I caught sight of my 'dead' mother and father standing under the archway. They were younger than when they died. They stood there in the prime of life, very much alive and well, and *young*—not old. My dad was wearing a smart grey suit, and my mother wore a neat black frock with lace collar and cuffs. Dad was leaning on a walking-stick, something he always took with him on his long strolls.

I walked towards them—or maybe I floated, I can't fully recall that part—and when I got near I was overcome with joy. Dad stretched out his hand and put it on my shoulder, but my mother caught my arm in hers, and firmly said: '*Go back, Phyl—you haven't finished your contract yet.*'

Phyllis then awoke with a start, and all her surprised family were dumbstruck, mouths wide open. The shocked Ward Sister leaned over and asked how she was feeling, to which she cheerily replied, 'Fine thanks.'

Her staggered consultants couldn't believe what had happened, or that their prognosis had been wrong. But the spirit people knew more than they did. What's more, that psychic experience occurred over 10 years ago and Phyllis is still with us at the time of writing. Despite many physical illnesses which constantly beset her, including cancer, diabetes and a very weak heart, she's still on Earth working out her 'contract', as her mother said, while doctors had pronounced her all but 'dead'.

She's convinced her spirit family saved her; in fact, she often sees brightly-coloured spirit lights floating around her bed at night, especially when she's felt particularly poorly. The Two Worlds *interpenetrate* each other, and are so intricately woven together that it's often difficult to know where one world ends, and the next begins.

Sceptics might accuse Phyllis of a vivid imagination (something they trot out when perplexed): fine, but that doesn't account for her remarkable recovery which has defied medical science these last 10 years. No, we are surrounded by an invisible web of never-ending love, and if we would only open our inward sight, we would see it.

For instance, I've met many people who tried to commit suicide but mysteriously failed. Mrs Killick's case was extraordinary. She called one sunny May afternoon, a radiant woman of middle years, wreathed in smiles and smartly dressed in colour co-ordinated hues. To look at her you'd never have thought beneath that fine exterior she'd led a tortured life. 'Now', she said directly, 'whatever you get, Mr O'Brien, please don't hold back—just give it right from the shoulder.'

'But it might not work at all,' I said. 'Every link's an

experiment.' So we both settled back and waited, but I quickly established her mother's presence, named her and her manner of passing—both of which were readily accepted. Mrs Killick's mum was also right on target when she mentioned her daughter's personal dilemmas. But then came some shock comments which made Mrs Killick cry. 'Your mum says you've had a dreadful life, full of suffering and a blackness you never thought would end. It was then you tried to kill yourself—' I stopped dead in my tracks. Mediums should never transmit alarming information, that's one of our unwritten rules. But Mrs Killick replied, 'She's absolutely right. Please, go on—straight from the shoulder, Stephen.' So I did.

'She says you wouldn't be alive today if it wasn't for her. She says *she stopped your suicide attempt, even though she was on the Other Side when you took those fatal pills*.' I stroked my forehead in embarrassment. What on earth was I telling this complete stranger? I had no idea how she'd take the message, but, oddly enough, my tearful sitter perfectly understood.

'I *knew* it was Mum who saved my life. And now you've confirmed it,' was her astonishing reply. 'You see, Stephen, I did try to kill myself while my husband was at work and my 13-year-old son was packed off to the cinema. I locked all the doors and windows, went upstairs and took a massive overdose of tablets. I laid down on the bed, praying for the end, and must have slipped into a coma, ready to die.

'But the next day I woke up in a hospital bed, and went hysterical. I kept shouting, "*Why I am still alive? I should be dead*!" But do you know what happened after I took those pills? My son suddenly felt an urgent impulse to rush out of the movies and run home. To this day he doesn't know what came over him, and he ran as fast as his legs would carry him, only to find the doors locked. Somehow, he turned the key with a stick, and poked it out, then, with a thin twig, hooked it under the back door and opened it. He flew upstairs, and found me close to death on the bed.'

Mrs Killick stopped, filled with emotion, and slowly regained her composure. 'They only just managed to save me by stomach-pumping and heart massage. I was nearly gone. *I should be dead*, not sitting here talking to you, Stephen. But what you've just told me confirms my intuition. I always felt, deep down, that my mother in the next life impressed my son to save me. Now I know I was right. And I'm glad she did, because now I see that taking my life wouldn't have helped. And I'm much happier today than I've ever been.'

When I asked if she herself might have sent out powerful subconscious thoughts to her son to help her (a wearisome psychologist argument), she firmly ruled it out.

'No! I *wanted* to die,' she affirmed, 'and *made sure* they were all out. I had no intention of being discovered.'

Behind all this is an incredible lesson in tender loving care delivered by a spirit mother on that day. Death was no barrier to her love at all. How many other times, I wonder, has that Other World intervened in our daily lives, mingling its thoughts with ours to inspire us towards a more peaceful, loving existence? How many times has an inexplicable 'chance' thought led to a completely new direction in our lives? It certainly makes you think.

We're surrounded by Angels who envelop us with their love, and often we don't even know it.

Now, back to the Future. Perhaps the most surprising prediction I've been given came when I was feeling quite low. I was out walking, thinking, 'When will things brighten up for me?' when all at once a clear voice about three feet above my head spoke through the sunshine: 'When Thatcher goes to war.' I stopped and looked up into nothingness. Passers-by stood and stared, but hadn't heard those sounds from another world. Being, if I might say so, a very practical, sensible man, I shelved this prediction as 'only a possibility', not having heard of any troubles between Britain and other countries. But *two years later*, just as life was straightening out in my favour, the Falklands conflict rose overnight and claimed world attention. Britain sent a task-force to Argentina, and the prophecy was fulfilled.

How can this be explained? Perhaps the Argentinian Junta planned their attacks two years in advance—when the voice gave the warning. Or (and this is what I believe) the Future had been glimpsed by my inspirer.

White Owl has often taught:

> When people from Spirit transmit news of an event to you, they are not always certain whether it has already happened, is taking place now, or is just about to occur.
>
> This is because we deal with the Language of Thought. It relates differently to Time in my world than in yours.
>
> Thought exists in a dimension of its own, and different rules apply.

Being scientifically-orientated, as far as my thinking goes, I took part in some fascinating Time experiments at Stansted Hall College of Psychic Studies in Essex. As well as teaching and demonstrating mediumship, I willingly agreed to join three others in thought-provoking research. The test involved two of Spiritualism's best-known mediums, Mary Duffy and Gordon Higginson, and was undertaken in absolute secrecy. We gathered in the stately home's library one misty afternoon while the 100 students, from all parts of the world, knew nothing of the tests.

Eric Hatton, Vice-President of the Spiritualists' National Union, crept in to meet us, armed with a wicked grin and a tape-recorder. We had no idea what he was planning. 'Now, I'd like you all to tune in to the spirit world and receive one message each, then deliver it to this empty room. Place the connection where the Other Side direct you, picking out the exact seat of the recipient, if you can. I'll tape the messages, then we'll call the students together tonight and let them sit where they wish.

'When the tape plays we'll see if the links fall to the right people, in the correct seats. If they do, this shows the Other Side can see into the Future, who'll be attending, and possibly even where they'll sit.'

This thrilling challenge couldn't be refused, so I got the first message without any hesitation. It detailed the place of 'Tunstall' and a few family names, and that the recipient had 'lost' a son. Then came precise facts about family matters, including that my projected recipient had 'undergone surgery to remove the womb'. I normally wouldn't have mentioned that, but this was a special taped test and we were asked to be as specific as possible. Gordon and Mary then followed suit, each pin-pointing the exact seat of their 'invisible' target. But would we three be successful? Always ready with his wit, Eric announced, 'Time will tell!'

Outside the library that night, Eric had written on the blackboard: 'A Surprise Experiment in Time—Stephen, Gordon and Mary lay their reputations on the line.'

'He can say that again!' I said to Eva French, a witty cackling Londoner (and a regular feature at the college), as she grabbed some chalk and with raised eyebrow and comical grin scribbled underneath: 'Heads will roll!'

Then she shook the hall with her lovely guffaws, and we sloped off into the library, where Eva plonked herself down in the front row, knitting furiously, like Madame Defarge eyeing up the guillotine . . . I gingerly took my seat alongside Gordon, Mary and Eric on the platform and the test got underway. After Eric's explanations I suddenly felt my insides turn upside down when I glanced at the audience—*my target seat was empty*! I whispered to Gordon through the side of my mouth: 'You can smile, yours is occupied. Mine's vacant!'

But he grinned from ear to ear. 'We haven't started yet, Stephen,' he returned.

Just seconds before Eric turned on the tape, there was an almighty fuss at the back of the room as an elderly late student bumbled into the room; she was weighed down with shopping. 'I'm sorry I'm late,' she spluttered, swinging her bags all over the place as people ducked. 'Move along please!' she ordered, and everyone shifted up one place to let her in, and my seat was now taken! What's more, my message fell to the correct lady, in the correct chair, and, astonishingly, all the information was accurate. We were astounded.

She lived in Tunstall, the place I'd mentioned, had undergone a hysterectomy, and her son had passed on. The other personal details were also correct. Eva French dropped a few stitches, lowered her knitting and gawped up at me with her chin on her chest, then comically mimed in exaggerated silence, 'P'raps 'eads won't roll after all, Mr O'Brien!'

Gordon and Mary also had similar successes. It was far too startling to be a fluke. How could the spirit people have foreseen it? No one knew where anyone would sit that night. Could the next world have guided the recipients into the seats they wanted them in? Or had our spirit friends jumped forward in Time and seen the shadows of what was to be? I think they did.

Here's White Owl on the Mystery of Time:

Time, as you know it, is an illusion. You are trapped in a three-dimensional world, seeing events from only one restricted viewpoint. You are limited by the slow-moving physical brain and its sluggish perceptions.

It is therefore beyond your current abilities to appreciate the intricacies of Time in all their fullness. It is also difficult for me to explain, from my vantage-point, how Time is experienced by us. But I will try.

Time does not run in a straight line, from the Past to the Present, then on into the Future, as many with you suppose. Neither is it a question of the Past having gone, the Present being with you now, and the Future yet to come. Nor is Time a circle or a spiral. None of these geometrical figures describe it adequately.

Time is not a shape, it is an Entity, a Living Being, a Consciousness on its own, delicately interwoven into every facet of Being in every known and unknown world. It is Past, Present and Future, all combined into One. It has no fixed boundaries, no clear-cut demarcation lines, as many think. It is an integral part of Immortality Itself.

The Past is not dead and gone; it is alive. Neither is the Future yet unborn; it is with us Now. Understanding these concepts is not easy while you are still encased in flesh—realization dawns with growth and development, and only those with eyes to see can perceive these inner realities, when they are ready to see them.

Many spirit people know nothing of these ideas. To them, Time still remains a mystery, or a straight line: Past, Present, Future.

I cannot be clearer at present, for these truths can only be fully experienced by the true Seeker, who can release his Spirit and appreciate the workings of Thought.

The Dance of Time

Old grandfather clock
By the peaceful wall,
Tick tock,
Tick tock;
Clicking out your endless seconds,
Swinging out your days,
And smiling at the man who winds you
In his foolish ways.

Old grandfather clock
Tick tock,
Don't mock:
Time does not exist—
She's just a clever mind-trick
And you are her accomplice.

Old grandfather clock,
Don't mock—
Time like a Spanish Flamenco Dancer
Wears a scarlet frock, and spins and prances
Clicking castanets and swirling crimson skirts
In fast hypnotic dance;
Her sultry eyelids flutter and entrance
Till reason's locked and shuttered.
Then stamping out her flamenco rhyme
So rhythmically, so sneakily,
She clasps her victim fast:
To age and to decline,
To suffer and never know the wonder of
The freedom from Time.

Grinningly she's tricked you,
And wooed you with her Power
So that close to her gyrating dance
A boring minute's like an endless hour.

And as Spanish music swells with tensions
Trapped are you in three dimensions.
And Scarlet Time tosses her gypsy locks
And slyly turns the countless clocks
And spins the stars and marks your birth
And times you as your death unfurls:
Clicking and dancing, swirling and prancing;
Wheels within wheels,
Worlds within worlds.

> *'Come dance with me!*
> *Come dance, come dance!*
> *Come near and kiss your youth goodbye!*
> *Come shake a tambourine with me!*
> *Come count the days, come age and die!*
> *Come hold me close and grip me fast,*
> *And let me show that nothing lasts!'*

Then lured by her encircling palms
A fine young man fell into her arms,
And twirled and danced and became entranced
By Scarlet Time and her gypsy charms.
And around and around the floor they sped
As Spanish music upwards climbed;
And Gypsy Time, she stamped and rhymed
And held the youngster to her breast
And danced and spun without a rest,
Until her laughter drowned his cries
As his spinning flesh sunk on his frame and dried:
    And all the watchers near them cried
As the muscle-bound youngster aged and sighed,
And crooked his back, and lost his sight,

And forgot his name, and groaned and died.
Like an age-old corpse battered by strife
His dry flesh powdered to dusty life.

And Gypsy Time laughed as his skeleton fell
And she spun herself free to continue her spell—
Faster and faster and quicker she swirled,
Until she saw me—and then she called:

> *'Come dance, come dance!*
> *Come step with me!*
> *Come waltz and let me clasp you tight!*
> *Come age and die and twirl with me,*
> *Come hold me fast with all your might!'*

And into her arms she pulled my form
Against her body, soft and warm,
And tightened up her vice-lock grip
   As the watchers gasped and prayed I'd slip
   Away from her 'ere magic starts—
But the pounding music thumped my heart.

Then gazing into her sultry face,
Something within me started to race
And make me see she was just a 'mask'—
A shadow-dance
That covered a truth beneath her stance.

So I raised my angered fist aloft
And struck her painted china face!

And suddenly the music ceased;
   And the watchers gasped in the deafening peace,
Broken only by the glittering falling glass
As onto the floor her body smashed:
Time shattered to a thousand slithers
Like a broken Dresden doll with tousled locks:
Time turned to dust and sighed, and finally died—
   And all the watchers smiled
   At her empty dress 'neath the ticking clock.

Old grandfather clock, tick tock:
Don't mock.
Time does not exist—
She's just a clever mind-trick
And you are her accomplice!

I've broken the spell, I'm free at last!
And I'll give my truth to all who ask.
My life is cleared of apprehension,
No longer trapped in three dimensions.
I've broken free! I've seen the light!
I know there is no day or night;
No Past or Future yet to be—
Just this Living Moment Only.
And I'm free, my friend! At last I'm free!

And then, through the mist, the tick tock stopped,
And bellowing low came the voice of the clock:

> *'Break the spell, you surely did,*
> *But more than you know is currently hid:*
> *Now, ceasing all my endless tocks*
> *I'll give the secret Time unlocks.'*

And all the room fell deathly still,
The birds stopped singing on the window-sill,
And every soul held his breath and listened
To the mellow voice that glistened:

> *'Exist for* Now
> *And Time will smile on you,*
> *(For she knows well her lie)*
> *But break her face, and crack she will.*
> *Time measured by decay: Untrue!*
> *That is an Illusion,*
> *Which grins at those who fail to see*
> *And frowns at those who do.'*

Old grandfather clock, tick tock:
Tick away ever, I care not!
I'll not be bound by transient things:
In Ever-Nowness my song I'll sing —
And to my life I'll constantly bring
My Own Time.

And once again the clock-voice croaked,
Shimmering the stillness as it spoke:

> *'The Ever-present Now holds fast*
> *The ghosts of all the seeming Past,*
> *And the seeds of Future yet to be*
> *Floating through memory:*
> *For Past and Present, and the Now*
> *Are all One and the same;*
> *A marriage of All Three*
> *(Hard I know to see)*
>
> *But somewhere Now, you're dying.*
> *And somewhere Now, at birth you're crying.*
> *Can you follow me?'*

And instantly a bright light flashed my mind—
And suddenly I realized
What I sought to find
Was right before me,
And I'd been blind.

Old grandfather clock, tick tock,
Tick tock:
Tick away endless, I care not.
For Time is but the Ghost of a Great Illusion
And I'm no longer trapped by her Delusion.

15

Questions and Answers

Many thousands of intelligent questions have been asked of me over the years, and my northern meetings proved no exception. They were always lively and full of bright thoughts. While I'm the first to admit I don't have all the answers, I do try to share the knowledge I've found in my personal quest for truth.

So, by popular request, here's another varied, thought-provoking selection of questions, asked quite frequently:

How do you hear your spirit voices?
Within the Mind. Communicators don't have physical voice-boxes, so even when voices sound completely objective and as audible as mine is now, they're still heard within the mind. The same applies to physical sight and sense—everything's a mind experience. Our brains convey sound-waves to the mind, which recognizes them as speech.

Where is the spirit world?
Everywhere. There are many worlds of spirit, all *interpenetrating* each other. Just as TV and radio signals are passing right through us now, unsensed (when there's no instrument to interpret them), so the spirit worlds are with us here and now. But they exist at much higher frequencies than we do, that's why they're mostly unregistered by us.

Imagine the universe as a tank of water, and the Earth as a sponge submerged in the tank. The worlds of spirit are represented by the water: thus, the spirit worlds are around us, through us and all about us, at one and the same time.

We'll never be more eternal than we are at this moment. We are Spirit *now*.

Is reincarnation a fact?

It all depends on the mind you're questioning. Even in the Beyond they're divided on this: some claim it as a fact, while others hotly deny it.

I believe that with God all things are possible, and therefore these opportunities would be available. But you, as an individual, a personality, a characterized soul, will not reincarnate. But what *can* return to Earth is another aspect of your eternal mind.

We need to consider the differences between Personality and the Spirit. The Personality is everything you are in your physical consciousness—whereas the Spirit is the everlasting essence of you, the direct Life-Force which links you to the Great Spirit. So in your current individual form, you will not return, but pass into eternity, forever.

Yet, another portion of your Spirit, your Mind, might be characterized into flesh again, as a separate individual at some future time. This means that your survival as a personality is assured.

These are difficult concepts, which liken the Spirit to a many-faceted diamond, segments of which are personalized into Earth consciousness as individuals, yet all springing from the same Spirit Source. However, I don't think reincarnation can be successfully proved: there are many other explanations which can nullify facts concerning 'previous lives'. Neither do I think it's as common an occurrence as some lead us to believe.

If it happens, then the Spirit realizes that there are lessons to be learned or special tasks to be accomplished on this planet and, because of free will and personal responsibility, undertakes the incarnation itself.

Do children grow up on the Other Side?

Yes. They reach the full bloom of youth, then remain in young adulthood. The physical ageing process only belongs to the material body, it doesn't affect the spirit body.

When old people die, do they stay old?

No, the spirit body reaches the full bloom of youth, and remains that way. Although the earthly body wears out and decays little by little each day, inside there's a fit and healthy spirit body. When death occurs, they will be young again.

Then why have you described old people at tonight's meeting?

Because they came here from the next world *remembering how they were when you knew them*. They return as they were, for recognition only.

How can they assume their former appearances?

By the power of thought. They *think* of themselves as they used to be, then project this image into the medium's mind.

Are 'accidents' meant to happen?

I'm not happy about the word 'accident'. Everything is governed by Eternal Natural Laws. *Cause and Effect* rules supreme. If the brakes of a car fail, sending its occupant into eternity, there are reasons *why* this has happened. It's not an 'accident', it conforms to the Laws of the Universe: in this case, the cause is a mechanical fault.

We should also look at another element: Time. In mass tragedies certain people cross into the next world—why? Why were they there at that particular time? Why weren't *we* there? A set of causes has brought them to those precise effects, and their day to pass over had come. So in this respect, their death could not be viewed as an 'accident'.

Neither am I happy with the word 'coincidence'. I think the Universe is more highly organized than that.

I have prophetic dreams which come true. Where does this information come from?

Most likely from within yourself. Your own spirit can glean future events without being told of them by a third party; we are much cleverer than we at first might think. Certainly, in major instances, our own Future projects itself 'backwards'—so to speak—into our Present day, and we can see it—that is, if we've developed that special kind of perception. But it's worth pointing out that on many occasions what we see as a future happening is often only a set of future possibilities.

But never forget: *your Soul knows where it's going, why it's come to Earth and what it hopes to achieve.* If we get in touch with the Higher part of ourselves, those areas of Mind above our conscious thinking, we would never fear tomorrow, for we would see our pathway clearly before us.

How can I develop my psychic powers?

Firstly, look at your *true* motives for undertaking this work. If they're based on *genuinely* helping and serving others, that's a good starting-point. But if they're centred around the ego, then you're heading for humiliation, heartache, stress and trouble. Remember the Universal Law: *Like Attracts Like.* You draw people from the next life similar in motives to yourself. That's fine, if your motives are helpful, loving and sincere; but if they're not, you'll get what you deserve. That's the Law.

Those pursuing psychic development should be emotionally and mentally stable. Psychic and mediumistic work excites the nervous energies and delves into areas of Mind which can be best endured, understood and dealt with only if the adept is stable in all senses of the word.

If you still wish to proceed, join a group—don't develop in isolation; find a development class, preferably one conducted by a well-trained, respected medium, who's aware of all the dangers and pitfalls, and also the guidance you will most certainly need. There should be psychic centres or Spiritualist churches near you, where you can find such people.

Also, don't remain in ignorance—read as much about the subject as you can, sifting through the material and accepting only that which appeals to your intellect and intelligence. Question every teaching—accept nothing blindly. Even if information comes from the Other Side, this doesn't mean it is valid. *Question everything.*

Remember, it's easy to fall into self-delusion when unfolding your talents entirely on your own, without constructive, objective criticism and education. Like any other learning process, get yourself trained by recognized authorities. No one would think of re-wiring a house unless they were a properly trained electrician: the dangers are obvious. The same applies to psychic development—never meddle with the powers of the mind unless you are firstly strong-willed and self-governed, very disciplined, and, of course, emotionally and mentally stable; then get some proper training. Your medical history, and also respected teachers can ascertain your suitability.

I saw a columns of light and small coloured lights the size of a coin floating in my bedroom. What were they?

Probably a build up of psychic energies in the atmosphere, or a spirit person's presence. Broadly speaking, these psychic visions are manifestations of energy, as is lightning.

How can the spirit people walk through a wall?

Because they exist at a higher frequency than material objects. If the atoms of their spirit bodies were moving at the same rate as the atoms of the wall, they'd bump into it as we do!

One night I floated out of my body, panicked and couldn't get back in for a while. What should I do if it happens again?

Don't panic! Out-of-the-body experiences are very common. The spirit body, which is more or less an exact replica of your physical body, exteriorizes a little and you become conscious in the Other World. On returning, if you panic this causes strong whirling vibrations in the mind, momentarily preventing re-alignment taking place; returning is something best done gently. Next time, keep calm—there's nothing to fear; it's all under your control.

Do we have any privacy?

Of course! We don't always know what's happening on the Other Side, and they're not constantly aware of us. Unless either party tunes in to the other's existence, each world remains unsensed.

Can the Other Side see our thoughts?

Yes, if they've developed the ability. But even then I still don't think they see *everything*. But it's very easy to do, once you know how.

What language do they speak?

The same ones they knew in Earthlife. But the true language of the Spirit is *Thought*. When Thoughts are transferred from one person to another, language becomes unnecessary.

What work do they do Over There?

Anything they choose: healing, teaching, the arts and sciences—any pursuit the imagination can create.

Do they earn money?

No, there is no monetary system Over There. However, if certain people want some, they can have it. It's all a question of attitude of mind. But the only real rewards are the growth of your spirit and character, evolving through service. Service satisfies the basic need to feel a sense of self-worth and achievement.

Is it true we all have a guardian angel?

In a way, yes. We're certainly watched over by many from the next world, but I'm going to disagree with the Spiritualist Movement and traditional thought here, when I say I don't believe we have a specific soul to 'guard' or 'guide' us in any special way.

I accept the Law of Personal Responsibility, which states we're in charge of our own lives, their planning and execution. Though help is available whenever needed, I don't think we're led or guided every step of the way.

So what is your guide's task?

He's in charge of the work we're doing. I'm responsible for all its aspects on Earth, and he organizes it in the next world. Ours is a willing co-operation, never a domination. We're partners, good friends. Love and respect binds us together. He doesn't interfere with my daily life, nor I with his. However, because he loves me he does sometimes impart some very sound advice.

Will he use another medium when you die?

Why, do you want me to pop my clogs?! (Laughter . . .) No, I don't think he will. It's not easy for two minds to blend so closely, especially when they both live in different worlds. He's often said our work is a special mission.

I prayed my young daughter would recover from terminal cancer, but she died. Why was she taken from me?

No one 'takes' a soul away. When a body 'dies' the soul passes back to its rightful home.

We're governed by Natural Laws, one being *Cause and Effect*. Illness is the effect of a number of causes. Your daughter's body became unable to allow her spirit any more expression in this world, so 'death' occurred. But don't be saddened, everyone lives on into eternity. Keep cheerful, because your little girl is still alive.

As to your prayer not being answered—to die is not a tragedy for the person making the crossing; in many cases it's a blessèd release.

Can mediums foretell the future?

Occasionally—but the principal task of a medium is to relay evidence of survival from one world to another.

You teach that physical handicaps vanish upon death, but what about mental handicaps?

They don't exist in the next life: a balance is always struck. Mental handicaps are caused by malfunctions in the brain, which is no more than a physical computer, a fleshly transformer, a receiving and transmitting station for Thoughts born in the Mind.

The Mind is perfect: it is King. The brain causes malfunctions, but once that's out of the way, the individual's thoughts can freely express themselves.

Does cremation affect the soul?

No. Once death has occurred, you can do what you wish with the body—it won't adversely affect the soul.

My husband was buried in a mass war-victims' grave without a service conducted. Will he inherit eternal life?

Of course. Services and 'special ground' don't mean a thing: the soul survives death, that's the Law. Just send your husband your loving thoughts, and remember he'll be with *you*; he isn't under the earth.

My mother and I argued violently before she died. Do you think she'll forgive me?

Only your mum can answer that. But there's a good chance that time, and her new viewpoint, will help her to understand. Forgiveness is a jewel found in the soul who is progressing towards spirituality. Meanwhile, send her your thoughts and she'll receive them.

My father was Catholic and didn't believe in communicating with the 'dead'. Do you think he'll get in touch?

It's up to him. If he still believes it's wrong, then he may not try. On the other hand—and this is the stronger possibility—now he realizes he's still alive, he'll probably make the effort.

By the way, we can't communicate with anything 'dead'. Mediums communicate with the living! Catholics pray to their saints, and who are these but mortal beings who've passed over?

Is Spiritualism a dangerous cult linked to the occult?

No. Spiritualism is a state-recognized religion in Britain, registered at the Home Office, with its own ordained ministers who perform marriages, funerals and naming services (the Spiritualist equivalent of a 'christening').

It asks its adherents to believe nothing, but advocates they test everything with their own common sense and intelligence. It has no creed, no dogmas, no special book or set philosophies, and doesn't tell people what they should think or do.

But it does have Seven Principles upon which it's founded. They were given to the world through the mediumship of Emma Hardinge-Britten, and people following Spiritualism (which many claim is also a science and a way of life) broadly accept them as a basis for daily living. They are:

1. The Fatherhood of God.
2. The Brotherhood of Man.
3. The Communion of Spirits and the Ministry of Angels.
4. The Continuous Existence of the Human Soul.
5. Personal Responsibility.
6. Compensation and Retribution for all the good and evil deeds done on Earth.
7. Eternal Progress open to every human soul.

Many Spiritualists will only accept these as guidelines because they're open to liberty of interpretation, but most agree that the fifth principle, Personal Responsibility, might be the most important one. This teaches we can't blame anyone for our thoughts, actions or deeds, but ourselves. We must carry the burden of our mistakes, and rectify them. There is no 'vicarious atonement'; no one can remove from us what we have done, only we ourselves can do this.

Spiritualists find this morally sound and Just because it speaks of a Divine Justice which cannot be cheated in any way. It is the Law of Cause and Effect in operation: as we sow, so shall we reap. If we plant a rose, a lettuce will not grow. If we shine forth love, love will return to us—and similarly with all the negative aspects of hatred, anger, intolerance and selfishness.

What happens in a Spiritualist church?

There's usually some music—hymn-singing or songs—and a prayer, delivered spontaneously from the heart of the speaker, and sometimes there's a reading, given from any book on Earth of any faith, philosophy or teaching, or even the reader's own thoughts. This is then followed by a demonstration of clairvoyance: message-relaying from the next world.

Nearly all churches also hold separate services where spiritual healing is administered to the sick, by the laying-on of hands or by prayer.

Churches usually advertise in the newspaper, or you can get their addresses from your library. Spiritualists are quite friendly folk, and the church is a good place to start your investigations. I started mine there.

I had a vision of my husband while he was physically hundreds of miles away, but he was still alive. What did I see?

His double, or a 'phantasm of the living'. A person doesn't have to be 'dead' to be seen in another place, or even another time. What's seen is usually a thought-form of the loved one, or sometimes their actual spirit body which has projected out while the physical is resting. There are many documented cases of bi-coporeity, where the same person has been seen in two different places at exactly the same time. The two forms are even said to be able to carry on two separate conversations at the same time.

I attended a Transfiguration meeting, and while other people saw changes in the medium's features as spirit people purported to make themselves visible, I saw nothing. Why was this?

Because you didn't see a true Transfiguration medium. These exceptionally gifted people are extremely rare. But if the mediumship is genuine, *everyone* sees the changes as communicators build up their features on the medium's bone structure, and become physically visible to the witnesses. What you saw sounds like a poor imitation, or even worse—fraud.

How can a spirit person possess a human being?

They can't. The nearest they can get is a close proximity of the mind, and this cannot be achieved without the full consent and co-operation of the person on Earth.

Do the spirit people ever get things wrong?

Frequently! They're only fallible human beings, like ourselves.

There are a thousand people here tonight, but you can only give relatively few messages. Is it worth the effort?

Please ask me that question again, when you've been one of the recipients who was helped.

16
Reflections

Many northern people seeking truth said they'd been greatly helped by my teachings, and asked me to publish them. They wanted to read and re-read my lectures, too, along with many other correspondents across the globe who requested the same. I promised them all: 'One day I'll get them printed.'

So, by public request, here are some points to ponder, reflections culled from the millions of words I deliver publicly each year, through writings, appearances and the media.

God and the Natural Laws

God is a Great Spirit, a Breath of Living Consciousness—not a man, but a Power of Life Itself.

We are all Children of the Great Spirit, small sparks of the Great Spirit's Life-Force. This Divine Spark, which we each possess, motivates us, gives us conscious awareness of our own being and links us to the Creative Mind, forever.

We can never be separated from our Creator—the link remains eternally unbroken. We are Sons and Daughters of the Living Mind, and therefore all Brothers and Sisters.

How do we know that God is perfect? God may be slowly evolving just as we are.

We are governed by Eternal Natural Laws; not laws made by man—for they are transient—but the Natural Laws which are born in the Creative Mind, the Law-giver, which some men call God. The Natural Laws reside in all areas of Being: emotional, physical, mental and spiritual.

We are personally responsible for what we think, say and do, and no one in this world or the next can take away from us the mistakes we have made. We will have to eventually rectify them and hopefully learn from the growth-experience of facing our challenges and conquering them.

We have free will, freedom of choice, the right to govern our lives as we see fit. This knowledge, of course, brings with it personal responsibility for our thoughts and actions. But our free will is limited. For example, we can't drink the oceans dry in one gulp, even if we wanted to: there are Natural Laws at work all the time, restrictions if you like, curtailing our freedom. We can create beauty and joy, or wreak havoc and destruction. It's up to us— there is not a personal human-being-type God who will interfere.

There is only one eternity, but many worlds within worlds, within which we may exist. All these places *interpenetrate* each other; so at any one point in space, there could be millions upon millions of different worlds containing life-forms—all interpenetrating each other's existences. But each world is separated from the others because they all vibrate (exist) at different frequencies. 'In my Father's House there are many mansions.'

We are our own judges and juries; there is no celestial panel awaiting us when we pass over. Judgement is immediate. We shall confront ourselves with the vivid memories of our acts—'good' or 'bad'—and pay the price our conscience dictates; usually by seeking forgiveness from the ones we have wronged, and then by an inner urge to serve them and others until we ourselves feel that the records have been put straight and we can once again live in peace with ourselves.

Mediums, and others involved in the psychic fields, don't always find love and light in the Beyond. Everyone survives death, and there are places to hold all kinds of people in all manner of conditions. The Golden Rule is the Universal Law: *Like Attracts Like*. Those of a similar nature inhabit the same sphere of existence, broadly speaking.

What we think, we send out into the universe, and one day these energies (thoughts) will return to us.

Ghosts and Poltergeists

Ghosts are not the same as spirit people. Very often they're energy pictures held by the psychic fields of activity surrounding the very walls and atmosphere of a building, not real people making a visitation, but 'psychic snapshots' if you like. Many 'hauntings' conform to these patterns.

Thought-forms of people, or 'ghosts' (to give them their more popular name), cannot communicate with us in the way that a living, vibrant real spirit person can. Ghosts have no conscious personality of their own. Sadly, many mediums have not yet mastered the art of telling the difference between thought-forms and communicators, and therefore have fallen into the trap of confusing the two.

'Poltergeist' means 'noisy (or troubled) spirit', but most poltergeist cases are nothing of the kind! The supernormal movement of objects is usually caused by abundant psychic energies possessed by physical people living in the house. Very often at puberty youngsters throw off tremendous amounts of this energy.

Real poltergeists—troubled visitors from the Other World who are bound close to our Earth conditions by their powerful desires—are quite rare indeed. In a genuine case, the spirit person can only move objects by drawing psychic energies from individuals and life-forms in the vicinity.

Suicide

Taking your own life doesn't extinguish it, it merely terminates it here and places you in another world. If we can't cope with life here, we shall not be able to cope with life Over There, for we'll take this 'inability to cope' with us into our new environment.

Nevertheless, suicide victims are helped to understand that progress is always available. There are compassionate qualified specialists both in our world and in the next, happy to help people find a balance in living.

Peace of mind has to be earned by the soul who desires it.

I would most strongly not advise anyone to take their own life because the idea of life is growth. Growth cannot come only in the sunlight, it will probably occur better in the shade. (See *Visions of Another World*, page 217.)

The Animal Kingdom

People often ask if pets are psychic—the answer is: yes. Animals' minds are uncluttered and free of prejudice and social etiquette. Even the most humble of pets possesses a soul ability of sensing or seeing spirit people that most of us find difficult to register.

Man experiments on animals because he foolishly deems himself higher in importance than our fellow creatures. I think man would do well to remember that he is also an animal.

Humankind will never progress spiritually as long at it subjects animals to unspeakable tortures in the name of science or medical research. Abattoirs run red with innocent blood.

The horrors of vivisection and research laboratories add nothing to man's spiritual stature, for they do not speak of love and compassion. Even vanity and cosmetics make millions of animals suffer ignoble deaths and inhuman tortures. Help free our little brethren by purchasing only 'cruelty-free' products—and vegetarianism/veganism is a far healthier way of life. (See poem 'The Voiceless Ones', *Visions of Another World*, page 146.)

Animals are our brothers and sisters, and it behoves us to help them evolve their consciousness through contact with our own compassionate natures.

Many owners are distressed when their beloved pets die and are eager to know if their friends survive death. I can happily report that they do. I've lost count of the times spirit animals have returned to their loved ones through my mediumship. In most cases they bring a feeling of warmth and gratitude for the concern and love shown to them when on Earth. (See the chapter 'Animals Survive Too' in *Visions of Another World*.)

I feel deeply sorry for caged creatures. It must be a far from ideal life for them, all cooped up in those confined spaces. I know we wouldn't like it. We put people in small places like that as a punishment, but what have the animals done?

Soul power, or psychic power, is resident in every living thing, and animals in particular are extremely sensitive beings. They can register human emotions because their psychic abilities operate freely. They, like us, are spirits working through physical bodies.

Everything Man has done to the Animals, he has already done to himself.

The Spirit Body

The physical body only exists because it is built around the blueprint of the spirit body. Take the spirit permanently away, as in death, and the flesh decays because it has lost its animating force.

When we discard the physical, we register through a finer vehicle of expression—the spirit body. It is the counterpart of our present body, and in its own world it is solid and real: it can be touched, sensed, and it occupies space and dimension.

There is no physical or mental handicap in the spirit body, it functions in perfect health. If one loses a limb or suffers a deformity of the physical body, this will not affect the spirit body. You cannot harm it, as you can the physical.

I've seen the spirit bodies of many people I know who were physically asleep when I saw them. I knew they hadn't passed over properly, because they didn't carry a bright light with them, as permanent spirit visitors do.

Being Met at the Crossing

Everyone is met when they die, but not necessarily immediately or by the people you might think would be there to greet them. But no one is forgotten in the scheme of things.

There are people Over There whose job it is to watch for new arrivals, whether they pass suddenly or gradually. These watchers are especially evident in world disasters such as war or the dropping of atomic bombs or large-scale tragedies.

The Other World knows when a passing is to be taken, though not all spirit people have access to this information, and can be just as surprised as we might be.

Children in the Spirit World

I maintain that from the moment of conception, Life has begun.

Stillborn babies or children who aren't carried for their full term of pregnancy all survive death and grow up on the Other Side. There they're loved and cared for by people who dedicate their lives to rearing them, just as good parents do here. Most times, family members in the next life bring up the children.

Children grow up on the Other Side, reaching the full bloom of youth. Parents will know their offspring, because each night they meet in the greater world while physical bodies are sound asleep. Children are also brought to visit their families in the Earth home. There will be no separation as the years unfold, and one day there will be a happy reunion. Children attend schools in the Beyond, learn and grow, and are often brought to visit.

They won't forget their parents.

Spirit children bring feelings of light and energy; a quick, fine vibration of youthful enthusiasm. Their eyes are bright and open wide, and yet behind them there seems to be an inner knowing that very few Earth children possess. Spirit children often speak and play with youngsters on Earth. They're brought close by ties of family or friendship, and sometimes just to associate with and learn from our children.

Religion and Belief

All roads lead to God. The way we live our lives is more important than the name of the road we're travelling, for we shall change direction many times in our search for truth.

Religious beliefs carry little weight in the Beyond, where everything is governed by immutable Natural Laws which operate in spite of what we might believe. But never once did my spirit people decry anyone's religion, rather did they say: 'If it makes you a better person, then it is right for you. If it teaches you to love, then it is a good set of instructions.'

If you believe anything 100 per cent, then this is dangerous. It's unhealthy because your mind is then closed to any new possibilities.

The Other Side aren't one bit concerned with labels, religions or lip-service codes of conduct. They're concerned with people; Souls, not labels. Before I help someone I never ask them what religious faiths they hold. These are not the most important facets of our lives.

Thought and Prayer

Just like a pebble dropped into a still pool of water, thoughts are born and radiate outwards: they are living things.

Prayer is a stream of *spontaneous* living thought, born of desire—and someone, somewhere will hear those thoughts. People's prayers *are* answered—but not always in the way they wish or as immediately as expected.

The Universal Laws stipulate that by the very act of prayer, the very act of opening the heart, recognizing a Higher Source and seeking help from it, the person praying is making him or herself available to the great influx of inspiration waiting to be poured into the minds of all those who seek its help. In this way, prayer can be seen as a personal exercise of one's own spirit, seeking its refreshment, guidance or aid from those who are in attunement with it in eternity.

Mass prayers which are frequently recited or read have little effect upon spirit world denizens, because they aren't born in the heart and soul of the seeker. A prayer, sincerely felt and meant, born with emotion and desire as its parents, will reach further into the world of spirit, and bring a more fruitful reply.

Selfish prayers will not bring a good response from evolved beings

in eternity, whereas prayers for the good of others and one's self
will eventually draw the help which the seeker has earned by his
or her life, actions and thoughts.

Telepathy

Telepathy is a fact—I've experienced it too many times to deny its
existence. It is a Mind-to-Mind contact.

Critics of mediums accuse us of constantly reading sitters' minds.
They claim most of our evidence doesn't come from the spirit
world at all, but reaches us via telepathy. This seems rather
presumptuous. If only *one* case for survival is proven, then our
claims carry more weight than this.

In spirit messages, there are usually pieces of information
unacceptable at the time. These should be researched. If proven
correct, then the theory of telepathy on the part of the medium
has to be ruled out. Mediums can't read facts from a mind that
doesn't possess them.

We have a psychic link with those we love, whether they be in this
world or the next. It's a kind of magnetic link that can never be
broken, a thread of awareness that ties us to each other. When our
loved ones are distressed, a sensitive relative can register this, and
distance is no object.

Mediums can use their own soul powers (psychic energies) to
register vibrations of sight, sense and sound which don't
necessarily reach us from the spirit world. They can scan the
electromagnetic fields of swirling energies—known as the aura—
surrounding a person and become aware of all kinds of telling or
'secret' information.

Our psychic perceptions can be *wrong*, of course. When we
read a person's auric fields we must never ever deceive ourselves
into thinking we're right all the time, because we're not. It takes

years of careful development to perfect these skills.

Communication

I can't bring anybody back and make them communicate.

Firstly, they haven't gone anywhere—they're very near in a world interpenetrating ours. Secondly, no one on Earth has any power to force people on the Other Side to do their bidding. They have free will, like us.

Communication between two worlds, even at its best, is always an experiment; so many processes can go wrong. Communication is never easy. Mediumship has to be developed over a period of years, channelled correctly and watched carefully like a growing plant or delicate child. It has to be fed time and patience, and if undertaken, then it should be done so in a serious and responsible manner. To dabble with anything is unwise, to master anything is always fruitful.

A breakdown in communications is probably the medium's fault—though not always. After all, we're tuning in to higher frequencies of the mind, and that isn't easy. Mediums are rather like human radio-sets, but whereas radio tuning is more or less fixed, the medium's mind is trying to register constantly fluctuating spirit wavelengths. This registration is carried out by the mind, under strict discipline of the will-power.

Spirit Messages

The messages are prepared in the spirit world before they're transmitted. The spirit people know what they wish to say before contact is made.

Messages can only be fully understood by those receiving them and those transmitting them. What may sound trivial to the witnesses can convey a wealth of meaning to the receiver. For example, the link might contain certain code-words or even special personal references known only to the two persons involved. Who can say?

Most messages are direct and to the point. Sometimes they're simply worded, but on occasions can be so complicated that only the recipient can unravel them. The communicators bring whatever they can to be recognized and prove their survival. But they may also speak about parts of their lives or mention remote family details about which the sitter may know nothing. When this happens, people are asked to research and check if the facts are correct.

Often I catch everything transmitted by my communicators, but sometimes I miss small pieces of the message. It isn't always easy for them to make themselves heard in our world.

I've learned to trust and depend upon the voice of the spirit, and flow with the stream of evidence reaching me and not battle upstream by arguing over minor details which seem important to the recipient and mean very little to the spirit world.

A private consultation is just exactly that—private.

War and Peace

Wars are created by governments, not by nations. It would be a good idea to record your vote for the people you think least likely to destroy and most likely to create harmony and peace. The more people know about the horrendous effects a nuclear war will have and the untold misery it will bring, the more governments may realize that in a full-scale nuclear war, there can be no victors.

I don't believe 'might is right'. Materialism is a mental disease which leads to greed and selfishness, poverty and the breakdown of human dignity. Peace will only come into this world when individual souls birth it within themselves. Only by our *example* can we teach. Peace starts right here, right now, in our daily lives and dealings with other people.

Man is constantly at war with himself. The earthly consciousness battles against the Higher Self which strives to seek a closer union with Perfection and God.

Sceptics

Those who don't wish to believe will never accept, even if the evidence is so startling and correct that it takes their breath away.

It's a source of constant wonderment that sceptics pitted against me throughout my media career seem singularly certain that Life itself revolves around their own opinions. Every sceptic has a right to his or her opinions, but why *shout* them at me? They say 'empty vessels make the most noise', but please note: God has blessed me with perfect hearing.

Death

Survival of the consciousness after death is the natural birthright of all; every living thing survives.

Do not fear the Dark Angel called Death—for he isn't a Dark Angel at all; he's the Brightest One. Death is painless. It is simply the release of the spirit from the earthly body. I often think of it as a happy release for, in many cases, it is.

We 'die' every night in our sleep: just as soon as our physical body has relaxed, the spirit within starts to loosen from it and we leave our sleeping form and can travel out. But on occasions the spirit body only exteriorizes a little outside the physical, remaining close to it in a state of semi-sleep. This gives the spirit the chance to absorb cosmic energies from around it, and channel them naturally to the sleeper.

Every passing is different, but in each case no pain is involved. Pain belongs to the physical form only—it isn't present in the finer body. The physical body is the pain body, the spirit body is the energy body.

Sudden deaths, such as accidents, cause many people to go into a state of concussion. Just as the earthly body is knocked unconscious, so the spirit body suffers from a temporary state of sleep. But this soon corrects itself and consciousness returns.

After long protracted illnesses, the passing is taken more gently, and loved ones in the spirit world gather to meet the traveller as he crosses the threshold of death to life.

Death doesn't instantly change those who experience it; they're the same people one second after death as they were one second before it. Change is always open to all souls, of course, and they can progress if they so choose. But death does not confer upon us abilities and qualities of mind and character which we haven't earned for ourselves in this life.

People in states of coma are already passing in and out of their physical bodies. As the casket sleeps, the spirit is released into worlds beyond Earth. The same applies to persons on life-support systems; if the spirit vacates permanently, then the person has 'died' and the body is kept 'alive' only in a mechanical sense. It isn't animated by the spirit, but by a machine. Switch off the machine and the body ceases to function because the spirit is gone.

I have stood on the mountain tops of the Shining Lands and experienced countless visions of other worlds beyond death, and I am not afraid to die: for Death is the Great Liberator, the Bright Angel who leads all living things into an eternal life which is their natural birthright.

Evil

I'm not happy about the term 'evil'; misguided is a better word. One man's 'evil' might be another man's 'good'. It all depends on where you stand in the scale of spiritual development.

I don't believe in the mythical devil. If man wants to see 'the devil' all he has to do is look into a mirror. Man remains the most cruel animal in creation.

'Right' or 'Wrong'

I don't think in terms of rights and wrongs. Decisions are made according to our levels of understanding. What is right to one man may be obviously wrong to another. The acid test is the motive for performing our actions. When all is said and done we have to live with ourselves and answer to our conscience for the acts we commit.

If it's 'wrong' for a citizen to commit murder, how can it be 'right' for the state to do it? That's illogical.

Our minds are such wonderful instruments, I'm often surprised when people don't use them to think matters out for themselves instead of accepting another's opinions. After all, what is true for one man need not be true for another.

The Conduct of the Soul

What really matters is *how* we live our lives. When we pass over we shall gravitate to a sphere of existence which we have earned for ourselves by the building of our character and the growth of our spirit. (See *Visions of Another World*, page 209.)

All we take with us through the gateway called 'death' is ourselves. There are no pockets in shrouds, no status symbols or earthly aggrandisements on the Other Side. We shall simply take our mind and character, our soul-growth and moral attitudes and all facets of the true inner person.

Over There, we shall not be the person we think we are, nor the person the world thinks we are—but we shall be the person we truly are.

Over There we shall clearly see that the only things which mattered were:
- how we lived our lives;
- how we had thought;
- how we had acted.

Our problems are our own; they don't belong to the people in the next world, and therefore the solving of them is our responsibility.

All life is comparison. We must know tears and joy, happiness and sadness, pain and peace within. We must learn to cope with and grow from our struggles and hardships. It's not what happens to us that matters most—but how we deal with it that counts.

This world makes much of pomp and ceremony, and treasures public acclaim as a mark of importance. But in the Greater Life what we call ourselves is of little account. It is what we really are, what we have done with our lives which matters. These are the only eternal treasures we can possess.

When we stand on the shores of eternity and look back upon our experiences in Earthlife, we will notice how all the things we did happened in just the right places, at just the right times. And we shall say to ourselves: it is good.

Love

The greatest power in the universe is the Power of Love.

Love can never be dissected by clever scientists in their laboratories, or technically proven in any way: nevertheless it exists and, what is more, love is stronger than death. If you have tasted the joys of love—and I don't mean physical love, but the deeper true spiritual love—then be thankful, for you are fortunate indeed.

Only one single, final thought—just one code of conduct means more than anything else to me now. Without Love, we are nothing.

17

Homecoming

Two dreadfully long years had passed since I moved to Gateshead. Every night had dragged by, each day was endless and tiresome, and life was still incredibly hard and difficult, and getting progressively worse. I couldn't get out of the filthy catchment area, money was in desperately short supply, neighbours were threatening, arrogant and uncouth, and forever keeping me awake at night with their noisy TV and radio sets. Life was a great big pain and strain.

Then one day a strange spirit message came through during a table-tilt experiment I was conducting at a lecture weekend. The Other Side supernormally moved, danced, rapped and tilted a table in response to questions. Using one tilt for each letter of the alphabet, it mysteriously spelt out:

White Owl—Stephen's friend.

'Ask him what he wants,' said one of the 60 students.

'Get a message,' added another around the juddering table.

'Well, White Owl?' I said, more to satisfy the students than myself.

Home soon.

My heart lurched within me. Home? Wales..? I daren't breathe in case I'd heard it incorrectly. 'What did he say?' I nervously asked, my pulse racing, half-afraid to utter the question.

'He said "*Home soon*", Stephen. Can you understand it?'

Regaining my composure I softly answered, 'Well, I think so,' then half under my breath, 'I hope so . . .'

All at once, thoughts of beautiful green hills and mountains in my homeland moved majestically before my inner sight. I could see the clifftops of Swansea, smell the ozone as the rolling sea came thundering in upon the rocks; the faces of everyone I'd known since a boy appeared in my mind's eye, and I was filled with a surging desire to go back. But it was all a dream, too much to hope for, and another tilt of the table brought me smartly back into the room.

White Owl obviously knew of my dire loneliness, and homesickness—maybe he was saying another phase of my life was opening up. More service? Greater opportunities for soul growth which only living in Wales might bring? I wasn't sure, so with baited breath I awaited the conclusion:

Home soon. Home is where the heart is.

There was no doubt in his mind. But would events prove him right? What happened next was strange:

Swansea

Dear Sir,

I am writing to you in the Housing Department to respectfully request your assistance in finding accommodation in Swansea for my son, Stephen, who is now resident in Tyne and Wear.

Stephen is now registered under the National Mobility Scheme and if you could bring him back to Swansea it would be a tremendous help to me, as I am severely disabled and living on my own at present.

Yours faithfully,

Mr R. O'Brien.

Following through, I left Sooty 'on holiday' with Sheila, cut out buying food, ignored a final demand for an electricity bill and scraped together £47 for a rail ticket to go and see my father. The tedious seven-and-a-half hour journey gave me time to think back and reflect. Dad and I had never got along, yet all those ghostly disagreements have long been blown away by Time, the greatest healer.

But when I arrived, I got a shock—he looked terribly unwell. His chest was playing him up; he couldn't walk up hills so he'd been granted a car for mobility. His breathing was stilted and certainly worse, and the extra weight he'd put on didn't help his heart. He was now in constant pain and finding life a struggle. With agonizing arthritis, painful gout, and a 70 per cent chest disability, even my mother started sending messages from Beyond concerning him.

After tea and a chat came an endless round of calls on Housing Departments and eventually on Dad's doctor, who kindly wrote supporting his case. Then an interview at the housing offices.

'You're on Priority, Mr O'Brien, When something suitable's vacant, you'll be informed.'

'But my father's ill. How long will it take?'

'Maybe next week, or possibly two years.'

I walked out into the sharp air, grumbling, 'So much for the "Home soon" message.'

'Well, never mind, boy,' groaned Dad later. 'We've done our best, but I can't stand much more of these chest pains. Some mornings I can't breathe properly . . .' he wheezed. And, for all our stormy past, I really felt sorry in my heart for him, especially as he still missed my mother so much. Then we said our goodbyes and I headed back north, many doubts clouding my mind.

Sooty went bananas! She jumped up and down, ran like the wind through the rooms and shot up the curtains (!) then scrambled like a wildcat all over me and sat on my head, mewing with delight and slapping her furry tail into my face and eyes like fury! 'Did you miss me, sweetheart?' I laughed, tickling her stomach.

And then came a long, silent, red-tape wait . . .

One dusty evening while aimlessly wandering through Gateshead, deeply uncertain about my future and thinking about my past, I ended up sitting on the grassy Windmill Hills overlooking the River Tyne by moonlight. The eerie silver-blue sky and the majesty of the sparkling water dwarfed the black slums around its banks. My mind floated into the splendour of the scene, much as the evening breeze was drifting where it liked, when all at once the night was broken by a gentle spirit voice, heralding a new beginning for me.

'Finish the book,' it whispered.

'What? My life story? I only have scraps of paper with faded memories on them.'

But the voice didn't speak again. Surely I was in too upsetting conditions to have clear thoughts? Entranced by the glinting river, winding its way to the distant sea, all I could hear was the far off Newcastle traffic: I didn't hear another sound from eternity. Then, way over the glittering water, high above the horizon, some starlings squealed their cries, wheeling in the dying light of day. The sun was setting over the skyline, as I slowly rose and ambled back to the dreary estate—perplexed in thought.

Although recording my life seemed, at first, very arrogant (too many 'I's), I was told it would be of great service both to the Other Side, and people searching for knowledge in *this* world. Spirit friends also predicted that eventually millions would read it. And I kept remembering their strange message to me as a young man, 'Unto you is granted the Power of the Word.' So in the following cold, uncertain months, I obeyed their instructions, and my first book, *Visions of Another World*, was born; birthed amongst the poverty and unemployment of Gateshead town; written in the early hours between midnight and 3 a.m., when all the drunks had fallen senseless into their beds, the thugs were out in another world, and the night was at its quietest.

The prophecies were now fulfilled—I'd had many messages through other mediums to say I'd write a book—and I remembered thinking, 'Even if I die tomorrow, I've left something behind me to help others along the road.' It somehow made the struggles easier to bear.

I spent long and lonely nights writing that manuscript, sometimes typing way into the dawn hours, but it was very therapeutic, something to take my mind off my miserable surroundings. But it was only after I'd finished it that I fully realized how truly blessed by the world of spirit I'd been in my 30-odd years. Their love and guidance, protection and encouragement had been with me all the way. And through my link with them, I'd come to find my God. I'd been through the fires of hardship, and consequently was now much stronger, and more fitted to serve those in need.

Then the strangest things started to happen: *déja vu*. You know the kind of thing—someone speaks a very unusual phrase or you go down a totally unfamiliar street, when quite suddenly it's just as though invisible lightning strikes your senses dumb. You can practically mouth the exact words in perfect synchronization with the speaker, or describe what lies around the corner of that never-before-walked-down road.

Then Jeff rang from Wales: he'd seen an empty flat, but when I applied it had already been let. Dark fears of being re-housed in a high-rise tower block invaded my mind. Their noise levels are horrific; you can hear people talking, even lavatories flushing. There'd be no privacy, and I value privacy and golden silence more than anything. That night I selfishly prayed: 'I'd hate to leave my new friends, but if I must, please get me a decent house.' I was even cheeky enough to request two bedrooms and central heating! I'd have loved it; both my other places were perishing cold in the winter. But after that first refusal, I thought, 'Oh God, bang goes my central heating and I'll end up in a skyscraper!' Seeing I was disillusioned, Sheila and Graeme cheered me up by inviting me to Jarrow Spiritualist church.

'Come on,' said Graeme, 'forget your troubles and do a bit of work.'

'Take your mind off it for a while,' chipped in kindly Sheila, stirring the piping-hot tea she'd just brewed to combat the icy weather. 'Besides, we always need help at the church. Sometimes it's so full there aren't enough mediums to go round.' So I reluctantly agreed. Yet later I was glad I'd made the effort, for I got an excellent message from Barbara Marley, one of the resident mediums.

'Your grandfather's here!' she smiled, giving an accurate description of my mother's father, Grancha Price, even supplying his surname. 'Oh all right, dear!' she gushed. 'It's no good pushing, I'm going as fast as I can!' Then came: 'He knows of your application disappointment, but hold on and there'll be a move for you. He promises it'll be to your satisfaction. He heard your prayer, and the solution's coming. Can you understand?'

'Perfectly, thank you.'

That week another housing letter arrived. I was loathe to open it, as my faith in the Civil Service had long since dwindled like a popped bubble-gum balloon, and died. It was just a note to say they'd be in touch whenever something suitable became vacant. The bubble-gum hardened on the ground.

Again I couldn't sleep, anxious thoughts flying through my mind. In the end I sent up another prayer. 'Am I doing the right thing? Should I stay in England, or return to Wales? Are there people here up North I've yet to meet and help?' Then, filled with failing trust, I called out to my invisible friends, 'If it's in my Plan to go home, *give me a sign*.' Then I waited in the stillness for a light to guide me—but nothing came. Tranquillity bathed the dark room. I deeply sighed. There was no answer; the night was silent . . . No sign was given.

After this, weeks dragged by, and I'd forgotten all about my request when, standing at a bus-stop after my weekly visit to kindly Miss Smith, who taught me music for virtually next to nothing, I began chatting to a friendly north-east pensioner. She was charming, with a thick Geordie accent, but I was struck most by her unusual penetrating eyes. There was something strange about her bearing, her features. I couldn't say what, so we were just gossiping about the atrocious weather and the biting-cold snow lying thick on the ground, when suddenly she launched some amazing remarks. 'I'm from Wales, you know,' she beamed, her vital eyes shining bright.

'But you don't have a Welsh accent.'

'No, but I'm as Welsh as you are.' I was astounded at what a small world it is, and also that we'd never met before. Who on earth could she be? 'I catch this bus every week at the same time,' she added, looking rather surprised at my expression. I couldn't fathom out why we'd never seen one another, for I too had caught that very same bus at the same time each week for the last two years: same time, same day. Why hadn't we bumped into each other? It didn't make sense.

But then came the biggest shock: 'I'm from Swansea,' she announced, describing districts just a few hundred yards from my birthplace, adding, 'And I'm going back to Swansea in a few weeks.'

I couldn't believe my ears. She'd mentioned my home town, and returning to it soon. Then, out of the blue, a voice from heaven whispered inside my head:

This is the sign

I froze to the spot, the very core of me shaken. But who *was* this elderly woman who'd appeared on that snowy afternoon? And why hadn't our paths ever crossed before? Come to that, I don't remember seeing her on the bus when I looked around in my seat. In fact, I never saw her ever again. My blood ran cold. Could she possibly have been a Messenger, sent from Beyond? Someone charged with a message, a sign? Was she a visitor from another world made flesh in bright daylight? I've heard it said we often walk and talk with angels, yet fail to recognize them.

No matter—the sign was given, so I dashed off to the supermarket to collect dozens of cardboard boxes which I stockpiled in the bedroom, ready for the move. And I didn't have long to wait. Within a week the offer was on the mat and Grancha Price's spirit prediction was proven perfectly correct: it was more than satisfactory. I was given a two-bedroomed, centrally-heated place in a quietish area, near Dad. (I couldn't resist a wicked grin at the central heating!)

But now came the heart-breaking part. I underwent dreadful soul torment over whether or not to accept. My soul said 'yes', but my body screamed 'no'. I spent pounds I could ill afford ringing up friends in Wales begging advice. I wrung my hands in despair, paced the floors at night and cried buckets of tears, unable to get my mind together. It's hard to describe the deep feelings of the soul—only a faint shadow of the hurt, uncertainty, emotion and heart-wrenching can be conveyed. I felt that in leaving the North I'd failed to make a new life, settle and complete my work. Yet I also yearned to return to my nation. I was in a state of anxiety. Where was my place? What should I do? Where would I be happiest? Floating back into my mind came White Owl's message: '*Home soon. Home is where the heart is.*'

Then I became aware that it didn't matter where I lived, my heart went with me wherever I was. We have to be happy *inside* ourselves, not outwardly. So I decided to leave.

I knew I'd miss the North, beating with the great heart of its people. And only when I was leaving did I fully realize just how much I loved them. I knew I'd miss poor Gateshead, with its quaint streets and Metro trains whizzing across the River Tyne at lightning speed, and the warm kindness of all my new-found friends. I'd especially miss the spiritual people who'd gathered around me, much as lost children seeking guidance from their father—only I know *I* learned much more from them than they ever did from me. They were wonderful people who'd helped me so much in my time of need. They'd accepted me into their families as one of their own. And so, reluctantly and painfully, I accepted the new home.

Back at my flat, I couldn't bring myself to pack. Every time I touched a picture it was like ripping my heart out, and I just sat down and cried like a baby all over again. I'm proud to say it, for my tears fell in tribute to the love and respect I held for the northern people.

With just four hours to the end of my tenancy, I still hadn't thrown more than three things in a box. Emotionally, I rang Sheila and Graeme who both dropped everything and dashed over to my flat. Then pandemonium broke loose. Everything was chucked everywhere, willy-nilly—and within three hours my home was hidden in bags and boxes.

And so it was goodbye to Newcastle, the most difficult decision I've ever had to make. Even the thought of it now brings a wave of nostalgia and a lump to my throat. The silliest things kept crossing my mind, thoughts that couldn't be dismissed—mixed images, memories of all the happy northern friendships I'd shared, good days and bad days, all wrapped in emotion. I was even strangely haunted by the sadness etched on the face of the ragged old bird-woman who came each day to the city's monument to feed her cold and hungry feathered friends, and the vast black flocks of circling starlings screeching over cold city buildings at night. I'd never see them again.

But I could stay no longer, the voice of Wales was calling, and yet how heart-rending it was to break the sad news to my friends. What could I say? All I kept thinking was I had to do it gently, for I loved them all so much. The first I saw were my two dear friends, Keith and Elizabeth, the kindly people who'd brought my cat, Sooty, to me from the animal sanctuary. 'Oh Stephen,' sighed Elizabeth, her speech trembling, 'do you really have to go?' And she cupped her hand to her mouth.

'I'm afraid so,' I whispered softly, my voice quivering at the prospect of leaving them, especially after all the kindnesses they'd shown.

Elizabeth searched the floor with her eyes, then looked up into my face again. 'It's like losing one of our own,' she said softly, 'as if a part of our own family was leaving.'

And her husband, Keith, nodded sadly, and took my hand. 'I hope you'll be happy, Stephen,' he said rather quietly.

Everyone was upset to think I'd soon be out of their lives, but no one more so than me. 'I'll write and telephone,' I promised. 'And I'll never forget you. I'll always remember your kindnesses and value your friendship, forever.' I slowly got around to telling them all. Jim and Eileen fell silent; then came the time to see Moira and Adrian, good friends from the psychic circle in Sunderland. They both seemed very hurt, inwardly upset. They wished me well, but I could see in their eyes they were so sorry I'd be leaving their lives.

'Look after yourself, Stephen,' said Moira, glancing away.

Adrian was quiet for a while, but eventually said, falteringly,

'Watch how you go now, Stephen. And promise you'll keep in touch, won't you? We've really enjoyed your friendship.'

'I think the world of you all,' I said.

'Stephen,' returned Adrian, clasping my hand, 'it's been a privilege to know you.' Then I was silent; bereft of words, unable to speak. I lowered my head and felt sadness sweeping through me . . .

At the Tuesday circle Isobel cried; Joyce and Graeme couldn't find the right things to say. Great-hearted Sheila—without whom I would have starved in the North-east, and gone insane without her listening ear—assured me I'd always be included in her prayers. 'God bless you, Stephen,' she said, 'and always remember: be happy.' And we hugged, eyes misting over. Everyone had been so kind to me. I guess I didn't appreciate what I had until I was in danger of losing it.

But it was dear old Lily, Moira's mother, who wept freely and cried the most. She held me so tight, I could never doubt her love and concern. 'Take good care of yourself, love,' she said through her tears. 'Oh Stephen, don't ever forget we'll all be thinking of you and praying that God'll keep you safe. God bless you, son. And you know where we are if you ever need us, don't you..?' Then her speech dwindled into silence.

'Yes, Lily,' I sighed; my heart was so full, I couldn't speak another word.

'Come back to us one day, Stephen. Please come back, son . . .' The room was full of pounding hearts, and inward thoughts. 'You've done a lot of good up here. A great many people are thinking differently now. You've helped them, love, more than you'll ever know. Take care now, and God bless you, my handsome boy . . .' she said, her voice trailing away as she wiped her eyes . . .

And my last memory of England was the rented van bumping and trundling its way down dusty winding roads and out along the highways and off towards South Wales, 400 miles in the distance. As England faded out behind me, my eyes filled with tears and my mind spun with memories. Green fields blurred past the windows, and my thoughts ran free. I knew the hardships behind me were cocooned in soul-growth and smiling friendships. Through all the struggles, a part of my spirit had been slowly strangled, choked of air, and had finally died. This young man in his thirties returning to Wales was a new creature; someone older, wiser, reborn—all the richer for the love he'd shared with the North-east and its people.

Yet this man was also intensely sad in his deepest heart, as he watched England disappearing from view through the dusty truck windows, for he felt as if he had just kissed the Vale of Tears, and passed through the Valley of the Shadow of Death . . .

18
Touching Millions

Visions of Another World came out in September '89, and my first publicity engagement was a book-signing session, which turned out to be absolute bedlam. With just 10 minutes to the start, *no books had arrived*! Special copies were coming from London and were delayed on the roads. The bookstore manageress frantically rang local shops to borrow copies, but they'd all sold out! 'What am I going to do?!' she kept saying, slapping her worried forehead.

'Books!' shouted the delivery man.

'Oh, thank God!' she cried, eagerly shredding cardboard boxes and yanking copies free.

Meanwhile, restless queues were peeking around the presentation stands. 'Is he here yet?' 'Has he arrived?' 'Oh, he's lovely, you know!' I heard them say, as I descended the stairs, greeted by a horde of smiling faces and ringing tills, as copy after copy was seized, bought, clutched, and marched into line behind dozens of people wanting an autograph, a handshake, a smile and a chat. I wrote some inspired words in everybody's book. People pushed to the front, saying things like, 'Keep up the marvellous work, Stephen, you're one in a million!' 'We're so proud of you.' 'This copy's flying to Australia, and this one's for South America!' 'Will you sign these four, please? They're off to Germany tomorrow!'

One woman stepped forward loaded with *eight* copies! 'God

bless you, my darling,' she said, throwing her arms around my neck. 'Sign these, there's a love.'

Others began to cry as they neared my table. Emotionally overcome by our meeting, they poured out their hearts to me about tragic family losses and how much something I'd said on TV, radio or in the newspapers had helped them. 'God be with you, Stephen,' said total strangers, hugging me and clasping my hands tightly in both of theirs. People were so kind. I was deeply moved, utterly overwhelmed, and soon lost count of how many kisses I got on that day. I was presented with babies and children to cuddle too. It was a thoroughly smashing event.

The only black blot was another narrow-minded religious picket-line outside the store, but the police were called and they were silenced and disbanded, with the public shouting at them: 'Go and learn some kindness!' 'Call yourselves Christians? You're a disgrace to your religion!'

In fact, this particular shambles made news next day in *The Times*, no less! But I felt sad because they'd failed to radiate the Love of the One they claim to follow, someone for whom I have the deepest respect. Wendy, from my publishers, couldn't take it all in; shocked by the foray, she was even more overwhelmed by the powerful feelings of love and gratitude the public displayed towards me. 'I've been to book-signings before,' she said, 'but never one like this!' Taking deep breaths, she then gathered her composure, took some snapshots and informed the crowds, 'Stephen's on television tonight if you want to see him.'

Channel 4 had telephoned.

'Will you appear on the late night nationally-networked discussion programme, *After Dark*? It's a three-hour live debate called *Superpowers: All in the Mind?*'

'Of course,' I said, and before long I'd arrived in London, been given a slap-up dinner at a top hotel (£10 to step on the carpets), then chauffeured to the studios. The late show started about 11 and sometimes finished at 2. It was only cut short if debates got tiresome, but ours went the full run: millions watched and viewing figures kept rising. Topics discussed included the USA's latest craze, 'channeling' (passing information from Higher Minds in the Beyond via sensitives; Athena Pattengill had been flown over from the USA to participate), life after death, psychic work, fraud, charlatanism, and even delusions of grandeur!

The inevitable sceptics were a psychologist, and conjuror James Randi, whose screen credit was 'Charlatan', which I'm afraid I found wickedly amusing. My best volley of the match was delivered to psychologist Susan Blackmore, who continually dismissed the afterlife, saying we should let go of the people we've lost:

> *Dr Blackmore:* Perhaps if we grew in moral and spiritual stature we would no longer need the idea of life after death. If I'm just a biological lump of flesh, the best thing we can do is to admit that, and accept that 'the self' is just a construct, just something that the biological system's invented. And if you let go of that, and not cling to the idea that your self is so important—
>
> *Stephen:* Sue, have you ever lost anybody close to you that you really, really loved very much indeed?
>
> *Dr Blackmore:* I'm afraid I haven't, no.
>
> *Stephen:* Well when you *have*, come back and say that to me again.

As far as I was concerned, that was game, set and match, and I later got many letters praising this remark. But James Randi kept putting forward cases where he said 'fake' mediums had been debunked and proven charlatans. I pointed out that this didn't nullify *all* mediums as being genuine, saying to him, 'Anyway, that's only your opinion.'

'*I don't have an opinion*,' he rattled back.

'Then you can't be a human being,' I said. (Regrettably, another favourite remark with viewers.)

When balanced presenter Tony Wilson asked me to give messages live before millions, I brought a contact for charming guest Ivy Northage. Her late husband relayed specific details about her eightieth birthday celebrations and their two sons, named 'Twickers'—Twickenham, where she lived—and even that she'd changed her brooch and evening dress, having made her choice from three gowns and two brooches, just before leaving for the studios. These were specific details which, as Ivy pointed out, happened when she was completely alone. No one on Earth could have known them.

When we went off air, a middle-aged cameraman took me gently aside. 'That was wonderful tonight, Stephen. I believe in your gifts,' he said, 'and though I was behind the lens, I prayed you'd contact my dear mother who died recently. I can't tell you how much I loved her, Stephen. She was a lovely, wonderful old lady, and I miss her so much.'

'I know what it is to lose a great friend,' I said, squeezing his handshake in sympathy, remembering my own mother's agony as she lay dying of widespread cancer throughout her body. Thankfully, I was able to offer him a few words of hope and comfort, which seemed to help.

'I'll never forget her, you know,' he said, dabbing his eyes.

'No, no matter how long its been, you never forget . . .' I said.

After more congratulations, drinks and handshakes, I was bundled into a chauffeured car and hurtled home to Wales at 120 mph down empty motorways. I crashed into bed, totally washed-out, at 5.30 a.m.

So many people wrote to me after that show saying how dignified they thought I'd been when dealing with the sceptics— all bar one woman who penned, 'How you kept your hands off that Randi's throat and didn't throttle him to death, I'll never know. If I'd have been there, I'd have cooked his goose!' To which I replied, 'Mr Randi surely has a right to his opinions, and Love is the message I'm trying to give, not hatred, anger or intolerance. I've tried to live my life according to the Golden Rule: Love everyone as much as one can, and be as harmless as possible. Surely those who seem against us, stand in the greatest need of our love?' She didn't respond, so I think she got my point.

Travelling back and forth to London became a regular habit and I soon lost count of the media interviews I did, as well as welcoming journalists and photographers to Wales from magazines like *Woman*, *Chat*, and *Take-A-Break*. There were so many London trips (!) but one of the most pleasant was with *Daily Mail* journalist June Southworth. We ended up in a dubious Greek restaurant, where she conspicuously prodded at, and apologized for, the strange-looking unidentified food—but we shared such a happy hour together, and what a charming lady she is. 'Oh, Stephen,' she smiled, 'you make it *so* hard to write anything nasty about you!'

'Well, *that's* a blessing then!' I quipped, as we both laughed, making our way out of a taxi and into Northcliffe House, *Daily Mail* headquarters. My breath was taken away—it was so impressive, so vast, all made from glass and marble, with scenic lifts and waterfalls. My eyes scanned the tall expensive facades and just kept on going up and up, until I felt wobbly at the knees. And everywhere there was bustle and hurried activity, and no one was allowed entry without a computerized pass.

A similar press-lunch was given me by free-lance journalist Susan Marchant, but it was followed by a *very* unusual photoshoot. 'Come on, Stephen, follow me!' she said, whisking me off into the British Museum.

'What on earth am I doing in here?'

'Just stand over there!' She pointed hurriedly, and then took dozens of photos of me languishing against mummies and giant Egyptian statues, lined up alongside all the other ancient old relics!

Soon the road loomed up in front of me, and I appeared in 20 major cities, and did radio, TV and press features which all but practically exhausted me, and had me on my knees. But valiant to the end, I spread the news of everlasting life, touching millions, as I'd promised my spirit friends I would. And no sooner had those engagements been fulfilled, another 30 meetings were arranged. Gradually the media made me a celebrity (something I'd always secretly known would happen to me, since childhood).

This meant I met many famous people. We arrived at one concert hall just as famed tenor Luciano Pavarotti was leaving. Then the box-office told my manager, Jeff, 'Comedian Larry

Grayson would like to see Mr O'Brien's show and meet him afterwards. Is that all right?'

'Stephen would be delighted,' answered Jeff; and I was. I'd lost count of the times Larry Grayson had made me laugh in famous British TV shows such as *Shut That Door!* (his own peculiar catchphrase), and BBC TV's *The Generation Game* over the years. His gentle humour had endeared him to millions. After my evening of clairvoyance, the dressing-room door knocked and in stepped Larry Grayson.

'Stephen, how lovely to meet you. I really enjoyed the meeting—it was so emotional, a smashing night.'

We shook hands and were formally introduced by Michael, a reporter with the local newspaper.

'I'm very pleased to meet you, Mr Grayson—'

'Oh, call me Larry! I feel I know you so *well*. I'm a fan of yours!'

'And I've watched you on TV for years—'

'Hey, steady on,' he joked, 'I'm not *that* old!' And we all laughed, especially when he told us side-splitting stories about his comedy characters 'Apricot Lil' and 'Slack Alice'! Then he produced a copy of my book. 'I can't find out "Whodunnit",' he laughed, flicking to the back pages. 'Will you sign it for me?'

'Of course.'

We all had a marvellous time listening to Larry's hysterically funny stories—he's such an entertaining, warm human being. Whenever he opens residential homes for elderly folk, he insists on staying until he's personally met every single resident. 'He won't go until he's spoken to them all and made them cry laughing!' informed Michael. 'And by the way, Stephen, I was so moved by the meeting tonight. It was amazing—and that's praise indeed from someone like me, a newspaperman.' I coloured up red.

'You've got a wonderful gift, Stephen,' said Larry, whose rise to fame had been foretold by a clairvoyant the year *before* he became a household name. 'I've also seen my mother, you know. I was adopted, of course, but after my mother died she appeared to me, standing at the foot of the bed, and told me she was safe and well. It was very comforting.' He said he'd later told singer celebrity Max Bygraves about it, but Max tried to explain it all away. Larry countered, 'You can say what you like, Max, I'm telling you what happened, *and it was true!*'

'One personal experience is worth a thousand theories,' I said.

'I couldn't agree more,' added Larry, conviction in his voice. Then he mentioned his friendship with the late broadcaster, writer and humorist Arthur Marshall. 'Dear old Arthur,' he reminisced, 'I'd ring up and he'd say, "Ah Larry, dear boy, when are you coming down? I'll get a Battenberg!" '

After an hour of belly-laughter, Larry gave both Jeff and me his personal address and an invite to 'Pop in and visit whenever you're in the area. And don't forget I want news of all your meetings, 'cos I'm a fan and *I* shall be *there!*' he cried triumphantly. 'I first heard you on BBC Radio 2's *Anne Robinson Show*.'

Anne was so very charming, as soon as she knew I was booked she moved actress June Whitfield and gave the major time to me. (Sorry, June!) Between records, we chatted away animatedly, Anne saying with that famous BBC TV *Points of View* smile, 'Darling, they're lapping it up, loving it! All four million of them are now sitting glued to their sets.' I couldn't help but grin: it's always amazed me there are actually millions out there listening to the radio! The studios are so quiet, it's hard to imagine whole families tucking into salads and hanging on every word. I feel the same when doing a 'down-the-line' interview, where I'm phoned at home then linked live to thousands across Britain. What a spooky thought! But I'm used to it now: I think I've spoken on most major radio stations, and the reception's always the same—switchboards immediately jam with callers. In my several appearances on Greater London Radio's *Johnnie Walker Show*, poor Johnnie never once got the word 'telephone' out before all the lights started madly flickering.

On BBC Radio Wales *Level 3* show I had a smashing time with renowned authoress and colourful celebrity Molly Parkin, and even took part in a delightful comic sketch with stars William Franklyn and Nerys Hughes. I played the medium and they were the 'ghostbusters'! It was a great laugh!

And on BBC Radio 4's *Loose Ends*, I gave TV personality Emma Freud some taped evidence from her grandmother on the Other Side. Emma was most touched, but had to check two vital facts she couldn't immediately place. Her grandmother had said that the name 'Johnnie' and 'a rose placed in my hand' as she lay at rest were very significant. But upon asking her father, writer, politician and broadcaster Clement Freud, the evidence was placed as quite correct—ruling out telepathy on my part. A rose *had* been placed in her grandma's hands, and 'Johnnie' was the nickname she used to call herself! When the tape was broadcast there was absolute silence from all the guests. The show's main host, Ned Sherrin, referred to it as 'an awesome silence'! And, of course, letters started pouring in all over again.

Some people imagine my tours to be grand and glamorous, with my manager, Jeff, and I being accommodated in all the best hotels with five-star treatment—but they'd be surprised to know the truth! I've stayed at YMCA rooms and tiny guesthouses with no hot running water, and buckets balanced on the windowsills to catch the rain leaking in through the roof! At one cheap place I was just about to jump into bed when a spirit voice said, 'Lift the pillow!'—and there was a live earwig crawling underneath it!

Someone else Jeff never travels without is his faithful, battered (but bow-tied) teddy-bear called Ravenshaw. 'Rave' was rescued many years ago from a junk shop, and is now pampered beyond belief. He was always wrapped up snugly and put to bed in the afternoons while our entourage travelled to the venue. One night, when we returned, Jeff was furious! He dashed into my room holding Ravenshaw aloft and bellowing, 'I can't believe what that miserable landlady did! She made the bed and actually flung 'Rave' onto the windowsill!'

'So what? He's only a teddy-bear.'

'Yes, but you *know* he doesn't like it on the window!'

By the time the '89 leg of the tour reached southern Britain, I was completely shattered. Exhaustion had set in: my eyes were red, I had a nasty 'flu virus and long sleepless nights had physically run me into the ground. Fortunately, I was being hosted by one of my dear friends, Peggy, whose kindness and spiritual healing gifts are well known down South. Peggy had even once been reported in a local newspaper as being a 'certified' healer—the cause of much amusement, for it should have read 'certificated'!

'Stephen, you look all in, love. You've got big blue circles under your eyes. Why don't you lie down and rest? I'll wake you when our lift comes for tonight's meeting.'

'All right,' I said, 'if I can find the strength to get to the bedroom,' and I practically dragged my feet all the way and flopped down onto the soft bed and crashed immediately into black oblivion . . .

My next memory was slowly becoming conscious again, after what felt like a timeless sleep. The air in the bedroom seemed strangely still. I couldn't hear children playing outside in the park any more; there was an eerie silence all around, yet I knew I wasn't alone. Misty human figures gathered around the bed, gazing at my drowsy form. I felt the touch of their hands smoothing my skin, as coloured spirit-lights hovered in the air. The visitors gently alleviated aches and pains, while psychically emitting warmth and tender compassion. For several minutes, my skin glistened with perspiration under the heat from their rays, and the room was 'shivering' with life and energy.

My body was as heavy as lead, and I couldn't move a muscle. Smarting my eyes into focus, I saw five spirit forms standing, making an examination. Three wore white coats. Then I heard a woman speak. 'You need seven days complete bed-rest. You're physically and nervously exhausted,' she warned. 'You must rest *immediately*.' And with those words, I moved my legs a little, and the doctors faded out . . . She was right, of course, but there were more engagements to fulfil. I couldn't rest: the work had to go on. I'd never let the spirit people or my public down, people like that lovely old lady who showed such courage and devotion at Winchester Guildhall.

I'd just started the second-half messages when suddenly a policewoman marched in and shouted: 'A package has been found. There's a bomb scare. Everyone out, *now!*' British to the end, stiff-lipped and complaining, the audience reluctantly obeyed.

I stood and watched them go, saying over and again, 'I'm so sorry. I'm sorry this has happened.'

Just like a captain on a sinking ship, I was the last to leave, when out of nowhere a frail pensioner came to the stage, extending a bony hand. 'I'm not afraid,' she said in quivering tones, through sparkling eyes. 'I'll stay with you to the end, bomb or no bomb. May I stay with you?' A lump came into my throat, and I felt the tears starting to well, as she squeezed my arm.

'I'm not afraid either, my darling,' I said, deeply touched by her loyalty, 'but the police really do want us to go.' So we gracefully left the hall, side by side, hand in hand.

Outside on the iron fire-escape it was like a scene from *Romeo and Juliet*. Once the crowd spotted me, they all gathered around my feet, circling the stairs, clasping my hands through the bars, wanting their books signed.

'If we don't get back in—it's been wonderful so far, Stephen.'

'God bless you for helping us.'

'Can we buy books?' someone called out, and a young man from the crowd bravely ran back into the cordoned-off building and brought out the bookstand. I autographed more than 100 that night, and in 35 minutes the capacity audience were finally allowed back in.

'We're not leaving,' I said through the microphones, 'until we've had the meeting we came for.' There was instant thunderous applause and cheering, and someone whistled out from the gallery, as I picked up the very same spirit message exactly where I'd left it earlier. I'll never forget the audience's love and devotion. I was deeply moved; they really wanted to be there with me.

But without doubt, one of the highlights of my recent tours was my appearance at the Wembley Conference Centre, London, when on 31 March 1990 the Spiritualists' National Union celebrated its first 100 years. Some of the most eminent speakers, mediums and healers in the kingdom attended and, out of all the mediums in the country, I was invited to work with my good friend, world-acclaimed psychic artist Coral Polge. Feeling honoured to be selected, I really looked forward to meeting again some of the leading lights in Spiritual thought, such as Gordon Higginson, Mary Duffy and great thinkers like Sir George Trevelyan, founder of the Wrekin Trust, a spiritual charity. Although in his eighties, Sir George gave an excellent address which gained him a standing ovation. And the whole day was video-recorded and marketed to the public, for posterity.

Hours before the event, hundreds were queuing all around the huge Conference Centre, waving banners, singing, and clutching their tickets, thoroughly thrilled by the prospect of a whole day's celebration. There was a buzz of fevered excitement in the air, and every face was radiant. Over 2,500 people from Britain and overseas gathered in the vast amphitheatre stadium. Underneath bubbling conversations and psychic stories, there was a wonderful feeling of unity thrilling through the crowds.

Coral's eagerly-awaited psychic drawings were to be projected onto a massive white screen. After being wired with special radio-mikes, we walked on stage, instantly greeted by loud applause and dazzling bursts of light—not spirit lights, but dozens of clicking shutters as flashlights popped in all sections of the impressive auditorium. This was such a special day and people weren't going to let it pass without photographing it. While we were being introduced, several came down through the crowds. 'Give us a smile, Stephen!' 'May we take your picture?'

Well, what could I say? I obliged! Normally I don't like my quietness disturbed, but there was no way of stopping so many flashes exploding right, left and centre. Anyway, I must confess—I felt like a Hollywood film star on premiere night! *Psychic News* described the proceedings:

There was almost a tangible atmosphere of expectancy as world-famous psychic artist Coral Polge and Welsh medium Stephen O'Brien took the stage for what proved to be an excellent demonstration and a high-point of the proceedings.

Linking with spirit communicators simultaneously, they reunited one sitter with her great-grandfather, contacted a young boy killed in a road accident, and successfully proved the existence of life after death. As the mediums worked in perfect unison, you could almost see the crowds of spirit visitors excitedly queuing up to make contact with loved ones.

With a calm atmosphere enveloping the auditorium, despite the emotional content of the messages, there were many light points during the proceedings.

One woman concluded her message by mentioning the fact that someone had walked off with her brooch after her passing. 'She's waiting for them on the Other Side!' Stephen told a delighted audience.

Another elderly, yet comical communicator, who described himself as 'a man of many parts, some of them still working!' was jokingly asked whether he had donated any of his vital organs.

'He just told me they weren't very vital by the time he died!' Coral relayed.

Successfully reuniting an RAF pilot, shot down during the Second World War, with a surprised wartime colleague, silence then fell as the features of a boy began to manifest on the screen . . .

'I've got a young lad here,' Coral explained, 'who I believe passed on a main road. I have an explosive feeling with him.'

As the features of a bright-eyed youngster filled the screen, complete with a mop of hair 'that has a mind of its own,' a female registered her acceptance from the back of the hall.

'I have the name Owen; Margaret Owen,' Stephen offered. 'Can you accept that?'

'Yes.'

'He was hit by a vehicle of some kind.'

'He was hit crossing the road at school.'

Gently relaying information, the Welsh sensitive continued: 'He has come back to tell someone not to cry for him. He has not died. I can see a lady still taking flowers.'

'That's Margaret,' the recipient confirmed.

'I have the feeling his mother was not allowed to see the body. He received extensive injuries.'

'That's quite correct.'

Adding the finishing touches to the picture, Coral added, 'He appears to have been rather a forgetful boy, and had a habit of losing his coat rather a lot.'

'That's absolutely right,' the recipient added. 'We still have a blazer of his at home.'

Just about to move on to the next eager communicator, Stephen returned to say: 'Just before I leave you, does the *Chichester Arms* mean anything to you?'

Taking a few seconds to regain her composure, the sitter replied: 'My husband used to investigate and record coats of arms. He was working on the *Chichester Arms* when he died.'

Relaying messages of a consistently high standard, accompanied by Coral's accurate likenesses, the mediums left the stage to unanimous acclaim and deafening applause . . .

With enthusiastic cheering ringing in my ears, suddenly I was besieged at the stage by crowds of people waving copies of my book. It all started when I signed a disabled woman's copy because she couldn't climb the steep stairs to the foyer where I was supposed to give autographs, then before I could breathe, there were people *everywhere*. My official minder intervened. 'Stephen will meet you upstairs, ladies and gentlemen, move along now please,' he called, whisking me away through a rabbit warren of corridors up to a specially-placed stand. My eyes popped out on stalks when confronted with my name in flashing red lights, announcing my arrival! Not quite Broadway, but the next best thing!

Then came another shock: endless queues of chattering excited people! It took me over two-and-a-quarter hours to see everyone (I completely missed my tea) and I didn't realize *Psychic News* overheard one of my witty remarks:

An obvious and deserved success, quietly spoken Stephen was kept busy for hours after the demonstration as hundreds of people waited in line for an autographed copy of his best-selling book, *Visions of*

Another World. Stephen jokingly concluded, 'I shall have to receive healing for my arm after I've finished this lot!'

By the end of the '89 tours, I was flabbergasted—and £500 pounds in debt, having worked solidly without being paid one solitary penny for all the hard slog and sacrifice. So much for those who think I'm a squillionaire with my own country mansion, two white sports cars and a private villa in Spain. Rumours like that have been going around about me since the early seventies—but even following all the success that's come to me, not one of them is true. (If only they were!) I still get the bulk of my clothes from charity-shops and friends' 'hand-me-downs'.

But White Owl says: 'We never promised it would be easy, but your *needs* will always be met.' And he's kept his word.

I comforted myself that my '89 promoters promised 19 children's hospitals across Britain would receive donations from ticket-sales; I'd insisted on this from the outset. But as for me, it was back to rainy old Swansea with a huge back-payment of council rent to find, and the bailiffs virtually knocking at the doors. After receiving Notice to Seek Possession, there followed another council battle. So much for 'fame' and 'fortune' going hand in hand!

Only when I got home could I think of the wonderful times I'd shared with so many thousands of strangers nationwide: sometimes I'm a sentimental old thing. But I'd been touched by the public's love and support. As well as TV, radio and newspapers, requests from spiritual organizations all over Britain had poured in. I also had offers to work in the USA, Holland, Canada, and a chance of a private villa in Gibraltar for a week! But I was far too busy to accept any of them.

And I was certainly getting quite infamous! People recognized me on the streets, in supermarkets, on buses and in public places. I got quite paranoid at the finish and went out with dark glasses on, only to be stopped by a woman smiling brightly, 'Oh, hello, Stephen! You're looking grand!'

On another occasion two women in curlers were whispering

about me at an antiques fair one afternoon. 'It *can't* be him, you're mistaken. It must be a *lookee-likee*!'

As well as besieging me with letters, the public sent gifts to halls and theatres. One was a striking original pastel drawing of a spirit-woman in flight: it was beautiful. People also sent much-welcomed stamps to help me answer the many correspondents who don't enclose a stamped addressed envelope. I even had a tape of Luciano Pavarotti and some apple-tea purchased especially in Turkey! Everyone was so kind.

Journalists even came from all over Britain to attend meetings, some presenting me with flowers! And the public travelled hundreds, sometimes thousands, of miles to see me work. One group flew in from America, while others travelled from one end of Britain to the other, because I wasn't appearing soon enough in their area. And, bless them, they queued in all weathers, and sent so much love to me and my friends on the Other Side.

My public appearances drew huge crowds. At Cheltenham and Middlesbrough town halls, over 1,000 people turned up on the door! We squeezed them all in. At Middlesbrough I was still on-stage testing the microphones when suddenly someone opened the main doors too early. I'd never seen anything like it in my life! They stampeded down the hall to get to the front. First in line was a wizened old man on crutches. He came bombing down the aisle, hitting old ladies out of his way, right left and centre! But he got his first row seat! But sadly, many people were often turned away for lack of room, something which always upsets me. Because of the crush, at some meetings I was even given personal 'minders'. Well, I ask you! Who'd run off with me?

I eventually lost count of how many thousands of books I personally signed. I also autographed other peculiar objects—one woman produced an umbrella case! I didn't dare ask where the umbrella had gone! Whenever we sold out of books, Jeff came to the rescue: I signed sticky labels! As people kept coming forward, I had to wittily ask, 'Book or sticky label?'

'Sticky label please, Stephen!' And the whole queue rocked with laughter!

When the publicity fuss died down for a week (before it all started up again!) my guide congratulated me one sunny evening.

'Millions of souls have been touched,' he said, 'and we cannot place a price on this.' And he's right, you know—we can't.

Mind you, I did feel strange queuing for groceries in the supermarket after being such a sparkling celebrity everywhere else. But it was nice to get back into the swing of everyday living again. Yet strangers still called out to me across the baked beans counter: 'Hello, Stephen! Saw you on the telly last night! Great stuff!' After so many years of feeling ill-at-ease in this world, at last people were accepting me as one of their own kind—which brought me firmly back down to earth with a bump, thank God.

After all, I'm nothing special, only an ordinary man from Wales; 'our Stephen', the boy next-door, who sometimes just happens to hear voices from another world . . .

Part Two

Journeys into the Spirit World

Draw back the Curtains of Sleep
and pass into the Light,
through a myriad Planes of Living Thought,
Worlds within Worlds,
where Heaven and Hell are States of Mind.

Fly through your waking dreams
into Reality,
where Mind is King

When the Spirit is free, it drinks in Wisdom,
Power, and Life;
and through the Eyes of the Soul
it beholds
The Children of Darkness
and
The Children of the Light.

Stephen O'Brien

19

The Kingdoms of Hell

I

It was a moonless windy night. The flat roof above my bedroom
drummed out the hollow sounds of heavy raindrops as they
bounced off it. Curled up tightly under the bedclothes, I hid my
face and entered a troubled sleep: waking, sleeping, rousing,
dozing. I was still conscious at dawn when I heard an odd buzzing
sound, like a swarm of bees gathering in the distance. Then the
noise faded out . . . Silence followed, but the next instant I'd
suddenly left my physical body far behind me on Earth and I was
standing in the spirit spheres at the side of my guardian soul,
White Owl.

'Come!' he said. 'See where the selfish and greedy live. Behold
with me the kingdoms of hell.'

And all at once we found ourselves walking down the slopes of
a misty grey valley. The air was heavy dark blue and thick, no
warmth of happiness lived in that freezing, bitter place; even the
grasses were dank and bent under the weight of the insipid
atmosphere. All around us there was utter silence—not a pleasant
stillness, but a chill, cold unnerving deadness; no birds were
singing, no animals basked in the fields.

'Where is everyone?'

'They are near. What you feel is their minds, colouring the
countryside and darkening it. Souls here shed little light.'

Not fully understanding, I remained quiet, following where he led, feeling safe in his company. We walked towards a distant township. Through the heavy air, I just about recognized it as groups of shacks, made from something like tin sheeting. When closer, I saw the dirt encrusting the derelict, ramshackle hovels. 'Surely no one lives here?' I said disbelievingly. But White Owl gave no reply.

Along the dirt-track, just ahead of us, were some broken wooden hutches. Running to them, I saw underfed rabbits, kittens and a few hamsters inside. Loving animals as I do, I immediately went to release the poor creatures, but my hand was stayed.

'No. There is a reason. The people yonder show no love. These little ones are here in the hope that someone may pity and tend them. They are willing participants, so that dwellers in this place may learn compassion, and to love something other than themselves. Compassion fans the flame of spiritual growth. There is always hope.'

My mind jumped in amazement, and as we neared the sheds, a small plump woman ran out, then stood in a doorway. Her yellow-skinned brow was deeply furrowed, the corners of her mouth turned down through years of constant selfishness.

'Hello,' I said brightly. But she scowled hard, with piercing jet-black eyes, such a dreadful look. I immediately sensed her vicious nature, contained in the electromagnetic energy fields—the aura—surrounding her. Psychically, its colours were deep muddy scarlet, and murky green and brown. She stepped back from my eyes, and quickly slammed the door in my face, fastening her door-bolts and twisting the key in the rusty lock—a sickening, fearful sound.

'She is a typical dweller.'

'But why did I feel so cold next to her?'

'*Because all her thoughts centre upon herself*. The iciness betrays lack of love and compassion in her heart. She believes herself very poor, but far beyond the dark hills,' and he pointed them out on the horizon, 'live people who think they are rich; yet you would get a worse welcome there.'

'Outward appearances don't always reveal what's in the heart?' I observed.

'You have said it.'

I understood my lessons, but couldn't help wondering how long she'd lived in that state. My thoughts were instantly read. 'For 40 years as you measure time.' I was astounded. ' "In my Father's House there are many mansions." '

'I understand. There's a place for everyone.'

'Countless billions of mental states have produced an equal number of spheres in which to exist. Heaven and Hell are purely states of mind, not geographical places.'

'I see.'

'From now on, Stephen, we are invisible to our surroundings.' I suppose I expected a flash of blinding light to accompany his words, but nothing came, so I just accepted that if he said we were now invisible, then we were—though I could see us both with perfect clarity. We walked on . . .

I witnessed some horrific sights on this journey, some too upsetting to record: there were people with cracked and bleeding skin, their thoughts shadowing their spirit bodies because of extreme mental torment, and their 'injuries' self-inflicted. This, I learned, was because they couldn't love themselves: their mental perceptions of how they *thought* they looked changed their appearances. Our thoughts have a more immediate effect in the next world than they do here on Earth.

Some places were like nightmare cities—grotesque sequences of ugly images, each self-centred and vengeful soul living in a twilight of his own making, having extinguished all compassion for others from his being. In eternity, the more love and compassion a soul possesses, the greater the light it sheds over its surroundings; because the spirit body increases its frequency with each noble act and thought, and higher frequencies mean a brighter emission of light (just as electrical elements on Earth glow and shed light when their vibrations are stimulated by electricity).

I saw social misfits, the ignorant and the abusive. I saw

murderers hiding themselves away in dark caves, weeping for crimes they'd committed, unable to forgive themselves, even though the injured parties had long since understood their cruel acts and forgiven them. I saw a great deal more, all of which taught me that within everyone there's a Divine Monitor, the Conscience. This inner voice judges all our acts, and records each fragment of our lives and thinking; and these memories are responsible for the punishments inflicted upon us by ourselves— through the mirror of our souls. This is the 'Judgement Day'. When we pass over we become far more acutely aware of our lives, memories and thoughts than we are on Earth. In the next life perceptions are heightened, and we're confronted by our acts, good or bad, and the Conscience dictates the price to be paid— usually by righting the 'wrongs' through service, until peace returns to the troubled mind.

One wizened old woman was sitting on a riverbank, her ragged shawl pulled tight around her thin cold form. She was weeping mournfully, reproaching herself with bitterness. 'I killed it! I killed my own child,' she cried out in anguish, pulling her long straggling hair until some came loose in her bony fingers. Her tortured, twisted mouth was dampened by freely flowing tears.

Moved by her plight, I placed my hand on her shaking shoulders. 'Don't cry,' I said. But there was no reaction.

'She cannot hear, see or sense our presence,' White Owl informed.

'May I comfort her?'

'If she wishes it.'

'But she needs help. Why can't she see us?'

'Because she cuts herself off from aid. A cloak of anguish wraps so tightly around her mind and spirit, there is nothing anyone can do. She has chosen.'

'Please let me try,' I countered, placing my hands on her shoulders again, and whispering soft words of hope into her ear. But he was right. She was totally deaf to my influence.

'What *we* want is unimportant,' said my teacher, 'for her mind has created this prison—she alone is responsible. Not even Angels can help this woman, unless she desires it. It is similar on Earth, is it not?'

I sadly agreed, as another lesson hammered home. Then the woman pitifully cried out, 'I killed my baby, my precious little child! I'm not fit to live, not fit to breathe!'

'Neither does she know she has "died",' said White Owl. The whole sad tale made me reel. 'Ordinary guilts and regrets which plague the human mind do not have such devastating effects on the spirit as you see here. She is mentally and emotionally unbalanced to the extreme. Negativity thrives in these spheres. Normal fears and doubts would not place a being in these planes of thought.' That, at least, comforted me, for some of my own thoughts are far from spiritual on times.

'I'll pray for her,' I said.

'A noble thought, but I assure you, unseen hosts await the moment when she genuinely calls for help.'

'And what will happen?'

'Once the desire is born, she will be lifted up into the Light, out of this world and into another.'

'Because of *one* thought?'

'Yes. The Power of Thought is Mighty.'

'Please,' I begged him, 'will you allow me to be seen? Give me a chance to reach this soul.'

A long pause followed, during which I knew he took private counsel with some higher source, before granting: 'It can be done, but only for a moment. You are now visible to her.'

I gently moved in front of the poor woman, and quietly said, 'I've come to help you. Please don't cry.'

But as the words left my lips, she cowered to the ground in paralyzing fear, burying her head in hands and shawl and screaming out in terror, 'No! Leave me! Go away! Don't torture me! Punish me no more! Get away! Get away from me!' Her chilling cries both frightened and numbed my mind—so unexpected, such sudden dread. Then a frightening electric shiver coursed through my body, and I realized I was invisible again. The hysterical woman tore at her hair, weeping bitterly.

'Why am I plagued so? Haven't I enough to bear? Send the devil's child from my eyes! Send the spirits away!' I was stunned, but White Owl took my arm and led me aside.

'Her fear distorts her vision. Her troubled mind colours everything much darker than it really is. She feels threatened, and her eyes are clouded, distorted. The blackness of her mind caused her to see you as a ghostly vaporous figure.'

'I feel ashamed of myself,' I said, lowering my head, 'of causing her more suffering.'

'She is to blame; you offered service.'

'But who am I to relieve such misery?'

'One of God's Children, motivated by compassion. But she is not ready. You cannot help any soul, in any world, until it is ready. Only then will it respond.

'This woman is tortured by her own conscience. Not long ago on Earth, she brutally murdered her young child. Then, in a psychotic rage, a frenzied fit of uncontrolled madness, she cruelly dismembered it. Afterwards, she took her own life. Now she is haunted by her cruelty; her mind projects endless horrific scenes before her. She frequently sees her child's terrified expression, its gaping eyes, her own unbridled rage . . . She is the only one who can find her peace again, no other.'

'How?'

'First, she must learn to understand, and then forgive herself. From this new beginning she can go forward until she finds rest. Her future will involve service to others and, eventually, a reconciliation with her child. No one can escape their acts, they must all eventually be faced.'

I was utterly speechless, totally lost for words.

We slowly departed into the dark grey mists that divide some spheres of eternity from each other, as I glanced over my shoulder at the weeping form, murmuring to myself, 'May God help you to resolve your troubles, and find your peace.'

My thoughts were so confused, at first I hardly noticed our changing surroundings, so it was quite by surprise I realized the light had almost completely gone . . .

II

As I clasped my blue spirit robes tightly around me, they changed into a dull grey colour, perfectly blending with the dank surroundings. The chilling air was as sharp as a deep-freeze: there was no love-light in this place. Still astounded and shocked, I lowered my eyes—only to find we were hovering over a wide, marshy mudbank. When we 'landed' our feet sank into the mire right up to our ankles. Upon looking up again I saw some huge iron gates a little way off. Intrigued, I wanted to go nearer; and my companion read these thoughts and we approached.

'There are tyrants here,' he said, as we came upon the gates, unseen and unheard by the people within. Beyond the barriers hung an awesome feeling of hurtful vengeance, spiteful arrogance and cold selfish cruelty. I can't express the dreadful sensations lurking in that grim dark air, no words could describe those coarse vibrations of thought, which chilled the very essence of me.

At either side of the imposing gates stood a massive brown-skinned guard on duty, wearing only a loincloth and carrying a whip made of long thongs in one hand, and a razor-sharp spear in the other. Both were frightening, to say the least. Though the gates they watched were locked, I longed to know what secret was within. 'Can we pass through?' But White Owl didn't answer. Turning to ask again, I froze to the spot and gasped in fright. He was gone! Childish panic flashed through my mind and instantly flooded me with terror: abandoned in this dismal place, I was *utterly alone*. I feared the guards could see me and wanted to run like the wind in the opposite direction. But I fought my instincts, calmed myself until composure returned, and realized this was another lesson—one I must face alone.

Taking a deep breath, I bravely moved through the locked gates, unseen, but shivering. Behind me, the resounding crack of whips split the twilight, and in front of me were the soul-strangling cries of people in great distress. Curious, I peered through the freezing air, horrified to discover a great pit had been dug. In it were emaciated men and women, sparsely clothed in torn and weathered rags—pathetic creatures cowering in sheer terror, fearful of their captors. Circling the 'prisoners' were more venomous guards, subjecting their prey with jabbing spears, and shouting obscenities at them.

From nowhere, into my mind came the thoughts: 'Cruel minds seek power over the weak. This is their sport: frightened victims locked in thought-cages of their own making, held by negative fear, born deep within themselves. Escape is easy: they must banish fear, then take positive thought and exercise their will to seek another environment. This would raise them from oppression—*if they believed it possible.*'

'Who can help them?'

'Only themselves. Their own thoughts trap them. Many invisibles wait for just one to find the key to freedom. Look and learn.' And I did, and sadly my guide was right. These wretched souls *wanted* to be in the pit: perverted and unbelievable as it might seem, they revelled in their martyrdom; just like people on Earth who bask in illnesses, refusing to let them go, fearing they'd lose their false sense of emotional security.

'Couldn't we end this masquerade?'

'Why?' said his soundless voice. 'The guards follow their perverted desires, and the people have found their places. By their thoughts, both maintain them. Who are we to interfere?'

'Shouldn't someone try?'

'Bright Ones are filled with compassion and the right of the individual to govern his life. If Angels ended this by force, they would be no better than those perpetrating it. It is by our example that we teach.' Then his voice faded out.

Suddenly I felt frustrated, and somehow these coarse thoughts made me instantly visible to the guards, who quickly seized my arms in vice-like grip as sudden terror paralysed me. Sickening fear locked my thoughts in the same cage as the others, as they dragged me, stunned and struggling, towards the pit.

All at once, sheer dread forced me to assert my mind. Shutting my eyes tightly, I demanded freedom, *thinking* myself far from that malevolent place. In a flash of a second, I shot upwards like a fork of greased lightning, flying from that horrible world. But I knew I was being followed: I hurtled past stars and planets through pitch-black space and endless time, but I couldn't shake off that awful feeling of pursuit—someone was close on my tail, I wasn't alone.

Still plagued with confusion, suddenly my visions fell into a blur and all at once everything stopped dead—

With an electric jolt, I gaped my eyes wide open on Earth, to find my humble bedroom before me—as I sat upright, heart pounding hard in my throat, and the sheets drenched with perspiration. All around the bedroom was a sickening feeling of someone's unpleasant presence—someone who'd followed me back—but they couldn't touch me now, we were worlds apart. I was safe back within my body, thank God, and home.

And outside a small bird was singing his dawn song on the window-sill, as though nothing unusual had happened.

III

I became conscious in a small, claustrophobic, untidy flat above some kind of grocer's shop. Everything was dirty and the smells were vile: rotting food and human waste.

White Owl extended his straight arm and silently pointed into a corner of the drab bed-sit, where I saw a crumpled form, twisting and writhing in the bed. It was a woman of great years, thin and pale, with short-cropped greasy grey hair, and a tight thin mouth. Her hands were long and mean, her eyes like slits in her yellowy skin. In her troubled sleep, she groaned and wrung her hands. Her heart was giving out.

I sensed she was just about to die.

I watched her last breath, and then, slowly, she gave up her spirit, which vacated its bitter and twisted shell in urgency. Instantly she scrambled to her spirit feet and rummaged around the room, trying to lift papers and objects, bits of shredded matting and stained tea-cups.

'Searching for money,' said my friend.

'Of what good is that to her?'

'None whatsoever. She thinks she has woken from her usual sleep. She does not realize she has died.'

'The poor soul died alone,' I lamented.

'No—we were here.'

We watched as she scratched and pulled at objects, trying to find her banknotes, getting more flustered by the minute because her bony fingers kept passing through the furniture. Then suddenly she disappeared.

'Come! We must follow!' said White Owl, clasping my hand, and immediately we were walking through a neglected, overgrown graveyard. The night was pitch-black, only the moon lighting grasses and weeds through the scurrying clouds. 'She is yonder.' And he pointed towards a gravestone, where the bedraggled old woman was kneeling, scrabbling at the earth, moaning and weeping. 'The tombstone of her husband. She is childless.'

'But where is he?'

'Far away. Death for him was a grateful release from bondage.'

'Why is she here?'

'To recapture her past. She is lonely, frightened, afraid. And now, unsure whether she sleeps or has died. We must wait in case realization comes.' But no sooner had he said this, than she vanished once again. For quite some time we followed her. She called on people who owed her money, none of whom heard her or reacted, causing her further great distress. One young man was living in a derelict apartment she owned: she hurled wicked abuse at him for not paying any rent. But he clearly didn't live in the flat, it was too filthy, damp and unclean, and being homeless, he only sheltered there at night. But like the others, he couldn't register her belligerent ravings, which angered her all the more.

'Now she mourns, for she knows she has died.'

Then the scenes changed once again, her greedy thoughts instantly transporting her back to the dreary bed-sit. She was kneeling by the dishevelled bed, weeping profusely, not even noticing her 'dead' body within it. White Owl quietly bid me stay at one end of the room, and he stepped forward. In a twinkling of an eye, he raised an outstretched hand and all his body glimmered golden-white. He was now visible, and she looked up—then immediately cowered down in utter fear, as he spoke.

'Woman, why do you weep?'

'I think I have died. Or . . . is this a dream?'

'No, you have indeed crossed into the land from whence you originally came.'

'But I felt nothing, no pain.'

'God is kind.'

'God!' she suddenly spat at him. 'Don't talk of God to me! What did God ever do for *me* in my old age? I'm lame and weak and have no friends or lovers.'

'In order to be loved, one must first love others.'

'The only man who ever loved me is dead . . .' Then she stopped, realizing that she, too, had now joined him. Sudden panic gripped her. 'But where is he? Why hasn't he come for me, if there's a life after death?'

White Owl stood motionless, his kind eyes shining while full realization dawned. Then, having read her thoughts, he gently said, 'In your heart of hearts, you know he did not love you, and that your feelings for him were born of possession. Your soul knows that death for him was a happy release.' She immediately howled and wailed and buried her head in the dirty bedsheets, because he was right. He stepped a little nearer to her. 'Why not follow me out of this place? I will befriend you in your hour of need.'

'Go away!' she hissed. 'Get out of my house—leave me alone! All you want is to rob me of my things! Just like that good-for-nothing tenant in my flat! Get away! You're nothing but a bad dream!' And she tried to push him aside, but her hands went through his legs and he remained unharmed. She screamed and cried and ran from the room.

'Where did she go?' I asked.

'To a field outside, where she buried jewellery and semiprecious stones several years back. She now wants to retrieve them. Those who cry for their heart's desire which they have lost will presently seek to find it again. This woman is Earthbound. Her lust for material things binds her to these well-frequented surroundings, and she will not come away until she loses these desires, then wishes for a better life, one of giving and not always taking.'

' "Where your treasure is, there will your heart be also";' I quoted.

'Just so. There are many millions like this soul in my world, trapped by their greed and thoughts, "haunting" or frequenting places and possessions all over the Earth-plane. They do not wish to progress, even though it is open to them: many will not even accept they have made the transition.

'This poor soul believes herself old and lonely and unloved. She has trapped herself on Earth, until such time as she changes her thought-patterns. She will not find happiness until she does. No one can grant contentment to another soul: everything has to be earned.'

'I perfectly understand . . .'

IV

One moment I was resting in the armchair by a blazing fire, and the next I'd projected out into the Realms of Spirit, where my courage curdled as I gazed down at a thrashing midnight sea. Flying high above the oceans again, my friend and I marvelled at the wild waters smashing against the distant cliffs, sending huge spurts of screeching foam into the cold night air.

It was a dark and dismal night at sea, no soul would be safe on the oceans in such a hazardous thunderstorm. The cloudy skies had killed the moonlight and were split by fork lightning searing from heaven to a watery grave. Travelling incredibly fast now, we were way out over the unwelcoming deep and heading around a bend of dangerous coastline. It was like being in a terrifying nightmare. 'Tonight you will see another aspect of hell,' said

White Owl gently, his calm voice floating through my mind, above and beyond the roaring storm. 'Tonight we visit two people.'

Before I could question, all at once we came upon a distant point of light, twinkling in the darkness. It was an old lighthouse, and we were speeding towards it at such a rate I was sure we'd have a head-on collision—but instead of crashing mercilessly into the stones, we passed right through them in a flash of a second, White Owl saying, 'We are here.'

And we found ourselves standing in the small living quarters belonging to the lighthouse keeper. It was an eerie place; one solitary flickering candle barely lit the dark room. Clothes were scattered hither and thither, and old crates of beer packed with empty bottles took pride of place on every available surface. The whole room breathed an air of lived-in homeliness, except that the atmosphere was strange—not cold, but bitter; that's the only word I can think of to describe it, numbing bitterness.

White Owl silently lifted an outstretched arm and pointed at a miserable figure heaped over the nearby desk. The lighthouse keeper was obviously drunk, the broken bottles and glasses on the floor said so. I wondered if he was hurt, for he lay there groaning as if in some terrible great pain. I wanted to step nearer.

'He is not damaged, though his pain is very real. Can you not sense from the depths of his mind what ails him so?' And when I looked, I did uncover startlingly accurate facts.

'He's cut through with bitterness and regret,' I said, 'having given up his life ashore for this hermit existence. But . . . I can't see why.' And I tried harder to psychically gain the reasons from the photosphere of images and thoughts swirling within the sad figure's mind and auric fields.

My teacher broke in: 'He was once a successful politician, making his living from a world of corruption into which he easily slid. He smiled for the nation, but lied to himself. He projected a public image of stability and honesty, yet lived a secret life of emotional torment and deceit. Now he lives here, far from the public glare, rejected and filled with savage remorse. Here is a man who is thoroughly ashamed of what he has done. He cannot forget or forgive his past, and his conscience now pays the price. See how his memories torment him so?'

I then understood why the whirling images in his mind had upset me, and I took pity upon the poor man slumped over the table. He was ''haunted'' by one particular memory of a time he accepted illegal bribes which led to the death of an innocent young girl.

'I can now reveal we are not in the world of spirit, but on Earth. This man is alive in your world, and we are only visiting him.' These remarks stunned me.

The next instant I felt the touch of my guide's hand and we were outside again, once more flying high in the thunderstorm, slicing through the wind and driving rain. Where were we going now? Where would our second visit be? On Earth, or crossing over to the next world? There were no grey mists around us, just sheets of blinding rain covering everything in sight, wrapping us in a fast-moving shroud. The power of speech left me during our fantastic flight, all my concentration gripping my friend's hand to stop falling into the angry sea. Then he spoke within my mind, as we zoomed forward. 'For this next visit, you will need great strength and objectivity.' He sounded extremely serious. What on earth could he mean?

I glanced across at his earnest face through the deluge; his brow was dark and troubled, betraying a harrowing lesson to come . . .

V

All around, bright lightning forked from sky to sea; our speed seemed so great, even if we'd passed through a searing thunderbolt I don't think we would have been hurt. But White Owl smiled; I'd completely forgotten we were in our spirit bodies and no harm could befall us.

Beneath us, waves smashed wildly against each another as the rolling swells thundered, falling back into the murky waters. The pitch-black seas tossed and foamed like a crowd of savage madmen bent on murder. Everywhere as far as the eye could see there was liquid chaos and frenzied confusion: crashing and thundering; lightning and storm; rainclouds colliding and bursting; and the inky-blackness of seething oceans overruling it all, the deafening gale-force winds superseding every noise *bar one*.

Somewhere up ahead I faintly picked out the struggling sound of a chumming motor in the waters. A vessel? Surely not; not on such a dark and fearsome night—no one could be so foolish. But the valiant motor spluttered and choked, and then strangled, and suddenly died. And once more there was only the howling wind and rain. 'See there!' said White Owl, a finger piercing the gloom. 'See, the boat!' And I strained my eyes and beheld it. Amongst the storm-tossed waves was a brave little fishing-boat, the deck deserted, lit only by spasmodic moonlight and a tiny light in the cabin flickering towards its last breath. My heart almost stopped beating; surely there was no one aboard? If there was, they were certainly doomed to perish. I prayed to God it was empty.

We got nearer as each moment passed and still it heaved and fell under the mighty power of the sea. Like an insignificant cork it was flung into the air and once again received by a gaping, watery grave. Its rigging whiplashed against the water-logged timbers, its cabin roof had been half ripped apart by the winds: how helpless and fragile it looked, pitted against the mighty waters and raging foam.

My teacher's grip tightened. 'We are here!' And we immediately passed within the boat, and floated over to upturned charts and crockery in the cabin's corner. It appeared that half our spirit forms were inside the cabin, and half outside the timber walls—and though the violent waves pitched all the contents from side to side we were both unmoved, standing untouched and still, fully able to see the heart-breaking sight before us.

A frantic bearded man of middle years, obviously the captain, was fighting desperately to reach the battered ship's radio; yet each touch of its controls was useless, for the waters repeatedly threw him against the timbers. Many times he summoned all his strength and tried once more to transmit an emergency call, but failed.

'The radio is dead,' said White Owl, 'and the boat sinks fast—the crew is already gone.'

Then I saw black flooding waters seeping through a hole in the bow and my failing hope for the doomed captain suddenly overwhelmed me; his efforts would be useless: the sea was too strong and he too weak, and my mind prepared itself for the inevitable. But then, in a final determined bid for his life, the terrified man grasped hold of the radio yet again: '*Mayday! Mayday!* In the name of God, someone, anyone, please help me! Mayday! Mayday!'

And then the tipping boat hurled him against the opposite wall and to the floor. Frantically he scrabbled to his feet, struggling above the rising waters, and dragged himself over to the gaping hole in the bow where he tried with all his might to push his heavy coat into it to stem the rushing flow—but it was no use, the tides wouldn't yield but rushed in faster, quicker. Mentally, I heard my teacher say, 'Only in times of deep crisis does the soul truly find itself, and its God.'

Pitifully, the doomed fisherman fell to his knees and cried and sobbed, and in a half-dazed state between death and life he touched his spirit and found his Maker—and he began to pray in snatches, for some of the words wouldn't come: 'The Lord's my shepherd, I'll not want . . . Our Father in Heaven . . . forgive us our trespasses . . . Dear God, I'm dying . . . I'm dying! But not like this, not like this, God . . . Please help me! My wife and children . . . my little ones! Take care of my children, and my Elizabeth . . . Please help . . . help me, my God, I'm dying . . . I'm dying . . .'—and the cries from his heart shrunk away into his shaking form, wracked with fear and tears.

Then my tears joined his, and White Owl averted his gaze in helplessness and humility.

As the last moments came, they were mercifully swift for the fisherman, who fought to the end to catch the final fragments of oxygen trapped in an air-pocket in the cabin's roof, while the little boat whirled around and around in the deep currents, and filled with hungry black water, and turned on its end and sank beneath the foam without a trace . . .

His last cries will always remain lit within my mind; they were filled with sheer terror, and as long as I live I shall never forget his gaping fearful eyes. A man had drowned before my gaze and there was nothing I could have done to save him, nothing. But his eyes, that fearful expression—I covered my face in dismay.

In a matter of minutes the ruthless sea claimed everything in sight, not a shred of life was left anywhere, not even hopeful wreckage or spilled oil. The ocean showed no mercy. Then I heard White Owl say, 'Behold a form of hell.'

Then the North Wind howled and whined.

'But now comes the Light.'

Immediately there came a brilliant flash of golden light across the water, like a mighty burnished flame shooting high into the heavens, and out of the seas rose a glowing form—a Bright Angel of Light. There were no wings, just a vast aura of loving radiance, wrapped in a man's body of golden rays. And safe in his arms he bore the spirit of the 'dead' captain, unconscious and sleeping peacefully like a babe. As I watched in wonderment, the Angel sailed smoothly upwards into the troubled skies, and both he and the captain faded out from sight into the furious night.

'Behold a form of heaven,' I heard again.

And just for a moment, the storm didn't matter, and a deep sense of peace pervaded my being. 'Thank God his prayer was answered,' I gratefully sighed.

'But his life was done. Nothing could have changed that; we were powerless to prevent the transition because his time had come. In this sense, we too have visited hell tonight.'

'Let us leave this place,' I begged in sorrow.

And 'So be it,' were the last sounds I heard, for—

My eyes quickly opened, tears still brimming in them, and I was back in my armchair on Mother Earth again, before the dying embers of my living-room fire . . .

20

The Kingdoms of Heaven

I

In the darkness of my bedroom I watched as the grey ceiling slowly became transparent and faded away, revealing a deep velvet black sky speckled with white stars. An exquisite vision of great beauty, it made me want to fly into the depths of space. Then I saw a man's bare arm appear over my head, hovering in the dim room. A thrill of expectation swept through me. 'Take my hand, and come with me!' said a gentle voice. I eagerly gripped White Owl's strong hand and, as we touched, all sensations of Earth liquefied—and my awareness of another world strengthened . . .

Shooting upwards towards the stars, we travelled faster than light through space, then blackness, then blinding banks of thick grey clouds—the borderland mists, dividing Heaven from Earth. Then suddenly the rushing mists vanished, and my whole being quivered with joy as we shot out over the greenest fields I'd ever seen. The bright grass on the rolling hills seemed to have a consciousness all its own. And the blue heavens were filled with radiant energy, a healing force, ever available to draw upon. 'We are here,' he said. 'Behold the children!'

Under majestic giant trees, a short distance from us, was a small group of beautiful children playing and singing joyfully in a ring of fun and laughter. We both slowed down and as our feet touched the living grass, it almost seemed to kiss them. I stood entranced by these magnificent young spirits, revelling in their freedom. Then my friend spoke. 'See how carefree they are? If only all who walked the Earth could bask in the moment, with no thought for tomorrow.'

'*Could* we?'

'Of course! People allow pressures and stresses they have made for themselves to disturb their inner balance and break them down. Worry dwells within them. Fear corrodes happiness and eats away their joys. If men lived in the Ever-Present Now, they would be much happier.'

'But it isn't that easy.'

'Nothing is. Peace of the Spirit is a treasured prize which must be earned. It is not a gift.'

'But these children don't have the crippling difficulties we have back home.'

'True, but they know how to cope with problems.' His lips moved into a wise smile, and his dark eyes glistened. 'Creatures of the Moment, they take no thought for the morrow, for they know tomorrow never comes. But when obstacles do come—and we have many here you don't have on Earth—they deal with them, without poisonous black thoughts destroying their harmony. Do you see?'

'Yes,' I replied softly, my eyes delighting in the youngsters' games. They were throwing a bright red ball gleefully around the circle, and laughing when it was dropped by a clumsy boy. 'I do understand. But we must forward-plan; that's why we get distressed.'

'Man makes living so complex and unnatural. Simple needs and a life close to nature would bring him complete harmony of body, mind and spirit, and the treasured prize of peace.' There was sincere longing in his quiet voice. 'Watch now,' he said, then called a five-year-old coloured boy by name. They embraced like life-long friends, White Owl telling him, 'I have some news for you, Thomas. Your mother on Earth has been praying for you again. She worries over your sister in university.'

The little chap frowned. 'Not again! When will she ever learn? She still doesn't know about God's love, and that we're all safe, even when we're away from her.' And with that, Thomas threw his arms around White Owl's neck, kissed him, and ran off to join his playmates under the cool trees.

'There is much more to see,' said my guide; and in an instant we were flying high over sparkling crystal seas, brightly lit with sunlight, moving so fast through the skies—stomachs to the ocean and heads to the horizon—that my breath was taken clean away. 'Thank God we're high up!' I shouted.

'Do you still fear the water?'

'You know I nearly drowned as a boy.' And the very sight of the lashing, thrashing waves beneath us sent my head reeling and my insides turning upside down. There was water everywhere, as far as the eye could see, and not a foot of solid earth in sight.

'Look down!' insisted White Owl. 'See the rolling tides, how they smash and break.' But I couldn't; we were 300 feet above the raging blue, yet each passing second pulled us nearer to a watery grave. 'Look down!' he called again. So, reluctantly, I did. Childish fear immediately gripped me like a ghost from the past, sweeping my senses in an inky black cloud. And all at once I vividly recalled frantically gulping for air when I nearly drowned as a lad, helplessly sinking, struggling, with no ground under my young feet, nothing to give support—and terrible black fear pulling me under the water again and again. These spinning terrors strangely seemed to pull us closer and closer to oblivion. I clenched White Owl's hand with all my might—but still we descended, down, down, every passing moment nearer to the thundering blue waves.

'I'm falling! We're falling!' I cried.

'Then think positively.'

'I can't!'

'Remove the fear.'

'I can't!'

'*Think*—and we shall rise!'

'But I can't—we're going to crash into the sea!'

'*Only if you will it.*'

But fear won the day. Although knowing what to do—I couldn't change my negative thoughts. Then suddenly I felt a surge of encouragement from my friend, and I pitched a last chance to save us. With all my might, I defied my terrors—and vanquished them, willing us to soar from the perilous deep. Opening my eyes, I just caught sight of the skimming waves as we brushed their crests at rocket speed and shot up into the skies like two jet planes making for the sun.

'Well done!'

But I couldn't answer for sheer relief! I'd beaten the foe and asserted my mind as King. 'Never say die!' I laughed out loud.

'Lesson learned!' smiled my friend, as we zoomed out across the open sky—and then there was nothing but blackness . . .

II

The next thing I remember was standing beside him in a golden cornfield. Releasing my hand, he said: 'The Power of the Mind is Mighty. It is Ruler, not servant. And you control it. Dark thoughts are actualized, unless removed and replaced with Positivity. Come, I will show you.' Then he touched my skin— immediately the cornfields vanished and we found ourselves in a leafy woodland clearing surrounded by trees and singing birds. Before us, amongst the rushes and flowering plants, stood a red brick wall as high as a house. Perplexed, I gazed up at its 20-foot surface.

'If you believe you can do something,' said my friend, 'then you can do it. Come.' And he led me 30 feet away from the wall. 'Now, jump over it.'

My face must have said it all, but nevertheless I squeezed out: 'You must be joking! I'd never make it—not till the desert freezes over and the camels come skating home!'

'But you will—if you *believe* you can.'

'And that's the trouble,' I said.

'Remember, Thought is King, and can accomplish anything.

Now,' he smiled, 'jump over the wall.' Then he stood like a patient father awaiting his son's first few stumbling steps. I guess his trust moved me, and, not wishing to disappoint, I convinced myself to try. I sheepishly retreated a few more feet, believing I'd need a good run.

'Preparations are unnecessary.'

But taking no notice, I bent my body forwards, scuffed the brown earth, then pelted full stretch at the big wall. Quickly gaining momentum, I knew I'd succeed. But as I sprang upwards, sudden doubt streaked my mind and killed confidence stone-dead: energies failed me, and black doubts flung me hard against the bricks, 10 feet from the ground. I felt the shuddering impact of bones on cold stone—but no pain, cuts or bruises, as I fell twisting to the earth, stunned and shaken.

'You doubted,' he said, as I clambered awkwardly to my feet, dusting myself down. But no dirt clung to me, and there wasn't even a scratch on my bare feet. 'Fear robbed you of the power to win. Therein lies the lesson: *Think positively always.* Never allow fear into your being. It destroys equilibrium and ruins man's efforts—not only here, but even more so on Earth.'

I nodded, realizing he was right. 'Now watch,' he said, as he released positive will-power and floated into the air, and up and over the bricks without so much as a raised brow. An amazing moment later, he reappeared, walking right through the 'solid' wall at ground level and stood beside me, grinning from ear to ear. 'If a man has faith, he can move mountains. Now you!' he challenged.

Well, what could I say? Now believing myself capable, I mimicked him and rose into the air as easily as Peter Pan, striking a comical balletic pose and sailing regally over the wall like a cygnet from *Swan Lake*! Then I poked my head through the misty bricks, and together we rocked the trees with laughter.

White Owl placed his arm about my shoulders, and instantly I felt as if I was shrinking—dwindling downwards, melting away, our laughter still ringing in my ears. Strangely, the whole scene blurred and collapsed like a tent when the centrepost is whipped away—and everything turned as black as pitch. I remembered nothing more, until I woke up the next morning . . .

III

Back in the eighties when I had no money or food, at the time I was estranged from my father, I was feeling very sorry for myself. My flat walls and floors were cold and hard and no coins chinked in my pockets. Outside, the streets were white with torrents of snow, and inside—well, it was just as cold as it was outside! So I took to bed early, despondent and down-hearted, where I sailed into a poverty-stricken Christmas Eve sleep . . .

I soon became conscious meandering down a sunny country lane in the Beyond. The sun-kissed trees and flowering hedgerows seemed happy to feel my presence strolling idly by. My inner self almost knew they bid me welcome. In the lush green fields I could hear busy droning bees, and birds sang high in the mighty oaks. Radiant heat beat down upon my bare back, and I sensed my spirit body absorbing energies from it.

The country colours were so vibrant and full of life—much brighter and more intense than in any Earthly scene. The fields off the path seemed to beckon, so I ran happily through their living grasses and flowers, speeding down a sloping hillock, trailing my hands through the long stalks as I went. The plants enjoyed my touch—I knew they did, I felt their pleasure coursing back along my bare arms. They were alive; they had consciousness and feelings.

Stopping in the shade of cool beech trees, taking deep health-giving breaths which filled my lungs with electric vitality, I noticed some tall wild flowers on a bank. I approached in child-like wonder, never having seen their kind before. Their stems were two feet long, their petals translucent, like wafer-thin rainbow dragonfly wings, displaying shining, moving colours as they caught the light and nodded their large heads in the gentle breeze. Inside, bright orange stamens gave off a sweet perfume unlike any I'd known before, and when quiet winds caressed them, they made a musical sound—a strange tinkling noise like tiny Indian silver bells, all rung at once, and yet at different times.

How I wanted to pick one! It would have looked splendid adorning my bare flat on Earth. Tempted by their shining petals, I reached out—but then stopped dead. Words came to me: '*Much better to let flowers grow.*' So I stroked them lovingly, and sensed their gratitude as I passed them by. I don't know where those words came from—perhaps they themselves had spoken.

Then the whole scene changed dramatically, and I was now inside a pleasant airy building. It was some kind of hospital. I was in a waiting area outside a corridor leading to children's wards. I could hear the youngsters playing within, laughing and running around, no doubt with their nurses. To the right was a crumpled artificial Christmas tree and some sparkly decorations in boxes, and several unwrapped presents were piled up on old tables. There was a large fortress and fairy-tale castle with turrets among them—and I smiled at the pleasure this would bring some lucky spirit lad.

Though the children's voices were happy, I instinctively knew they'd 'died' having suffered at the hands of cruel parents and guardians: they'd been abused, or simply rejected. It was easy to register this in the vital atmosphere: the spirit body is far more sensitive than the physical. These children were resting—holidaying, while being cared for by nursing staff whose job was to heal their broken trust and show them that adults *are* capable of unconditional love and genuine affection.

Just to the left of the swing doors I noticed a tall cupboard. Being naturally inquisitive (some would say 'a born nosey-parker'!) I opened it. Inside were three strikingly fine feathers: two-and-a-half feet long, looking like a cross between ostrich and peacock plumage. I ran my fingers through their floating delicate fronds of blue and green, with speckles of yellow intertwined, and confess I couldn't help wondering how nice they'd look on my naked flat walls back home. It was then I wickedly thought I'd take one. After all, there isn't any money in the Beyond and weren't these beauties created to be enjoyed? And the children already had dozens of Christmas gifts, so I convinced myself they wouldn't be missed. Even now I blush at the impish thought. But nevertheless I reached out and took one from the shelf. I was only going to 'borrow' it, when all at once I felt a piercing hard stare stabbing me in the back. I immediately swung around, and there in the doorway stood a formidable plump matron, in full outfit, scowling with displeasure. She leaned against the door jambs, hands folded tight across her ample chest, head tilted to the side, and a smug smile on her lips. Words were unnecessary, an aura of annoyance and her expression said it all: 'So you're *pinching* it, are you?'

Dreadful guilt flooded me. Caught in the act, sudden shame made me want to escape as fast as I could, and that thought instantly pulled me backwards—like a rag-doll on a stretched piece of elastic—right out of the hospital and threw me ungraciously in a heap, on a riverbank in the country.

Bump!

Ruffled and shaken, I stood up by a bubbling mountain stream, pondering on those brilliant feathers. Although I wouldn't get them, at least the children would have a lovely Christmas. Then a gentle hand touched my shoulder from behind.

It was White Owl, resplendent in the clear summery sunshine, bronze skin glistening and eyes bright with smiles. It was obvious by his wicked grin that he'd been watching me all along. Lifting up a clenched hand and opening it, he revealed a shining object resting in his palm: a delicately engraved silver box. The hinged lid swung open and inside was a thick roll of well-thumbed banknotes fastened by elastic bands. 'Treasures,' he said, immediately snapping the lid shut and flinging the box headlong into the fast-moving river. It sank beneath the waters and bounced up and down, clinking over sharp rocks as it disappeared quickly downstream. Then he touched his chest and spoke again: 'Earthly treasures are transient, but the soul is eternal. What a man builds into his soul and spirit, remains. The treasures of the heart and mind, only these matter.' And I knew he was right.

'Yes,' I responded, as a sheet of muslin blackness fell before my eyes, obliterating the landscape. For a moment I was confused, but when I looked again—I was lying in my bed back on Earth, just awakening in the middle of the night . . .

IV

I'd only slumped onto the big sofa for a moment's rest, when quite remarkably a voice whispered, 'See your new vocation.' I turned over and tried to forget it. But very soon, I became aware of standing in the middle of a brightly-lit pleasant room Beyond. There were a dozen or so small infants' chairs placed before a blackboard. It was some kind of schoolroom. 'I am with you no more,' said my guide, as I sensed him withdraw.

All at once, the doors swung wide open and in ran eight young children, bustling and shouting for all they were worth. I was pulled to the ground as they clambered up over me, yanking at my hair and playfully slapping my back and legs. Brimming with glee, they called out my name and comments like: 'Hurray! He's back!' and 'It's been too long, Uncle Stephen!' And in a flash of recognition, I remembered who these six-year-olds were. I'd sat patiently with them while they were dying, on Earth. At that time, *they* were physically alive and *I* was physically asleep. In my spirit body, I'd nursed them and watched over them in my 'night-time life' until they'd passed into eternity. That was my old job, to care for dying children and help them make the crossing into Light, often from the darkness of cruelty.

Here were some of those very same beautiful children who'd passed over so tragically. One passed after her parents had beaten her to death, another was a battered baby, and another had died in a coma in hospital. She was little Louise. I'd sat beside her as she lay in her half-alive state, just waiting for her to become conscious in Spirit. Then, I'd be waiting to greet her. 'Let me die,' she'd plead. 'I don't want to go back. It hurts too much. I want to die; please say I can be here forever, Uncle Stephen.'

'In a little while,' I gently reassured, 'just be patient, Louise, and the Angel will come for you.'

'And I'll never have to go back?'

'No, you'll be safe with us. There'll be no more pain, and you'll never have to go back.'

The young child threw her arms about me. 'Uncle Stephen, pray for me. Please ask God to let me die soon. I want the Angel to come and take me, for nobody loves me on Earth.'

Humbled by her innocent plea, my eyes filled with tears. 'I'll pray for you, my darling,' I said, holding her close and cuddling her tiny form. 'It won't be much longer now, then you'll be free of all your nasty pain, and safe with God, forever.'

Louise couldn't wait for death, when the Angel of Light, a Bright Soul, would quietly stand beside her as her battered body released a grateful spirit. 'Soon now,' I softly whispered, 'very soon.' And she settled down after this.

If only those who fear the end could have heard her cries, her plaintive requests to forsake Earth and move on into Heaven, mankind would view the afterlife as a blessing and reward for toiling long upon the Earth. Now here, in the schoolroom, were all my little friends.

But more surprises were yet in store. As well as the wonderful greetings I'd already had, there would be another visitor. I knew this. I felt and sensed them approaching. But I didn't know who it would be. Maybe a Shining One coming to show how best to teach my new charges? I just had to wait; but my heart began to pound, as though some greater part of me already knew the visitor's name. And then the classroom door suddenly swung wide open—

'Stephen!'

'Mam!' I cried, as I ran across and into the arms of my beloved mother. A glowing aura of love-light surrounded and wrapped us in a cloak of love and respect. It was so wonderful to see her again, this woman who'd been the very centre of our family on Earth, and who'd suffered the torments of terminal cancer and died an agonizing death at just 49 years old.

'Welcome to your new work!' she said in those old familiar warm tones. 'I see the children have already greeted you!' And a loud cry of delight rose from the small crowd. The little ones pulled at my robes and laughed with all their might as my mother put her arms around me once again, and gazed into my full eyes. The whole air seemed filled with the bright sound of care and happiness, and in the midst of it all I heard my mother's comforting voice speak softly to me through her tears: 'This is the Kingdom of Heaven,' she smiled.

And the children gathered around our feet and cheered and shouted for joy, as this wonderful moment faded far, far away into nothingness. I could remember no more. My visit was over, but certainly not forgotten . . .

V

As I became conscious, White Owl and I were moving together towards a vast impressive building made of marble, or something similar. The huge dome-shaped roof was held aloft by several tall pillars. The whole magnificent edifice might have been transported direct from ancient Athens itself. Its colourful columns were shot through with living blues and greens, and violets and pinks—a wonderfully striking visual effect.

When our feet touched the vast stone steps, I noticed their coolness, despite the raging sun. The towering building was immense, about as high as an Egyptian pyramid. As we passed under the open archways leading to its centre, soft breezes and a gentle summer air enfolded us. 'This is one of the many Halls of Healing,' my teacher said. 'Here the spirit can be refreshed and replenish its vital energies, relax and find a greater, deeper sense of its own Being and worthiness. Here one finds a fuller realization of unity with all living things, and the all-pervading Creative Mind, the Great Spirit.'

Wrapped in velvet peace, we moved through the cavernous hallway to be greeted by the most wonderful sights and sounds. All around the circular walls of cool marble, people were seated or gently resting; some lying on brightly-coloured couches, others sitting on the floor with their backs against the walls. All were totally at ease with themselves, emitting auric feelings of inner contentment and harmonious peacefulness.

High above us, in the vast circular dome, beautiful music was playing; nothing was orchestrated, and yet it was such a refined blend of wonderful sounds, delighting the ears of all who listened. Music is one of the great loves of my life, filling my days with joy. I play the piano, compose, and appreciate the works of the great past masters, but not even Mozart, Beethoven, Bach or Chopin have ever created such a moving symphony of magical harmonies as I heard under that pulsing, translucent dome. Imagine if you can a million different silver bells and chimes all tinkling in concord and discord, as though heard from a mile or so away. Their gentle rhythmical pulsing continually created light within the dome; moving rainbow-light, myriads of different colours, mixing, blending, gently swirling. Then the coloured lights and mists gradually descended, almost with dignity and grace, gently undulating. Those resting in the hall lifted their faces and breathed them in, bathed in them, sparkling and glowing in their pure radiance. Standing or kneeling, they allowed the glistening colours to cascade over them, through them, around them, as if showering naked under some vast celestial waterfall. Absorbing the rays, they revelled in their caress and responded by being refreshed and renewed.

'The Healing Lights are Thought made manifest,' said my friend, 'as indeed everything is. It is gathered energy, projected by many Bright Ones whose self-appointed task is to bless troubled minds with peace. Those being healed are grateful.' And I could actually sense their gratitude permeating the air: we can't hide our feelings in the Beyond as easily as some can on Earth.

As we watched, a sleeping woman was carried into the centre of a photosphere of vibrant light. She was a new arrival, someone who had recently 'died'. Her two attendants gently set down her unconscious form on a bright yellow couch, then knelt one at either side. White Owl continued: 'See how troubled she is?' And it wasn't difficult to sense this, for she carried it prominently in her aura. 'She worries needlessly about her young family, her life, her money, and much else. If there is nothing for her to worry about, she creates something. That is her mental state. And though she has now "died", her worrying persists. Death cannot change what she has built within her own thoughts. Only she can do that.'

Noticing her toil-worn face and twisted form, I became aware these were reflections of an over-anxious mind. Then something quite extraordinary happened. While gazing at her, I suddenly perceived her innermost thoughts. I knew she'd left two small babes and a husband back on Earth, but since her passing he had deserted the children and placed them into care. She couldn't come to terms with this, or her death, and a mixture of all these circumstances was responsible for her present state. Aware of my thoughts, my teacher said, 'Correct. She is also very bitter towards the Deity, believing God has been unkind. But now, Stephen, be still awhile, and watch and learn.'

Gradually, two Bright Ones in shining raiments appeared within the rainbow lights encircling her; one placed a hand on her brow, the other touched her feet. These two men had developed compassion to the point where it could be seen and felt with deep intensity, and its power to heal made great. After a short while, the lights strengthened the woman's form and, quite by some miraculous power, it was just as if a completely different person appeared in her place before my eyes—so great was the transformation. The twisted, bitter woman had gone, and now she seemed peaceful, almost child-like in sleep, much as one feels when some great burden or pain has finally been removed. She was still a worried spirit, but now her countenance shone with tranquillity.

One moment later, the couch, the woman and the Healing Ministers blurred and then vaporized from sight: not an uncommon happening in the spirit world. 'She goes now to a place of rest, where full recovery will come. Upon waking someone will help her to readjust. She will learn that her prayers for her babes have all been heard.'

'What's happened to them?'

'They have been adopted by a good family.'

'But won't she fret over this?'

'At first. But every night she may nurse them in her arms like any other loving mother. While her babies sleep, their spirit forms can rock gently at her breast.'

'Will she approve of their new lives?'

'No, for she is vengefully possessive. She displays this as black-reddish tones in certain sections of her aura. But as time unfolds she will be more content. The new family offers her children more than she could have done.'

'Materially?'

'No—opportunities for spiritual growth.'

'Are they poor?'

'Yes, but this provides exactly what her children need to achieve growth as spirit beings. A pathway of roses and constant sunshine will not test and try the spirit or help the soul to expand its beauty and touch its deeper levels. Such a life may be deemed by some as 'pleasure', but nothing of any lasting value to the developing Mind will spring from it. Their lives will not be easy.'

'But you said they'd be taken care of.'

'Spiritually, yes. Challenges faced and overcome make the soul richer in experience. How can you appreciate the suffering of others, if you yourself have never endured agonies of the heart and mind? How can a soul serve those in desperate need of care and education, if it has never struggled to free itself from mental and emotional darkness?

'From Darkness we travel towards the Light—and appreciate it all the more. Only when the cup of human experience has been drained can the soul say, "I have learned." The little ones knew all this, long before they chose their mother and new family.'

And there we had to leave the matter, for I felt as if the land was about to be whisked away again, but I was wrong: what I'd sensed was our departure. We walked slowly out of the Healing Temple into the bright sunshine, and continued in silence for quite some way along a country road, rich green fields and bobbing flowers surrounding us on all sides. About a mile later (at least, it felt as far as that) we stood before our next destination—

VI

Sauntering into what appeared to be a small country house set in its own extensive grounds, we moved through the open french windows. The room we entered was pleasantly arranged like a hospital ward, but without all the fuss and squeaky-clean chemical smells, neither was there any machinery or medical charts. There were six beds in this light and airy drawing-room, and in them were six sleeping forms; one was the worried woman we'd just seen at the Healing Temple.

'This is a Home of Rest,' said White Owl.

'Are they sleeping or in comas?'

'Unconscious. In deep sleep, they rest.'

'But the spirit body functions in perfect health.'

'Those who pass after long periods of stress or strength-sapping illness sometimes need recuperation. The best way is to rest.'

I somehow 'knew' these were New Arrivals.

And as we walked on I sensed his powerful healing energies automatically transmitting to the sleepers. 'This man died quickly in a car accident,' he said. 'And this woman had a brain haemorrhage after many months of suffering with cancer. And that young girl was killed by being pulled into machinery, whereas these twin boys were gassed to death in a home tragedy. The troubled woman you already know.'

'How can you tell these things so accurately?'

'By reading their minds. It comes with practice and experience. In this world nothing is hidden, all is known, providing you have the eyes to see it.' And I knew he meant awareness, rather than sight. He continued, 'Just beyond this room is a special area. Come with me.' And the very next instant we were standing in the adjoining 'ward'.

'Who are these people?' I queried, my eyes beholding further unconscious forms.

'The stubborn ones.'

'What do you mean?'

'Take a long look at their minds. Can you see their reasons for sleeping like this?'

'No,' I said, after scrutinizing.

'None of them need rest. Do you agree?'

'Yes,' I said, looking at their minds again.

'They do not wish to wake.' For a moment I was nonplussed.

'You mean they *choose* sleep?'

'Yes—they know they have "died", but wholeheartedly believe they must rest until some distant resurrection day.'

'So their beliefs close their eyes?'

'What are beliefs, but Thoughts? Those who think a man's beliefs do not matter have not yet learned that they colour his Thought, and Thought leads to Action. What we believe binds or frees the human spirit. Beliefs are important, and should be founded upon Truths. These souls sleep because of their Thoughts. They have chosen.'

Strangely enough, I wasn't then surprised, for I'd already made the unfortunate acquaintance of many on Earth who feigned to be wide awake, yet were mentally unconscious. '*The Mind shapes Everything, whatever world we inhabit. What we think—we are.* Now let us proceed.' And we left, knowing the sleepers would only rise when they wanted to. I couldn't help thinking how easy it is to ruin the quality of our lives.

In the next room was a man I instantly recognized—my recently 'deceased' grandfather! Grancha Price, as he was known, was sitting upright in a comfortable bed, perfectly well, but looking quite tired. 'Hello, Grancha!' I called, running to his bedside and embracing him.

'Stephen! How lovely to see you! You're only visiting, I hope?' he asked, his brows knitted together.

'Of course. I'm not dead yet!'

'No, but I am!' he laughed. 'And it doesn't hurt a bit!'

'Were you surprised to find yourself still living?'

'Well, not really. I never said anything before, but I used to get an odd experience myself, now and again. But I couldn't tell anyone, could I? They'd think I was mad!' A broad grin lit up his face. 'Been very far?' the tired old man asked.

'Everywhere, Grancha! But not alone.' And I glanced across at White Owl, who exchanged eye-winks with my grandfather.

'Yes, I know your pal very well. One of the first to meet me when I died, he was. Oh, that cancer! The pain was shooting right through me—and they weren't feeding me right either! They kept giving me soup and all I wanted was a three-course meal!'

'But that would have fed the disease.'

'I know that *now*, but I was desperate for a bit of dinner and the beggars wouldn't give it me!' We both smiled with him. Then he became thoughtful for a moment, and lowering his voice, said, 'It was the cigarettes that killed me, you know.'

'Yes, I know. But even on your death-bed you had a little smoke.'

My grandad smiled, then yawned wearily, whilst nodding in agreement; he was plainly quite exhausted. 'Well, we're all human, I suppose,' he said. 'But if I had my time over again . . . (yawn) . . . I'd leave the ciggies well alone, my boy. They ruined my chest, they did. Great big patches of cancer stopped me breathing. Tell me . . . (yawn) . . . did Mary-Ann get the money?' he asked. I assured him the coal-dust found in his lungs meant my grandmother had received compensation, which really pleased him.

'It's only fair, see. I worked all my life down that pit; those mines were no joke, I can tell you, boy.' Then a flicker of sadness moved across his eyes. 'Although she comes to see me when she's asleep, she can't remember when she wakes in the morning. That happens to many people, they say.' And the old man's face was troubled; he loved my grandmother so very much, and he didn't need me to tell him how broken-hearted she'd been since his passing.

'Never mind, Grancha,' I said, squeezing his shoulder, 'one day you'll both be together again, just like the old days.'

'Ah, the old days . . .! (Yawn) . . . marvellous times they

were . . . They've all, gone now. Aye, boy . . . all gone now . . .'
And the old man gently slipped away into a wistful dream-like
sleep. How angelic he looked as I kissed his forehead, and left him
quietly to rest. As I reached the door, in a half-dazed murmur I
heard him whisper, 'Tell them all I'm alive . . . won't you?' And
he was soon sound asleep again, like a baby in its cradle. White
Owl and I walked out into the flowering gardens.

VII

Outside the Rest Home, there was no time to discuss my
grandfather's new life, for suddenly my guide spoke in urgency.
'Something is very wrong,' he said, and then a second later a flash
of red colour exploded above his raven-black hair. 'Someone
calls! We must be quick!'

It was a message, and instantly we were travelling, his hand in
mine, soaring upwards faster than a lightning bolt. I couldn't
make out any shapes as everything streaked past, all I knew was
we were now crossing the mists—those fog-banked clouds which
divide parts of Heaven from Earth. Accelerating more and more,
we were going so fast I could barely think straight. Then a
millisecond later we began to lose speed, as though a powerful
magnet impeded our progress, until eventually it felt as though
we were dropping through the atmosphere like two heavy stones
sinking to the ocean's bed. This was the slowing-down effect
Earth's magnetic pull has on spirit bodies.

Peering through the fog I saw nothing but waste land before us.
But here and there amongst the greyness some makeshift tents
were scattered, and everywhere were lines of homeless natives:
some as weak as kittens, crouched on blankets, but most lying
helplessly close to death on the dusty brown earth. They were so
thin and hungry, so emaciated, they looked barely alive. We'd
arrived in Cambodia, that strife-torn land of famine, death,
drought, neglect, war and want.

We found ourselves next to an ailing mother and her dying
baby, separated from the group. It was obvious the little one was

moments from its passing: I could sense this, and the mother was beside herself with fear and grief. The auric light around the child's lungs was a dark muddy-brown, shot through with black streaks. Death was near. 'This child must live,' said White Owl.

'But it would be better if she came to spirit.'

'No, she must *live*. She has very important work to do in these parts of Earth. The girl must not yet cross to us.' Still puzzled by his urgency, I watched as he spoke quietly with two spirit people standing close to the mother and child, who were huddled together on the dry ground. I overheard their conversation.

'What is wrong?' asked White Owl of the first man.

'The baby has a fever, from polluted water. We've tried everything, but can't break its hold on her life. We need your assistance. Her body almost releases her spirit, and this prompted our call.'

'Then join with me now, and we'll do what we must.'

And I stood back and watched as the three of them fell silent, closed their compassionate eyes, then linked their minds. Next, from nowhere, came a swirling white mist—glowing translucent light. It circled the three, then the mother and her babe: and as it did so, it brightened and condensed. It was pure energy, light, healing, the essence of living life-force. I was spellbound, and also a little light-headed as the treatment took place. Slowly the rays gathered around the baby's lungs and chest, encompassing her tiny body in their radiance, penetrating the very flesh itself and glistening the child's spirit under their powerful influence. The baby's body and aura glowed like burnished copper, shot through with blue and white electric sparks, and I began to gently sway. Her lungs were breathing easier now, and were psychically strong, the God-Force having re-energized them.

Soon it was over; the shimmering mists melted into thin air, leaving only a battery of radiant energy within the sick child. The healing was complete. The three men opened their eyes and smiled in satisfaction: their work was accomplished. It had been a success. White Owl addressed the second man: 'All is well. The fever breaks, and she remains on Earth. Thank you.' The three operators touched hands and my teacher moved over to me.

I felt I had to ask him, 'What special work does she have before her?'

'I cannot say; but her starved pathetic body houses a great and noble spirit. She will be most influential in this war-torn country when she reaches maturity. She will have a great love for her people. Her life is destined to touch many others; her gifts of organization and deep respect for humanity will affect many lives here. And your presence has helped us to conquer her illness.'

'I helped?'

'Your powers were drawn upon. Did you not feel them leave you?' And I confessed I did. Then I turned and saw the dying and the sick all around me in that terrible mournful field, and I wondered if they were all lovingly tended in such a way.

'Yes,' spoke my teacher. 'Not one is neglected; no genuine cry for help from Earth is ever overlooked. That is our promise to all God's Children still clothed in the flesh.'

For a short while longer, we walked amongst the needy and the dying, unsensed by fleshly nurses, helping here and there wherever we could, administering healing light to all in need. Near one group of desperately sick children cared for by an American nurse, I stopped and gave whatever energy-rays I could muster, concentrating so hard that I supported my swaying frame by holding on to some nearby tentcloth. Puzzled as to why I could feel it in my grasp, instead of my hands passing right through the fabric, I suddenly awoke—clutching my pillow with all my might, beside my sleepy head.

It was early morning, and I was back on Earth.

21

An Angel's Promise

Sitting in the peaceful room were six good friends. This was an evening meditation class where we gathered to recoup our strength and perhaps make contact with the Other Side. Little did I know what would happen on that night. Just when I began to relax, the mists rolled aside and I was suddenly caught up in the spirit.

But where? And what was that bustling noise in front of me? When my vision gradually sharpened I found myself floating vertically in the air, suspended above a vast market place. There was a gathering of about 500 people, pushing forward, pressing to get close to a raised platform at the front. In the brilliant light I perceived a man standing before them. Now no more than a few feet from his form, I was gazing down upon him. Undoubtedly, he possessed great wisdom. I sensed he was known as a Teacher of Righteousness; and though just a slender body of a youth, he was an ancient soul. There was something startlingly unusual about his striking presence. Of middle height and clothed in a long white seamless shift, his deep brown eyes were solemn, yet bold and full of fiery bright compassion. His slightly bearded slim face radiated a deep sense of concern for those reaching out to hear him, as the jostling crowd pushed further forward. The Power of the Spirit was strong with him.

Then, in that odd way spirit vision operates, suddenly my sight telescoped, and I was staring at his profile—close up. Searching his eyes I began to wonder, was this the man they had once called the Nazarene? Could it be? But what did *He* look like? No portraits of Him exist. And if this was Him, what was I doing here in a Past Time? Or was it a Present Time in the spirit world? Could I actually be witnessing this event *right now*, or was this an image of what had once been? It was all very confusing.

In a twinkling of an eye, he turned and ceased speaking, staring right up at me. Even though I knew I was invisible to the crowd, he had found me. 'Behold,' I heard his thought-voice say, and the visions altered, shifted quickly away, and the market place had gone.

Now all I could see was a dark wooden table, old and well worn, and upon it was a yellow-with-age scroll made of wax-like parchment. A pair of hands slowly began to unfold it, and as they did, I saw revealed at the bottom of the paper, the words:

Your Map of Life.

The parchment gradually opened a little more, uncovering drawings of boulders and obstacles on a winding pathway, against which someone had written:

Challenges.

And further along the many bends in the road I could see the words:

Happiness and Sorrow.

Then his thought-voice spoke again. 'Your path is long-since written, but only revealed one step at a time. Just take each step as it comes. Everything is progressing as it should.'

Instant recognition of the message brought immense relief to my anxious mind. Then the parchment misted over, and the vision vanished, and I was once more gazing into the arresting eyes of the Teacher in the market place; but the strangest thing is that although minutes had passed while I'd received my personal message, it seemed as though I'd never moved from his face, and that no time was lost at all.

Just at that moment, I heard someone speak in the distance back on Earth—a pale insignificant voice compared to the powerful orator before me who kept the multitudes enthralled.

Then, all at once, I was aware of hurtling back down through nothingness again, and I couldn't contain my words; my restless spirit cried out loudly to him: 'I don't want to go! I don't want to leave you!' Yet the travelling continued, pulling me nearer and nearer to Mother Earth, until my flight was surprisingly stopped—some unseen power had arrested it, and now held me fast in its invisible grasp.

All around me was the deepness of space, unending infinite blackness, pierced by bright star points of light. And again the compassionate voice spoke within me. 'See there, beneath you!'

And when I looked down I discerned the planet Earth—the Great Mother who houses and protects us. Silently her great blue and milky-white orb revolved on its hidden axis, in mystery and wonder, as the Teacher said: 'Many sleep peacefully there tonight because of what has so far been achieved. But our tasks are not yet over. There is still much more to do, and few to do it. We are engaged in constant conflict against the Powers of Darkness: selfishness, greed, hatred, anger, jealousy, vested interests, the possessive god of materialism, and the lust for power over the masses.

'*Your* part in the Brotherhood of Light continues. But never despair. Keep your spirits high, and know that the Power of Love and the Might of God is with you. Go forward then, and open the Mind of Man to his Origin, Purpose and Destiny. Touch his soul with compassion, and bring as many as you can with you into the Light of Love.'

'Yes,' I responded, thunderstruck by the sheer, utter beauty of His Words, and the pulsing Great Mother beneath me.

'The road is long, my son, but never spiritually lonely. We will not forsake you. We shall never desert those who serve. We will guide and bless, forever, and ever . . .' said the voice.

Then the greyness of the planet again pulled me towards it at an alarming rate, and once more sensations of Earth drew near as my spirit groaned within me for the visions now slipping from my grasp—'But I want to stay longer!' I cried. 'I don't want to leave you!'

And as soft as a bird's wings rising in graceful flight, the gentle Angel Voice sounded its Eternal Promise deep within my heart, my mind, my soul:

> *'Lo, we are with you*
> *Always—*
> *Even unto the end of the world . . .'*

Tape cassettes by Stephen O'Brien: all enquiries to:
Voices Management (Dept B2) PO Box 8, Swansea SA1 1BL, UK.

No reply without a stamped-addressed envelope.